100 DAYS ON

100 Days on Holy Island

on

Holy Island

A Writer's Exile

Peter Mortimer

MAINSTREAM
PUBLISHING
EDINBURGH AND LONDON

This book is dedicated to the memory of my father,
Alex Mortimer, 1915–2001.

First published in Great Britain in 2002 by
MAINSTREAM PUBLISHING COMPANY (EDINBURGH) LTD
7 Albany Street
Edinburgh EH1 3UG

ISBN 1 84018 407 8

Reprinted, 2005

A catalogue record for this book is available from the British Library

Typeset in Footlight and Stone Print
Printed in Great Britain by
William Clowes Ltd, Beccles, Suffolk

AUTHOR INFO

Peter Mortimer is a poet, playwright and editor, hidden away in the windy north-east coastal village of Cullercoats. He has written plays for most of the region's theatre companies, and his poetry collections are for either children or adults, though it's not always clear which. He is occasionally moved to such inadvisable forays as this book; previous examples are *The Last of the Hunters* – six months at sea working with North Shields fishermen, and *Broke through Britain*, a 500-mile penniless odyssey from Plymouth to Edinburgh. He is the founder/editor of IRON Press, and the founder/artistic director of Cloud Nine Theatre Productions, both highly active on the north-east arts scene. When asked, he will clown around with serious intent as a writer-in-schools. His new poetry collection, *I Married the Angel of the North*, is due in 2002 from Five Leaves Press.

ACKNOWLEDGEMENTS

Not everyone on Holy Island was totally delirious at my plonking myself down there for 100 days. For the many people who *were* able to offer me help and support, I am heartily grateful. Thanks to Angela Wright for once again offering me a Whitley Bay sanctuary to write the final draft, also the Riverdale Hall Hotel, Bellingham, and John Cocker for vastly reduced accommodation rates when I was about the same task.

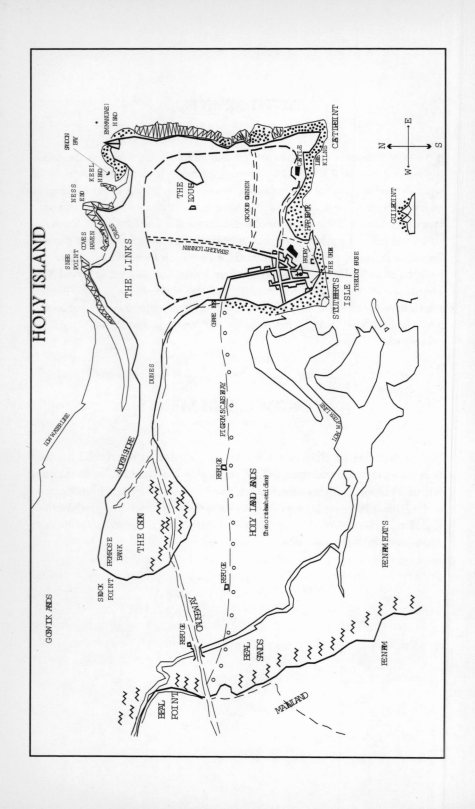

HOLY ISLAND

AUTHOR'S HEALTH WARNING

Readers wanting an historical book about Holy Island should look elsewhere. Such books are legion. For a quick condensation of the main historical points, try below. After this, history is secondary to my purposes.

St Aidan founded a community of Christian monks on Holy Island, a small and remote settlement off the north-east coast of England, in AD 635. This was at the request of King Oswald of Northumbria, whose desire was to convert the pagan Northumbrians.

The island's Norman name was *insula sacra* (sacred isle). The name Lindisfarne is said to have come from the Old English 'lindon', meaning water, and 'faron', meaning island – though no one is certain. Druids lived on the island before Christians.

Aidan was followed by St Cuthbert, under whose influence Holy Island became one of Europe's most important centres of Christianity. Cuthbert died in AD 687, and when his body was dug up in 698, it was found to be 'uncorrupted' i.e. had not decayed. The small island off Holy Island is known as St Cuthbert's Island (aka Hob's Thrush), a place the saint went for isolation and prayer, later exiling himself to the even more remote Inner Farne Islands.

Frequent Viking raids forced the monks to flee with Cuthbert's body in 875, and after much wandering they eventually settled in Durham, where the great cathedral was built in his honour. The famous Lindisfarne Gospels were also created in Cuthbert's honour around AD 698 by the monk Eadfrith.

Benedictine monks rebuilt the old wooden Priory in 1082, also from stone, and again in honour of St Cuthbert. The Priory was destroyed by Henry VIII in the sixteenth century, and the distinctive Holy Island castle built from the Priory stone as a fortress in 1570. The castle's neglected remains were rebuilt in 1903 by the new owner, Edward Hudson, to designs by the famous architect Edwin Lutyens.

Nothing of huge historical significance has happened on Holy Island in the last 500 years.

The visitor passes through a place,
the place passes through the pilgrim.
Cynthia Ozick

Only earth and sky matter.
Annie Proulx

I was better with the sound of the sea
Than with the voices of men
And in desolate and desert places
I found myself again.
 Hugh MacDiarmid

[Holy Island is] an afterthought of land.
 Melvyn Bragg

INTRODUCTION

The idea to spend 100 days on Holy Island took root in February 2000 when my partner, the writer Kitty Fitzgerald, and I rented a cottage on Lindisfarne (the island's alternative name) one ferociously windy winter weekend.

Holy Island lies off England's north-east coast, nine miles south of the market town of Berwick-upon-Tweed, and the Scottish border. It is part of Northumberland, England's fifth largest and least populated county. Historically and culturally (as well as geographically) this has been an isolated, fiercely individual region, one in which I'd come to live for a couple of years in 1970, and found myself unable to leave.

Both Kitty and I live 50 miles south in the large conurbation of Tyneside and, like most residents of the north-east, we found that Holy Island sat quietly in our consciousness as a special place to visit occasionally; simultaneously famous and remote. It is known as the cradle of Christianity.

In summer, the island teems with visitors – the main car park is almost as big as the village itself. The visitors' time on the island (like much else here) is dictated by the tides which twice daily sever Holy Island from the mainland. In those final minutes before the causeway is swallowed by the sea, a production line of cars makes its way westwards. Some leave it too late and are stranded. People have been known to get caught and be drowned.

Being on the island when the tide is 'shut' leaves you strangely possessive about the place. There *is* overnight accommodation in the few hotels and bed & breakfasts but the vast majority of visitors are daytrippers. The streets fall quiet, the pubs' atmospheres change, the island takes possession of itself once more, and you feel strangely superior to the thousands who have just left.

In winter, visitor numbers are greatly reduced, often to almost none. The cold and the wind are great deterrents. The small community seems to huddle into itself for survival, the few shops and other facilities are mostly closed. Many of the holiday properties sit empty.

As our winter weekend progressed, Kitty and I walked the island shoreline in a howling gale. We plunged across the empty sand dunes. In our ignorance, we'd brought little food, and found there was little to buy. The four pubs/hotels seemed dark and shuttered. The island was in hibernation, the odd hunched figure scurrying along a village street.

I was intrigued. I'd always found the idea of a 'holiday paradise' somewhat tedious; indolence on white sands next to a blue sea, interspersed with the odd tequila slammer, would drive me mad. Holy Island was harsh, in many ways unwelcoming, and these were the very reasons I wanted to spend a winter on it.

It's a small island, its shape somewhere between that of a tadpole and an amoeba about to separate into two. All the inhabitants are huddled in the village, shaken down into the bottom south corner, like balls in a bag. Strangely, the village has no name.

The island's giddy, improbable castle (the most famous landmark) is perched on Beblow Crag, a piece of rock which twirls upwards like a Mr Whippy ice cream, and lies to the east of the village. Its 100 ft height is accentuated by the snooker-table flatness of the land around.

The only other altitude of note, and part of the same Whin Sill geographical fault, is the Heugh, a 50-ft-high outcrop behind the ruins of the Priory – Holy Island's second most famous landmark, pillaged by Henry VIII in the great monastery dissolution.

There are two sheep farms on the main eastern 'lump'. The island narrows to a wasp waist, then grows bulbous again for the western section where the land deteriorates into sand dunes. This houses only two inhabited buildings, Snook House and Snook Tower – more of these later. The causeway runs along the southern edge of these dunes, and finally parts company with the island on its final stretch to the mainland. A motorists' refuge box is halfway along this stretch.

An important chance meeting during our weekend was with Ross and Jean Peart, who run the Open Gate bed & breakfast and retreat house. They invited us for Sunday lunch, where I explained my germinating idea of living on the island for a winter. Their enthusiasm and offers of help went a long way to cementing my resolve, and they became among my closest friends during my stay.

I knew Holy Island was a tight-knit community and that by nature such communities were conservative, often suspicious. I realised the sudden appearance for three months of a noisy writer (for noisy I am), may not be greeted with total delirium. I knew too that a great deal had been written and filmed about Holy Island and its historical and religious importance. Before and during my stay I would read and view most of it. I knew its history revolved around its brace of Saints, Cuthbert and Aidan, and how they helped rekindle Christianity in a 'heathen' land. And I knew film-makers were attracted by the unique terrain – Roman Polanski had shot *Cul-de-Sac* and *Macbeth* here. But little seemed to have been written about living on this island around the turn of the millennium. Holy Island was identified by its past more than its present. Its image in people's minds had more to do with its history than its reality. This seemed a strange state of affairs. How did it affect its population?

Not long ago, this population had been 600, but had now dropped to around 150. Much of the fishing industry had gone; the dozen pubs that had once catered for the thirsty sailors from the many visiting ships had now reduced to four. There were few signs of employment outside the tourist season, the ugly Lindisfarne Mead factory apart. Four new houses had been built, and one pub had been converted into an airy and attractive Heritage Centre. That apart, the island seemed to have changed little in decades.

Despite the influx of summer visitors, there were no take-aways, no amusement arcades, no caravans or tents, no jukeboxes, no crazy golf, no candy floss, no fairground rides, no fish-and-chip shops.

In winter, the pubs seemed more closed than open, as did the small village store. The castle shut up shop till the new season. The Heritage Centre and the Post Office, though, opened daily. There were three churches, a tiny school, the odd Celtic craft shop. What *was* Holy Island – urban, rural or seaside? I couldn't decide.

With Jean and Ross Peart's help, I arranged to rent the Cuddy House for my 100 days, which would start early January 2001. This was an old stone cottage in Fenkle Street (the middle of the village), owned by the painter Wendy Harman, who'd had to move off the island two years previously when her husband died. I met up with Wendy at the cottage in October, driving up the A1 in Kitty's old Morris Minor. It was as if, even then, I was to be reminded of the island's tidal disciplines. The car broke down and the delay meant I missed the tide, and faced a six-hour wait.

I'd written to Lord and Lady Crossman, whose family once owned virtually all of Holy Island and could still lay claim to large chunks of it. They lived on Cheswick Estate on the mainland a few miles north of the island, and I wanted to visit them. A few days after sending my letter my phone rang.

'Lady Crossman here,' said the cultured voice. This was the only time in my life I'd been phoned by nobility. What's more, she invited me up to see her. I sat in the large drawing-room with a cup of tea on my lap. My socialist instincts always wanted to storm all upper-class barricades and raise the flag for a classless society. But the other part of me hung on the every word of the aristocracy.

The Crossmans' influence on the island was considerable and in my 100 days I never heard a negative word expressed about the family. Lord Humphrey Crossman was an ex-military man. A stroke had left him partially paralysed, his speech badly affected. Lady Rose explained how the family had bought the island in the nineteenth century for £16,000. In the 1940s, faced with huge bills to install running water in many of the properties, they'd decided to sell many of them instead. Lady Rose was elegant, refined, kind, hospitable and had that slight sense of upper-class remoteness. The couple had lost their son David in a plane accident three years earlier and in that elegant room, with its deep windows, fine furniture and sense of exclusiveness, there was an accompanying sense of sadness that neither privilege nor position could negate. Grief cares little for class.

I talked with Lady Rose for half an hour, at which point she stood and moved to sit in another chair. I knew instinctively this was a sign our audience was over, metaphorically touched my forelock, and took my leave.

As the time for my 100 days approached, I grew more apprehensive. Unlike when I was working on my book *Broke through Britain*, which involved a daily shifting landscape, here I would be confined for three months within a very small area. Would it drive me mad? Or would the islanders succumb first?

My resolution at this stage was not to leave the island. But how about visitors? My son Dylan's 17th birthday fell during my stay. I'd want him to come up. Kitty? I wasn't sure. My 100 days needed in some ways to be an 'exile'.

Mad ideas ran through my head. I would go to St Cuthbert's Island and rebuild St Cuthbert's ruined cell, where the saint would go for solitary prayer and contemplation. I soon discovered that tinkering with such holy ruins was not on.

On the Holy Island website, I found details of St Cuthbert's Way, a 65-mile walk from the south-western Scottish town of Melrose (home of the saint's original monastery) to Lindisfarne. I decided to walk it as a way of easing myself into the island. Curiously enough, this is one of the few journeys from Scotland to England where the destination is further north than the starting point.

I also decided to write to ten northern authors. I would ask each to select from their shelves a book (not written by themselves) that they thought might amuse, divert or challenge me during my stay. For the ceremonial handing over of the books, I threw a party at my Cullercoats house on 17 December (my birthday). Nine of the authors turned up with a book and the party came and went. Christmas, too. The date of 5 January 2001 loomed nearer. I had never been away from my home for such a length of time. I was a confirmed urbanite going into a tiny, isolated, self-contained community with the conceit of writing a book about my stay. As to the shape and nature of the book, I had little idea.

I am grateful to the Society of Authors for financial assistance towards my stay. Also to New Writing North, who gave me a 'Time to Write' award to work on the book on my return.

What was I running from, or towards? What had prompted me to plonk myself down on this bleak, windswept location for more than three months?

And would anyone talk to me?

I had no answers. But I would have 100 days to find some.

SUNDAY, 14 JANUARY 2001 – DAY ONE

Bereft – Bereaved

The new year started dramatically. In the three days before I was due to set off to Melrose and the 65-mile walk to Holy Island, two major events happened to the Mortimer family in Rotherham.

On 3 January, my father died, aged 85. The previous day my 27-year-old nephew Matthew required an emergency operation for the removal of the large intestine. He had developed ulcerative colitis and the potential consequences were dreadful. With my partner Kitty, I travelled the 130 miles south to Rotherham. I visited Matthew in hospital where he lay emaciated, deathly pale, virtually inert. He was strung up with tubes like strings on a puppet.

From there we went straight to the morgue for the shock of seeing my father's body, which still had to receive the 'cosmetic' treatment. He was a waxen collapse of flesh and bone, his toothless mouth horribly open in a silent scream. Our third call was the nursing home where my mother was wailing inconsolably at the loss of her husband of 60 years. At such times you operate on autopilot. It was bad for me but worse for my brother Alex – the blow for him was as a father and a son.

Twice more in the next few days I visited from Tyneside. On the second occasion the family drove down from Rotherham for my father's funeral at their erstwhile home town of Nottingham. We stood in the cold Catholic church waiting for the undertaker's hearse, which arrived 20 minutes late, 20 minutes in which the poor organist exhausted her repertoire. I'd prepared a printed sheet about my father for the congregation. As with most funerals, the priest began with the words 'I never actually met Alex Mortimer but . . .' Thus our mechanical rituals. I delivered a slightly choked valediction.

These events delayed, and almost aborted, my Holy Island exile. I abandoned the idea of the 65-mile walk, and stared down at my brand-new walking boots and the two pairs of 1,000-Mile Blister-Free socks. The delay also brought practical difficulties with the renting of the cottage. The latest I could arrive on Holy Island was 14 January. Which meant setting off two days after my father's funeral.

Another problem was my mother. The decision to 'shelter' her from the true length of my absence, to be vague about my return time, now consumed me with guilt. Plus the fact I was abandoning her when she most needed me. I walked away from her, alone in that chair in the glum lounge of one of those institutions where we conveniently shuffle off the old, visiting them as we can fit it in. In addition, my nephew was still seriously ill. And in these circumstances, I was planning to plonk myself long-term on a remote piece of rock, surrounded by a community I didn't know and probably had little in common with.

If my motivation for the trip was less than all-consuming, it was at that moment that I fell back on the ruthlessness of the writer, that necessary but often disruptive instinct that powers him or her on, often to almost indefensible lengths.

I hugged my son Dylan goodbye. His formative years and never three months absent from his father. Everything I knew seemed to be disappearing over the horizon.

Kitty ran me to Holy Island. I felt the need to cling to her like a limpet. The day offered a perfect cobalt sky, a brilliant blue, the sun's weak winter fingers just barely stroking warmth into a north-east January.

We drove mainly in silence, as I resisted strongly the desire to shout 'Stop. Go back!' I wanted the reassurance of the familiar. I felt ill-equipped for the shock of the new.

The 50-odd-mile drive north was akin to entering a new galaxy. Holy Island came finally into view, an offshore presence, as someone once wrote, like a submarine cutting through the waves, a misty silhouette, a crouching secret place that had dragged itself away from the life of the mainland and was now, for reasons unclear, dragging me with it.

You turn off from the A1 and within seconds the sense is of a world closing behind you. The road meanders five miles, dropping slowly towards the vast sand flats which spread themselves before you. You finally leave the mainland for the causeway and it is as if, at that moment, all defences are stripped away, as if you are now utterly exposed. Everything you think you know counts for nothing, as the tiny dot of you traverses that huge empty landscape.

And the reason I was doing this – the only reason I could be certain of – was that I am a writer and it was this instinct that pushed me on.

The causeway met the western extreme of the island and hugged the shoreline as it curved towards the distant village, squatting on the skyline like a painted theatre set.

There was me, Kitty, her dog Polly, and Dylan's dog Jess, along with Wendy Harman, who was waiting for us at the Cuddy House. That made four females and me.

But soon there would be only me.

The cottage had thick old beams, slanting attic roofs, thick stone walls, deep recessed windows; a blazing fire was in the grate. *Homes & Gardens* would have approved. Except I had a sickness in the soul, a deep sense of unrootedness and loss. Like most people, I had long wondered how I would react to the death of a parent. My father had been very different to me, a council house shop-worker who started his own small business and was proud to move into the middle classes and shed his Nottingham accent. He'd been fleeced by business sharks but bounced back. His values were not mine. With family that wasn't the main thing.

And what was I doing in this place, two days after he was put into the ground?

Wendy gave us tea, after which Kitty, the dogs and I took a long walk across the dunes. The sky was a metallic turquoise, deepening on the horizon to such intense scarlet that it reflected the sea almost blood-like.

The breaking waves were not white but blushing pink, and round 360 degrees the sky was clamped to the earth like a giant lid. Kitty chatted on. I knew her motive was to cheer me. We walked on the path Crooked Lonnen where a string of dramatic hawthorn bushes, blasted to crazy emaciated angles by the wind, trapped in their arthritic branches the skeletons of rabbits which presumably had sought refuge from predators but found only a tomb.

Back at the cottage Wendy explained island practicalities. A coalman came once a fortnight from Scotland. On Tuesdays, the vegetable man from somewhere else. On Thursdays, the butcher's van from the village of Bamburgh a few miles down the coast. Also the bin man from the border town of Berwick. The fish man (it appeared all these traders were male) was said to come on Wednesdays and Fridays but in my 100 days I never even saw a sprat on sale.

Most islanders, said Wendy, travelled the 20-mile round trip to the Berwick supermarkets for food. Once a week, for those without cars, the island mini-bus made the journey.

And what about scheduled buses?

Naturally. One went to Berwick every ten days. Depending on tides.

I had with me a few eggs, bread, bacon, tea-bags, some chicken pieces and milk. I was watching the clock every few minutes. I was dreading 9.30 p.m., when Kitty would have to leave ahead of the tide. I was dreading the thought of being alone. Wendy went off to stay with friends on the island. Kitty and I took our final walk, up past the ruined Priory and on to the Heugh, that 50-ft-high outcrop on which, say some, was built the first Holy Island church.

The night was totally silent, the sky above us light-pollution-free, jet black, studded with fiercely burning stars. We walked along Sanctuary Close towards the cliff top; as the village light behind us melted to darkness, the two black dogs ran quickly in the long grass to invisibility.

Rarely had I so desperately felt the need for Kitty's love and support. And her with less than an hour left.

Back in the cottage, I busied myself to distraction, lining up on parade my washing and shaving kit in the small bathroom, folding shirts and trousers into place, strategically placing round the house my transistor radios, seeking to take root, make an identity.

On the mantelpiece I placed the three angels given me for good fortune by the members of my theatre company, Cloud Nine.

The time had come. I drove with Kitty to Chare Ends, the start of the causeway. A final close hug, a goodbye, and for several moments I watched her tail-lights grow weaker, more distant as she was sucked back to that mainland, taken away from this strange place that I was to make my home for 100 days. Then the night had swallowed her. There was only the blackness and the silence, and me in that terribly lonely spot. Tears ran down my cheeks.

Bereft. Bereaved. I turned and walked back through the silent dark village streets. Not a sign of life. Except one. Bizarrely. In a small pool of weak light thrown down by one of the lamp-posts stood a woman. She was protected against the crystalline cold by a fur hat and coat. And she was talking loudly into a mobile phone.

I entered the cottage to the strong smell of cloves from the simple chicken meal Kitty had cooked. The smell, and the last supper it evoked, flooded me with sadness. Proust and his madeleine, me and my chicken cloves.

And I could not bear to sit alone in that cottage. Instead, I walked round the village. The Manor House was dark and shuttered. The Ship was closed all winter. The Crown and Anchor was open. I peered through a bar window, to find a man glaring back at me with such an intensity I scuttled off into the night and could not bear to return.

I found some refuge in the small secreted bar of the Lindisfarne Hotel. A sparse huddle of locals eyed with some unspoken curiosity the entry of this total stranger at 10 p.m. on a freezing January night, with the tide shut.

The small bar was curtained and seemed shut against the world. Its walls sported various contraptions, lobster pots, dangling seaweed, sepia prints of old fishermen, white beards the size of doormats. Behind the small corner bar were stacked more than 130 single malt whiskies in tiers steeper than the San Siro stadium. I didn't count them. I asked the owner, Clive Massey. With his wife Sue, he had been on the island 29 years.

I had been on only six hours. And it felt intolerable.

Someone asked me who I was. My contact with the islanders had begun.

MONDAY, 15 JANUARY 2001 – DAY TWO

Art and Gardens

For 99 per cent of the time, 99 per cent of Holy Island visitors (and residents too, come to that) stay in the east. Indeed, so much is the east part considered the entire island that in Karen Scammell's popular guide is the phrase 'you can walk around the island in an hour'. This is patently untrue. When I walked round the whole island it took me almost four. The island's western section – almost all sand dunes, with only the mysterious Snook Tower and House as signs of habitation – is virtually ignored by human beings.

My first full day on Lindisfarne. A dull grey sky, the strangeness of the house, banana sandwiches for breakfast, a fitful night's sleep, images of Kitty, Dylan, my dead father.

And at 9.30 a.m., a knock at my door. My optimism led me to expect a small welcoming committee, mulled wine and hot scones, a wee speech hoping my stay would be a fruitful one.

It was the washing machine repair man, sent by Wendy Harman.

He would be the only human being to cross my threshold for another ten days, such was the rush to see me. Indeed, in these early days the impression often was that I dragged in my wake on this island great surging waves of indifference.

The village store opened briefly, its winter shelves as sparse as those of Moscow shops in 1812. The fire had gone out. I drifted round the village, read a public noticing advertising an arts & crafts class that afternoon. I thought I'd go. Also advertised was a parish council meeting the next Friday. I'd go to that too. If my diary was free.

There were five women and me at the arts & crafts. No one seemed particularly surprised to see me. I made a collage.

In the Post Office, where I'd opened an account (no banks on the island), Malcolm Patterson was unsmiling. In the Manor House pub, licensee George Ward never stopped smiling. He reminded me of a ventriloquist.

I sat at the bar, looking out across the harbour at the bobbing boats. The castle was in the middle distance. The Priory lay just to one side. Picture postcard stuff.

George gave me some bad news. The Manor House would close for a fortnight's renovations. The Lindisfarne was closing for a winter break. The Ship was already shuttered up. This left the Crown and Anchor.

'Probably open weekends,' said George

I needed something to do. I had no function.

'You could dig the Manor House garden,' said George. Thus was born an unlikely relationship that led to blisters, poetry and the odd free potato.

I was the only customer in the Manor House that night. I walked home at 11 p.m. The village was dark, deserted, and as silent as a meditation class. The odd plume of smoke was tugged from the stone cottage chimneys.

It was silent in the way cities were never silent, silence not as a brief interruption from the traffic, the humans, the incessant noise of civilisation, but silent as a way of being. What lay beneath the surface of this small settlement I had no idea. But on a bitter cold January night in 2001, it offered up silence as a totally natural state.

TUESDAY, 16 JANUARY 2001 – DAY THREE

Icons and Expeditions

Food supplies were small. Tuesday was vegetable man day. I had no idea what time. I drifted down to the far end of Marygate, the village's main thoroughfare – downtown Lindisfarne. It took me three minutes.

The village school, a small white-washed building, had reopened the previous September. It had two pupils. When the tide was shut, that was. When the tide was open, teacher Caitlin White took them to the vast Howick school on the mainland, where pupils ran to double figures.

Caitlin, whose refined southern accent seemed slightly misplaced in this terrain, had come from teaching in Paddington, London, which was a bit different.

A two-pupil school – was there a dinner lady, did they call the register? Was there a parents' evening? School assembly?

I'd worked a good deal as a writer-in-school, many of them faceless sausage factories turning their pupils into dull functionaries and their teachers to mogadon. I fancied working here. With a minimum of bureaucracy or red tape, Caitlin and I fixed up a storytelling session for the following week.

The school had one classroom, one corridor and a playground big enough for 200. In times gone by, it had housed almost that number.

I padded out more territory, past the harbour, towards the castle, collecting my first driftwood from the stony beach. Every Holy Island tree, with the exception of those sheltered in the village, looked emaciated, given no mercy by the fierce winds which rarely seemed to take a day off.

I decided to be cheeky, knock on doors. I'd done it for a month for my previous book *Broke through Britain*. The worst scenario was a door slammed in the face. I could survive that.

I knocked at The White House in Fenkle Street, home of Anne Burden, who'd run the arts class, and her husband, retired Berwick vicar, Mike.

The God Squad, so called, made up a sizeable minority of the population. Me and God weren't on the most intimate terms. But I'd give him ample opportunity to state his case on the island.

Mike Burden's retirement had brought a second wind. He now created driftwood icons from beach material. The Burden back garden, with a fine view of the castle, had a forge, a painting shed for Anne and a sprinkling of Mike's metal sculptures. At night it came alive with light.

'I was meant to come here,' he said. 'You were too.' And they gave me a cup of tea. His theory was that Holy Island was now more isolated than in centuries past, when constant nautical traffic called.

'Why not come to matins with me tomorrow?'

'OK. What time?'

'Seven-thirty a.m.'

Blimey. OK.

I caught the vegetable van. Barry Cochrane drove it.

That afternoon I took a five-mile walk to post a letter at Snook Tower. The owner, Sue Ryland, visited the island rarely, and when she did I wanted her to invite me round. I walked along the Shell Road causeway, the vast Holy Island sands to the left, and beyond, the Northumberland hills skulking in mist. I heard the lonely whistle of a train, the occasional muffled thud betraying duck shooters somewhere out on those ghostly flats. Endless varieties of birds scudded across the sands. Holy Island plays host to around 300 species any year and I knew maybe six.

The flooded track to Snook House was frozen stiff, the ice creaking beneath my feet. Both Snook Tower and Snook House were shuttered more securely than Fort Knox. Posting a letter was an impossibility. I carried my missive back home from that isolated spot, secreted 300 yards from the road in a bare patch between the dunes.

Two village buildings caught my eye on the return journey. The Lindisfarne Hotel, an imposing edifice which seemed the only unfaced brick on the island, and the Island Oasis Café, an ugly dark brown tin shed without a single external redeeming feature. It had once been an undertaker's.

I left the Snook letter c/o the Post Office, where I also stuck up the following advertisement: 'Writer on island seeks odd jobs. Incredibly cheap. No reasonable offer refused.' I declined to mention my appalling lack of practical skills, sat back and waited for the offers to flood in.

That evening I sat in the cottage and ate alone to the loud clink of fork and knife. I was on the island. But I wasn't – if you know what I mean.

'I'll need to go to Berwick in the mini-bus on Friday for food supplies,' I told myself. This was probably true but what I really meant was I could get off the island for a few hours. And only 72 hours on it.

That night I sat alone again in the Manor House bar. A young couple wandered in and began some serious drinking. The man came over.

'You ran a poetry workshop in our school,' he said. This seemed a good enough excuse to go back to their holiday cottage and get drunk. He was called Adam, his partner Sarah, and they were in the Herring Houses, a small settlement near the harbour, reached through inky blackness with the aid of a torch.

We drank and played music till 2 a.m., when I decided to make tracks. In the back yard I stumbled about, unable to find the exit. Adam came, stumbled about too, and also failed. I then gave up and stretched out on a bed in the spare room, the only person ever unable to find their way home on Holy Island. It was 2.30 a.m. I'd promised to be at 7.30 a.m. matins.

WEDNESDAY, 17 JANUARY 2001 – DAY FOUR

God at Dawn – Crowning Out

One of my talents is telling myself when to wake up. It has been unacknowledged for 58 years.

Dawn was still far off at 6.45 a.m. The moon was out. I left the two lovers deeply entwined and found the yard exit. Where now? I plunged across a field which was waterlogged, mainly (I was later to learn) through being below sea-level.

I had an appointment with God. It is well known such encounters are not best handled in wet shoes and socks. I went home and changed, then walked to St Mary's Church in the half-light.

This was the main Holy Island church, perched on the cliff overlooking the mainland and the small St Cuthbert's Island. Matins in winter wasn't a big crowd-puller; only Mike Burden and me present, plus the vicar, David Adam, a slight figure of a man with a shock of white hair and a mischievous face unusual in a cleric.

My plan to snooze on the back pew was stillborn. The service, in the choir stalls, had Mike and me within halitosis distance of the vicar (who luckily didn't have it). He said stand, we stood, he said sit, we sat, he said kneel, we knelt, he said pray, I mumbled.

At 8.30 a.m. he dismissed us. I went home, collapsed on the settee and was woken by the postman Dick Patterson (brother of the Post Office man, Malcolm). Dick was reputed (along with Snook Tower) to have no letterbox at his house. Why would he need one?

I'd planned that morning to begin my gardening career. Instead I went for a run, out through the village, past Chare Ends and on to the vast sand flats, often ankle deep in the receding tide. Legions of birds screeched above me as I ran past the poles of the Pilgrim's Way (where the devout had trekked for centuries). I was a dot on the landscape. My insignificance was splendid. And everything around belonged to me.

Running always did me good. Bad things flowed out of me like water down a drain. I lit the fire and sang out loud. Then went walkabout again, called at the United Reform Church for no particular reason, and had a cup of tea with Barry Hutchinson. He'd been on the island several months. Still hadn't settled. His brochure spoke of a UK church culture that had 'clearly run out of steam', a contemporary culture 'desperately searching for meaning, depth and purpose'. This cheered me up much more than the usual platitudinous religious guff.

At the village's East End, I walked down Jenny Bell Lane. It was low tide. I was able to cross to St Cuthbert's Island, a rocky outcrop where the saint had come to commune with God and fight his devils. It seemed pretty isolated to me but for Cuthbert it had eventually become far too busy, as the odd soul waded over to ask him the meaning of life. Cuthbert retreated even further to the Inner Farne Islands, a few miles out to the south-east. No interlopers here. Just his windowless cell, God and the devils.

St Cuthbert's Island was to figure a good deal in my 100 days. It had few tourist attractions: the ruined foundations of Cuthbert's first cell and an imposing oak cross erected 60 years previously, gnarled rock, tufted grass. No point coming to this place looking for distractions. You needed other reasons.

Back home I eked out my meagre rations, sitting down to an evening meal of mashed spuds and a fried egg. Mmmm!

The face at the window had frightened me off the Crown and Anchor on Sunday but now I felt fearless. Like all the island pubs it was lo-tech – no jukebox, no one-armed bandit, no pool table. It was nevertheless an attractive white-painted building in the market square, facing down to Sanctuary Close and the Priory, and within winking distance of the Manor House. The small curved bar had two outside walls, two entry doors. On a night such as this (freezing), it reminded me of those Victorian ghost stories where no matter how high the fire is built, the room remains chilled. Same here.

This was my expectation: I would walk in, the locals would slap me on the back, invite me to the bar, stand me a drink and show endless curiosity about my character and quest.

In fact, I stood at one end of the bar while six middle-aged, male regulars stood at the other. Occasionally I would lob a small nugget of conversation in their direction. The reply would normally be mono- or maybe duosyllabic, after which they would engage themselves once more in their own talk. Twenty minutes. Another lob. Another syllable.

The barmaid was called Kirsty Bevan. I couldn't work out if the regulars' frequent putdowns to her were merely ritual or intended. Kirsty swiped them back as effortlessly as a Venus Williams backhand.

I drank three pints of Smith's bitter and wondered how to make my exit in a seemingly nonchalant manner. At 11.30 I shouted an over-hearty 'Goodbye, then!' and walked out looking totally unnonchalant. Back in the Cuddy House my fire was still pulsing out its heat. I switched on the telly and watched Newcastle inevitably exiting the FA Cup.

THURSDAY, 18 JANUARY 2001 – DAY FIVE

A Worm Apology – Clinker

So the locals weren't exactly coming out with the brass band, the bunting and the welcoming speech from the mayor. Fine.

It was my brother's birthday. I ate my last egg in celebration and stared out at the cold porridge sky. I'd ordered a daily paper from the Post Office, where I was bright, cheerful and chatty to Malcolm Patterson. In return he was taciturn and serious-looking. Fine.

Gardening day. In wellies, thick blue jumper and old trousers, you might have taken me as a Holy Islander. The village was again quiet, empty. A symbol of how it was transformed in summer came with the bench outside Town End View Cottage which had PRIVATE painted on it. Rebel that I was, I sat on it for three seconds.

The Manor House garden was spectacularly set; on one side the churchyard with St Aidan's statue (he seemed to be holding either a dildo or a Mr Whippy ice cream), on another the Priory ruins. The garden looked out to sea via the harbour and across flat land one mile to the castle, again rising up a bit like a Mr Whippy. It was also part children's drawing, part Gothic dream (or nightmare) and had little to do with reality.

Mortimer the Gardener walked through the Manor House entrance, whose rainbow arch mimicked that of the Priory, supported on two pillars of weather-beaten sandstone slabs resembling sucked lozenges.

George Ward handed me a small garden fork.

'Will that do?' he asked. Only for eating chips, I thought. I rummaged about, found a monstrous item with curved prongs like dragon's teeth. At the first contact with soil, the handle fell off. I eventually found a medium-sized fork in the greenhouse.

I was a totally inexperienced gardener. I watched none of the 5,000 weekly gardening programmes and suspected no one who did ever got off their fat arse to emulate the activities, just as I'd never met a soul who'd taken up a recipe from a telly chef.

Each time I turned over a worm, I felt strange. I paused to write a haiku.

Apologising

to every dug-up worm

the new gardener.

The patch I'd been given to dig was the length of a bowling alley.

At first the digging was tedious, the shaking out of the weeds. After two hours, I took some enjoyment in it. A lobster boat chugged into the harbour. Through the gateway the grassed market square was peaceful, deserted. A low wall separated me from the churchyard which had only two visitors all day.

'Be quiet,' said the mum to the whingeing little girl dragged in her wake, 'or there'll be no *Teletubbies* later.'

By midday my influence was apparent. A small square of previously weed-infested soil was now dark, moist, fertile. I looked around for an appreciative audience. There was none.

My wages were grub in the bar – chicken korma and a pint of John Smith's. The only other occupant was Jen Ward's dad, Tom Storm. Each day he whizzed through the *Daily Telegraph* crossword. He'd been on the island 11 years and was 91.

I dug till 4.30 p.m., then wandered round the graveyard, which was no less nor more noisy than anywhere else. There, in the Crossman family plot, was a recent stone for David Lindisfarne Alexandre Crossman – the dead son whose loss had imbued the family with such sadness on my visit.

Holy Island had a population of about 150. So far I'd spoken to about six and occasionally they had spoken back. That night I took another hopeful tour of the village pubs. Ship shut, Lindisfarne shut, Crown and Anchor shut.

Back to my local, the Manor House. Back to George's grin. And another customer, Jimmy Brigham, known to all as Clinker for reasons never quite apparent. Clinker was the kind of character most Holy Island books fastened on: he'd been in as many documentaries as Elton John. With his craggy face and his local accent, he fitted all the media's easy stereotypes as to what a Holy Islander should 'be'. London directors swooned over his raw ethnic appeal, his indigenous authenticity. Clinker was the conduit through which they could relate to the island.

None of this seemed unduly to bother him. A recovering alcoholic, he showed steely determination in sticking to his Lucozade and ginger beer, often when the island indulged its ferocious thirst.

I befriended him. I think he liked the idea I wasn't just looking for a quick fix. He called me 'the left-handed book writer'.

Clinker's wife was called Joan. In 100 days I never set eyes on her, one of the considerable army of what I came to call Holy Island's invisible women. Why did they never appear?

FRIDAY, 19 JANUARY 2001 – DAY SIX

Escaping with Hector – Matters Politic

I once wrote a story where a man came back from the dead to find all ghosts were in a 'time-slip'; their lives one second removed from the living, with whom they could have no contact.

I felt a bit like that.

Which is why I decided to go on the Berwick supermarket mini-bus. That and my empty larder. The service was operated by Hector Douglas, the bearded incarnation of an old sea-dog. I'd missed the meat wagon through gardening duties. No sign of the fish van.

After a morning spent gardening (my wheelbarrow technique improving all the time), I jumped in the mini-bus. Only two other occupants, Eddie Douglas and his wife Jen, who became the second Holy Island invisible woman. I saw Eddie virtually every day; he collected for charity at the village junction, sat on a village seat, talked incessantly to passers-by, took photographs of the island. I never saw his wife again.

Eddie's Holy Island accent was thicker than Geordie, tinged with Scots, guttural, living most of its life in the throat before making its strangulated escape.

There was a ritualised sense to this expedition to Berwick, Hector Douglas providing each shopper with a reinforced shopping bag big enough to hold three Sumo wrestlers and their immediate family. I imagined the Holy Island mini-bus shopper was a distinctive Berwick sight – huge bag dragged along the floor.

Already it was obvious that, for most Holy Islanders, most money was both earned and spent off the island, a state of affairs making for a fragile economy.

Even after just six days, the supermarket seemed strange; the ranks of Chardonnay, the stacked tuna, the announced 'bargains of the week'. Berwick, a small market town, seemed amazingly cosmopolitan. And I was out on bail.

We drove back in the slatted rain, the growing gloom, the island already being taken by the dusk, the weak village lights barely penetrating. Across the causeway and the island seemed to belong to the sea, consumed by the horizon. It had little to do with the mainland I was leaving.

I'd spent £80 in Berwick. My bag was half full.

Up a small lane at the edge of the village was the Reading Room. It was small, wood-panelled, and it was here that Holy Island democracy flourished, here that the spectacularly unspectacular meetings of Holy Island parish council took place.

There is a good reason why attending council meetings is not a national spectator sport. And there is a certain accuracy to the British view of local councillors as (a) dull functionaries; (b) pocket-liners; or (c) pompous oafs. Local councils are not sexy and mayors are slightly ridiculous figures.

What united these four councillors, and indeed the audience of three, were the huge topcoats. The room's temperature was slightly above that of a Bird's Eye freezer compartment, which gave the discussion of causeway erosion and public toilet maintenance a certain urgency.

The councillors were Sue Massey of the Lindisfarne Hotel, Dick Patterson, postman, Tommy Douglas, fisherman, and chairman Ian McGregor, ex-postmaster and strong island activist.

Over the 100 days, I would attend three council meetings. At each one I would be a vastly different animal.

My island friends, Ross and Jean Peart, had returned after a week's holiday. I'd longed for their smiles and laughter. Ross beamed. Jean looked unsettled.

'I love it here,' said he.

'This island's supposed to bring spiritual calm,' said she. 'It often brings turmoil too.'

Of course. Why should it not? Unless you simply believed in picture postcards. But the Holy Island image, the stereotype, was of peaceful bliss. As if any humans, anywhere, lived in such conditions.

In their spacious Open Gate bed & breakfast and retreat, situated on the village's main junction, Jean and Ross fed me fettucini, every mouthful observed by their nervous pooch Penny, for whom even a suddenly raised eyebrow could precipitate an outburst of barking. At that moment I felt the most settled I had been.

That night I sang my head off. Jen Ward of the Manor House was organising the third annual music evening. Could I watch rehearsals?

'You can come and sing,' she said and fixed me with a look that scared me to death. Jen was a formidable woman. The couple's nickname in the village was 'George and The Dragon'. I know. Jen told me.

I came. And I sang. Rehearsals were in the down-and-out village hall, built in the 1930s by the then castle owners, the de Stein family. Inside it was painted in those sickly dead colours beloved of local authority offices and hospital outpatient departments. Five ancient metal blow heaters, that no doubt once warmed the Home Guard, hung from the walls.

'Warmed' might be optimistic. The heaters were eight foot from the ground, blissfully unaware of the principle that heat rises. These antediluvian monstrosities operated only on old 50p pieces, fed one end, removed from the other and fed again. A bizarre piece of recycling.

The building probably had the warmest ceiling, and coldest inhabitants, in Britain.

I found myself, swathed in topcoat and scarf, belting out 'Unchained Melody', 'Love Changes Everything' and the like, under Jen's stern eye and with piano accompaniment from Derek of the Marygate Hostel.

I noticed that, in these sub-arctic conditions, Jen Ward was wearing sandals and no socks.

About eight warblers present. And I was beginning to put names to faces. Mike and Anne Burden. Jean and Ross Peart. Barry Hutchinson of the United Reform Church. All these people, I realised, had connections with God. I put the thought out of my mind.

That evening I rang my mother in Rotherham. How long would Holy Island take, she asked? I wasn't sure, I lied, thinking of her sitting alone in that nursing home. Most times I was quite fond of myself. But not at that moment.

SATURDAY, 20 JANUARY 2001 – DAY SEVEN

The Word Never Spoken – Brought to Book

My first small spat with an islander. Not that much, just enough to niggle away, to chip at the fragile foundation on which I was trying to build my island relationship.

First – my day. A breakfast cooked on an electric cooker whose rings responded to required heat changes with the speed of a sloth in treacle. A walk with Ross Peart up Straight Lonnen, where the sight of a pot-bellied Vietnamese pig (belonging to St Coombes farm) brought up the island's forbidden word, P – I – G. I'd heard islanders never spoke the word but took this as tourist board island myth.

It was true. Animals of a porcine nature were referred to as 'guffies', a custom said to have dated from a fisherman stumbling over a – well, guffie – prior to a sea trip that ended in drowning.

When Jean and Ross had first arrived, they'd innocently stuck an ornate guffie outside their house. Next day it had been dumped by persons unknown in the rubbish bin.

'Look,' said Ross, 'where else would you see so many curlews?'

Later he pointed out a huddle of distinctive black and white birds.

'Oyster-catchers.' Only 298 species left to identify.

Our walk took in Sanctuary Close, an open path that linked the village to the Heugh – that 50-ft-high rock outcrop.

'The path was built for the visit of the Queen in the 1950s,' said Ross.

I realised how to get things done. Don't sit muffled up in endless cold local council meetings studying minutes, proposing motions and accepting amendments. When you wanted a posh new footpath laid, just invite up the Queen.

I spent the afternoon gardening. I was getting better. Being Saturday, the island was slightly busier. Several people stopped and peered over the wall as I turned over another sod or wheeled another barrow of weeds to the dump, which was rapidly becoming a mountain range at the plot bottom.

People stopping to watch me dig the very soil of Holy Island in some strange way confirmed my being here, became part of my justification. I reminded myself of this as, in fading light, I returned to the Cuddy House and ate another solitary meal. Seven days and no island inhabitant had knocked at my door.

This would have suited a loner. I wasn't one.

In the Lindisfarne bar that night, fisherman Tommy Douglas and oil-rig worker Stuart McMurdo were discussing guns. Holy Island has no police and probably the biggest per capita gun ownership in the UK. Islanders love wild-fowling, shooting birds from the sky. Some called it sport but only one side took any pleasure from it.

I'd never handled a real gun. One of my proudest boasts in life. I sat and supped my beer, listening to the gun talk, said nowt.

Anyway, the afternoon spat was niggling me. In the Manor House bar Jen Ward had said, 'I hope we're going to see what you write about us before it's published. We do have our privacy. And we didn't invite you here.'

Behind the bar husband George, smile ever-present, chipped in.

'Pete will be happy to show us the book proofs, won't you, Pete?'

Have you seen the film *The Wicker Man*? As I left the bar, I knew how Edward Woodward's character felt. As if some cold, clammy embrace was tightening its grip on me.

SUNDAY, 21 JANUARY 2001 – DAY EIGHT

Half Cut and Stone

Jen Ward was right. No one had invited me here. By what authority did I plonk myself down in this small community and observe them, like animals in a zoo?

None at all. Except I was in the zoo as much as them. And if writers waited to be invited, hardly a decent book would be written. If Jen mistrusted me, I knew others would. I wanted to tell them I wasn't a tabloid journalist, I wasn't looking for exposés, the sexsational truth behind their lives.

I wanted to tell them the book would be about me as much as about them. This sounded self-centred, though, and for the time being I wouldn't tell them anything. But the unspoken, as I moved among the villagers, was often the size of an elephant. As a playwright I should have loved all this subtext. But it unnerved me. I was insecure.

My supermarket visit saw me spoilt for choice food-wise. A breakfast of fresh grapefruit, followed by egg, bacon and tomato. The brief brilliance of yesterday had given way to another grey sky.

Later that morning I went for a run. My hip hurt. My medical ignorance led me to conclude I could run the pain off.

I enjoyed being swallowed by the vast sands. As if they accepted me without question. I ran long and far, noting how even here the tide was fringed with detergent. And how come we could forecast the height of the tide to the millimetre centuries ahead, yet had no idea if any particular tide would be a millpond or an aquatic inferno?

Sunday was traditionally a big drinking day on the island. For the first time three pubs were open simultaneously, reason enough to visit them all. I supped in the Crown and Anchor, the Lindisfarne then the Manor House. More booze with a gang at the house of Joyce Watson, mother of village store owner Gary. And always the sense I was hanging round the periphery, that slight awkwardness of the guest unsure of his position. That feeling would never quite leave me, the 100 days long.

In the Crown, fisherman Keith Kyle told me of his 25-ft boat sinking under him a few weeks previously. He'd been hoisted off by the Boulmer rescue helicopter. Interesting stuff but I felt like an interviewer. I wanted to be a normal human being and to be taken as such by the islanders. Some hope. I was a writer on the island. A curiosity to be wary of. Accept it. Get on with it. Don't make bogus claims, like so-called 'reality TV'. Don't be fatuous about capturing 'real life'. Just write the damned book.

That evening I leapt a cultural chasm. Daytime had been pub talk, fishing boats, football scores, mucky jokes. Now suddenly I was sat in a black hessian chair sprinkled with red cushions, sipping chilled white wine, in the flickering light of a giant candle, breathing in the heady scent of an oil burner. I was listening to Kid Ory, Sidney Bechet, Freddie Keppard – a musical jazz soirée.

This was at the Stables, the home of Chris Holbrook and Derek Pollard, overlooking the market place. They were island 'incomers', Derek a retired academic, Chris an aromatherapist and masseuse, callings that often fitted uneasily into this tight-knit, conservative community.

I gobbled down the culture like a welcome bag of chips. I took in curious facts; Louis Armstrong was once a coalman, Jelly Roll (as in Morton) was an extremely rude phrase. Sidney Bechet was chucked out of England on rape charges. There was once a band called Spike's Seven Pods of Pepper.

Soirées were almost unheard of on the mainland. Here they were a part of life, musical, literary. Lots of incomers took part. Not islanders.

I noticed a large piece of sandstone in the fireplace.

'We carried it up from the beach,' said Chris. An idea fermented in my mind. It was to do with me being – at least temporarily – a part of this island. And to leave a legacy. I would find a large stone. I would carve a poem on it. I would plant it in a prominent position. How exactly? I had no idea. Except the idea. That was enough for now.

I lay in bed in a state of feverish excitement. Jumbled in my head were my plans for a stone poem and the sounds of Spike's Seven Pods of Pepper.

MONDAY, 22 JANUARY 2001 – DAY NINE

A Giant in a Tiny School – The Wind's Lament

Maybe I needed to relate to something inanimate on the island, something that passed no judgement. Like a stone that would accept my carved letters. I had never carved letters on stone. I had no stone. I had nothing to carve with. I had nowhere to plant it. None of these seemed major obstacles.

Or maybe I needed human beings who came with less luggage. Small ones. Young ones. Today was school day.

A fierce wind sobbed and moaned as I ate my breakfast porridge and from the kitchen window I saw a flock of birds hurled across the sky in a blur of speed. The island felt like a boat riding out a wild storm.

And often there was that sense. A small community huddled against the elements and, unlike urban humans, aware how misplaced was any sense of superiority, any belief that long-term we were in charge.

The wind cut through clothing, through skin, through the soul. I cancelled the planned gardening, staggered like a drunk to the Post Office, where George Ward and I exchanged notes on the difficulties of standing up.

Back home I spent 40 minutes nurturing the fire, then sat at my small inlaid desk and wrote, as the wind shrieked and rattled the windows.

The grocery van from Beal honked its horn, the driver and assistant somehow serving from an open back without the onset of hypothermia.

Monday morning. No commuters driving their Mondeos to the office, no rush hour, no exodus, no nine-to-five culture. What dictated matters here were the tides. I had thought the tides were a necessary inconvenience for the islanders. I was slowly realising they were a protection against the outside world.

Not once this day did the wind draw breath, its wild and lonely lament sobbing round the cottage's two exposed sides. My coal stove, which when shut usually dozed in a soft red glow, this day sparked and fired in restlessness.

And after the morning's writing, my first work visit to the Holy Island Church of England First School (pop: 2).

And guess what – there *was* a school register. This was how Caitlin White called it.

'Molly Luke?'

'Here, miss.'

'Joel Raine?'

'Here, miss.'

Joel pointed outside to the madly swirling day.

'Whirlwind,' he said.

Having only two pupils, while still preferable to a class of 35 howling malcontents in a concrete inner-city comprehensive, wasn't a total dawdle. Keeping them stimulated without a normal class's interaction could be a problem.

But would a concrete comp simply allow parents to turn up and join in? Like Debbie Luke did?

I read and performed my story 'Blubberloop', about a baby-eating giant. Would four-year-olds be terrified? That was the plan.

Joel and Molly beat their chests, stamped their feet and roared like wild animals on request. As did parent and teacher. Suddenly I was in touch with Holy Islanders.

I read from my book of nonsense poems. Molly pointed to the cover illustration.

'Read that one,' she said. It was called 'The Woof Pig'.

'This poem,' I said, with a thought for Holy Island harmony and tradition, 'is called The Woof Guffie' – and I duly (mis)read it.

The session finished. I was forced back out into the real world.

Holy Island village is a small series of grid-like streets and stone buildings, and though the sea is a dominant presence, it is visible virtually nowhere in the village. In the howling gale, I called again at the Post Office to post a letter to son Dylan.

The collection box had a metal disc with '1' written on it. There was only one collection a day. I wondered if this disc was removed when mail was collected and another, also number '1', put in its place. Or was the same one replaced? And what purpose did it achieve?

Thus far, my cottage had been an islander-free zone. Day Nine, and not a single soul had been moved to knock at my door. I was a gregarious animal, a man who needed company around him. I was adapting to the opposite.

A knock at the door. Ross Peart from the Open Gate. A devout Christian but, more important for me, a lively spirit without caginess. He shouted above the wind, 'I've just walked to the castle – and back – brilliant!'

There was something about Ross's enthusiasm, his flushed healthy face, his hunger for this island's natural delights. I felt a soft townie, retreating before weather I should have experienced. I pulled on my coat and strode out.

Thus far, I was relating more to the inanimate. Digging the soil made me close to the island. Gathering driftwood. People were more difficult. I thought of the poet's dictum, 'no ideas but in things'.

I returned to a power cut of 15 minutes. Power cuts were not irregular on the island. Locals became stoical about them. The electricity came from Scottish Power, making Lindisfarne one of the few places to get its energy from a foreign country. That lurking apprehension that the power might fail, added to the island's sense of fragility.

That night in the Manor House I gave Jen Ward a copy of my book *The Last of the Hunters*, which is about my six months working as a fisherman in the North Sea. Would it convince her of my genuine motives? Or was I just eager to please?

TUESDAY, 23 JANUARY 2001 – DAY TEN

Castles, Cats & McGregor

There was something unnatural about a person such as me suddenly being here for 100 days, arriving from nothing, as if I'd dropped from the sky, popped up from the ground. Plus the expectation of an immediate warm welcome. Maybe if I'd been here to lay the drains, build houses, renovate the castle . . . But to write a book about the island?

None of this meant a damned thing to Molly Luke or Joel Raine. I returned to the safe cocoon of the school. We did more storytelling and they opened their café. I liked the prices: ham sandwiches 5p, crisps 1p, chocolate cake 3p, fruit 1p, lemonade 2p. For 20p I pigged out.

Then I made my first trip to Holy Island Castle. The wind and rain had given way to glorious blue and the white sun wobbled over the mainland hills as I took the one-mile stroll from the village, approaching the extraordinary edifice which stood in half-silhouette, across a flat treeless terrain which only accentuated the castle's sense of fantasy.

And if the island's reality was proving hard to adapt to, not so the fantasy. On the approach to this dramatic castle perched on its strange twirl of rock, I was a medieval foot soldier, a fairytale prince on a maiden rescue, an adventurer out to pierce the vampire's wicked heart.

As I climbed the path, the castle's sheer cliff rose dizzily above me. I imagined boiling oil poured down and on the castle ramparts espied Vincent Price in swirling purple robe, driven mad by the memory of his long-dead Leonore.

Shrieking fulmars plunged down like kamikaze pilots. At the path's top I noticed how the castle's rear, rarely photographed, was as ugly as an elephant's arse.

The path took me down the castle's other side, where the stone was faced in a strange blushing pink (more of that later). And more fulmars. Ross Peart had identified them for me as the country's longest living sea-bird (up to 50 years) who laid only one egg, and seemed to have invented mascara.

The castle was shut and barred for the winter. But I, brave Mortimer, would plan to gain entrance. Though not today.

And back to my Manor House garden, where the plot was almost two-thirds dug. I'd filled more than 20 wheelbarrows (or the same wheelbarrow 20 times) with weeds. The activity brought a zen-like concentration and softened my sense of solitude.

In the bar, I ate and drank my wages (a pint of bitter, a chicken korma). The only other resident was Tom Storm, immersed in his *Telegraph* crossword. We exchanged three syllables.

I am a man accustomed – probably over-accustomed – to filling his days with activity. I make lists. I whizz hither and thither. I am the stage plate-spinner, ever-frantic that one plate might wobble, slow and crash.

Mainly, Holy Island did not operate this way. And Holy Island was where I was living.

Next on my list that day was calling on council chairman Ian McGregor. He shared a name, but little else, with the Thatcher bully boy brought in to destroy the miners' union.

Ian and Helen McGregor lived in Crossgate, one of the island's first council houses, built in 1972, a small settlement with surrounding wall.

Despite a curvature of the spine which now affected his breathing and left him needing an oxygen respirator eight hours a night, Ian McGregor was a man of huge energy and ideas. When I knocked at his door, the clear day had given way to a steady and drenching drizzle. He opened the door and gazed at the raindrop which fell from the end of my nose.

He'd come to the island from mainland Northumberland at the age of 18 and had helped establish the new Heritage Centre, the 1,200-vehicle car park, and the terrace of low-cost houses reserved for islanders to combat the holiday-home blight.

Among his other ideas were Holy Island bottled water, a wind turbine to bring power self-sufficiency and a revival of the commercial mussel beds, which lay mainly unharvested. His own enthusiasm for these schemes wasn't often matched by the islanders. Since his arrival in the 1960s, he'd seen control of many of the island establishments pass to non-islanders – the pubs, the shops and so on.

Did he resent it?

'Why should I? If the islanders have lost interest, let the outsiders run things. Either that or we simply become a retirement island.'

What was it about Ian McGregor that appealed to me so much? Maybe the mix – he was an intrinsic part of the island but the island did not put him to sleep.

I walked home as the wind flapped the rain across the street, a wind direct from the harsh North Sea, a wind that tore at buildings and trees and froze on impact. The sun had gone down. The wind became colder, lonelier.

I walked into the cold stone house. The wind and rain had combined to cause mischief in the small kitchen. The former had blown open the door, the latter had flooded the floor and now the wind was rippling the surface of a small but widening lake.

Few people on the island locked their door against intruders. Now I would need to do it against the elements.

The house was cold, empty, the fire unlit. As I stood in my flooded, wind-blown kitchen, a chill descended on me, a depression of a man needing the kind of solace this island could not provide and with almost 90 days still to come.

In the middle of that desolate scene, unashamedly I sobbed.

WEDNESDAY, 24 JANUARY 2001 – DAY ELEVEN

Claiming the Island – Still Invisible

I was beginning to see the nature of this exile. In my recent book *Broke through Britain*, though my penniless state through 500 miles had been physically and mentally draining, I had passed through a moving landscape, each day affording new subject matter, new horizons, new characters, new writing opportunities.

I would suffer no similar physical deprivations on Holy Island. But for 100 days I would be confined to a tiny island, the same people, the same landscape, the same house. I had taken this on board as a general idea. But not as a reality.

I'd had no response from my Post Office advertisement. The islanders were less than hungry to use my services. In the Crown and Anchor, they'd mentioned a leaflet for the forthcoming Caribbean evening in the village hall. I'd offered to stick it through letterboxes. No response. The next day one arrived through my own letterbox.

I dug on at my garden. My retreats were the garden and the school. I had calculated, for no discernible reason, that the plot would need 700 fork insertions. I also calculated I'd already done 500. If that wasn't cause for celebration, what was?

From the garden, I studied the wide landscape. Without the castle, the place would be flat, fairly featureless. Which was like saying that without Stanley Matthews the 1953 Cup final would have been mundane.

My wages this day were plaice and chips in the Manor House. At the bar was Jimmy Brigham, 'Clinker'. I mentioned my idea for carving a poem on to a stone.

'The's bin rock slides near Chare Ends,' Clinker replied. 'Plenty good stones there. Take a look.'

I didn't know why but this small piece of advice, this offer of help from a native islander, made me feel like singing.

And I needed to 'claim' the island itself. What I had not walked, I could not lay claim to. I needed to experience every cove, every footpath, every inlet, every sand dune. I had to gain an intimacy with this island, however reluctant a lover it proved to be.

The resolution put a spring in my step as I strode out that afternoon, heading out on the Straight Lonnen path due north to the little-visited North Shore's coves and bays.

The island was wetter than a dripping sponge, with waterlogged fields. Winter mercifully brought no risk of the pirri-pirri burs, said to have been brought over on New Zealand sheep fleeces, which in summer stuck to dog fur, clothing or long beards, like limpets.

I skirted a puddle the size of Ullswater, across the ghostly, unnerving sand dunes of the links, onwards till suddenly I was on the lip of a giddy perpendicular cliff top at Coves Haven, plunging to rocks and sea below.

The wind, I realised, was at my back.

On the return journey, I caught the profile view of Lindisfarne Castle. This was so dissimilar to, so less dramatic than the usual, much-photographed and painted front view that I felt guilty, like some illicit audience member who's sneaked back-stage and now observed the action from the wings.

The terrain was still treeless. The few skeletal hawthorn bushes were so brittle that the merest brushing cracked off their branches. Only one human and his dog seen on this walk; it was Clinker and his Labrador Susie.

I'd been in two island churches. Now a third, up the little used Green Lane. St Aidan's Catholic Church had none of the normal pomp and ornamentation; it did nothing to revive those uncomfortable childhood memories of force-fed Catholicism. It was a humble hut, rows of tubular alloy chairs, a simple altar on a raised stage whose slatted wooden walls were curiously painted in turquoise emulsion. I almost warmed to it.

It was Wednesday. The Crown and Anchor would be open. The same group of middle-aged men was clustered at the bar. I was a rival cluster at the other end. The same put-down banter with barmaid Kirsty Bevan. I stood again as the invisible man, downed my two pints of John Smith's, coughed, adjusted my jacket, slung the bag over my shoulder.

Well, goodnight, then. Nice seeing you all again.

On the phone to my mother. How much longer would I be there, she asked.

Dunno.

It wouldn't be as long as another 11 days, would it?

Not sure. Sorry.

I stood staring at the replaced receiver a long time.

THURSDAY, 25 JANUARY 2001 – DAY TWELVE

Buns, Runs & Dog Swallowers

My small cottage was slowly accommodating me. Each day its walls absorbed a bit more of my presence. It was used to fleeting visitors, holidaymakers, come-and-go merchants. I was made of more serious stuff.

My mood was more upbeat at breakfast. I almost whistled as I cleared the table after porridge and toast. On a shelf I took down a mystery tinfoil package. Inside were a dozen small nuggets of soda bread made for me by Kitty. They'd gone stale.

The sight of those small, honestly made buns flooded me with longing for my partner. Into the bin with them.

Slowly a shopping pattern was being established. George Ward had already offered to get me some food from Berwick and now the retired Berwick vicar Mike Burden chipped in. I vowed no more mainland shopping trips for me and in a symbolic act returned the vast Sumo wrestler sack to Hector Douglas.

George had lit a bonfire at the far end of my Manor House garden plot. It was cracking its knuckles and swirling its smoke in pursuit of any nearby humans. These included a crocodile of Priory schoolchildren dragging themselves after their teacher's droning voice, a group of surveyors busy with plumb-lines on the Priory walls, and stragglers on Sanctuary Close. I stood and invited the smoke to consume me, which it did, taking me back to childhood.

I'd been over-optimistic about finishing the plot. Its final border seemed to recede ever further, as if, like some Greek myth, the islanders at night were secretly pushing it back, the quicker to drive me mad.

Smoke had tired of me, had lollopped away to surround St Aidan's statue.

I'd been shown more kindness: a loaned bike from solicitor Tim Hardin, who had a weekend cottage on the island. I cycled to Chare Ends. The tide was shut, the causeway covered. As I paused, I encountered another man who would feature prominently in my 100 days. Cleric and author Ray Simpson, who ran the society of St Aidan and St Hilda's, was a bearded bright-faced man who always wore a large wooden Celtic cross round his neck. He was a controversial figure on the island, as I was to find out.

High tide was still one hour distant but the thin strip of sand between sea and dunes made it passable for a cyclist or pedestrian (not a car).

And the entire terrain was mine; silence except the soft whoosh-whooshing of the tiny waves as they inched their way over the last tarmac. A unique experience, cycling across a slowly disappearing terrain, a landscape being swallowed by sea.

Above me, like a Farnborough Air Show formation, a black mass of birds, which, on sudden change of direction, flashed brilliant white underbellies. Pale-bellied Brent geese – seen in flocks of up to 3,000. Only 296 species left to recognise.

I returned home to find the coalman had delivered. No back yard entry. He simply trudged through the house bearing sacks.

I took another solitary run, despite the painful hip. Twilight, two miles to the castle and return. At sea the flashing lights of the Farne Lighthouse, down the coast a twinkle of light from Bamburgh Castle, and perched dizzily on Beblow Crag, Lindisfarne Castle, sucking me towards it, the soft pad of my feet.

These were the moments. When solitariness didn't matter. When there wasn't anything else, just the experience and the castle and me.

I decided to surprise myself for the evening meal. I cooked cauliflower cheese, placed it on the table, left the room, returned and said, 'Gosh – what a lovely surprise! Cauliflower cheese.' I tucked in, thinking where else could you go for a run and see two castles simultaneously?

That night in the Manor House bar, talk was of an island day visitor who'd lost her Border terrier in the dunes. Even the dog's Labrador mate couldn't find the scent.

'It happens,' said George Ward. 'The smaller dogs go down the rabbit holes and when it's wet the sand caves in.'

At the bar Jimmy Clinker nodded. He'd lost two dogs that way, one leaving behind four pups.

Holy Island – swallower of dogs.

FRIDAY, 26 JANUARY 2001 – DAY THIRTEEN

Poetry on Tap – God Underground

Idreamt of my father, pulled this way and that in his coffin by over-active mourners. What could it mean? I tuned in to *Today* on Radio 4 to banish the images. I was in a society where no one had ever met my father. Any talk of him, to any of them, was an abstract. Often I talked to myself.

A letter from my sister-in-law Helen in Rotherham. Little change with nephew

Matthew but my mother had got it into her head I was forced to dig for potatoes to feed myself (I'd found a few in my plot) and had sent me a tenner.

Another contact with my previous life was in the nine books given me by northern writers. I'd finished the first but its effect on me was far from comforting.

Novelist Andrea Badenoch had given me *A Vaudeville of Devils: Seven Moral Tales* by an American writer Robert Girardi (who I'd never read).

There could be no greater contrast with Girardi's world – which spanned the globe – and my own current present confinement on a tiny island. The writer's stories were set in Jerusalem, Japan, the USA, Aden, Australia, Italy.

A man is obsessed with a giant stone face at the ocean bottom; an SS officer's contact with a decadent artist changes his life; a lawyer stakes his career on defending a loathsome gangster against murder; a man trades five years of his daughter's life for a flourishing vineyard; a multi-national take-over is set against Saladin's wars in the Holy Land.

I loved the man's writing, hated how it intensified my claustrophobia. I took an almost childish delight in finding a factual error, when he writes of a character wearing 'a Manchester United rugby shirt'.

I pictured Girardi with huge wings that swept him effortlessly round the world, from where he peered down on a wretched figure locked in a cramped cage. But didn't I know there could be a universe in a grain of sand? And that travel was in the mind?

Course I did.

That afternoon I returned to the garden, lit my own bonfire to destroy the cancerous lump that was blocking my progress. Sometimes the smoke was like thick cotton-wool, other times like wispy grey hair. I danced in attendance at my bonfire, like primitive natives round their island volcano. Some of the lump burnt. Some parts oozed unspeakable liquids, hissed and stayed put. In the Manor House bar Jen Ward, who had started my fishing book, was speaking of island habits.

'People don't go into other people's houses enough,' she said. 'They tend to meet only in pubs.'

This would gave me an idea. If the residents wouldn't come to my house under their own volition, then I'd give them a little nudge. It was time for Mortimer's first Holy Island party.

My meeting with Ray Simpson led to my second island task – painting his bathroom. The paint colour he'd chosen was appalling and I agreed to do it only if he'd allow me to paint a haiku on one wall. He agreed and my series of island poems on unusual surfaces was under way.

Why was Ray Simpson controversial? His society of St Aidan and St Hilda already owned the Open Gate Retreat and bed & breakfast (run by Ross and Jean Peart) and had plans to buy another adjacent property. You might have thought such a move would have been welcome on a place called Holy Island. Far from it. A tension existed between the so-called 'God Squad' and many other inhabitants. The sacred and the profane, and most of their neighbours, lived cheek by jowl here. Tensions had nowhere to go, except rumble under, and occasionally break through, the island's thin crust.

Ray Simpson lived in Marygate, the main street, in a small cottage which included a wee retreat room. His books were about Celtic Christianity. This had lost out during St Cuthbert's time at the famous Synod of Whitby, at the expense of the Roman brand. It was now making a bit of a comeback, 1,300 years later. What *was* Celtic Christianity exactly? A less formal version.

The second meeting of the singing group – renamed by me as the Holy Island Howlers – took place that night in the village hall.

The British are terrible at singing. We mumble semi-tunelessly to hymns we don't know or chant the numbingly tedious 'Here we go, here we go, here we go' at football matches in a way to turn the composer John Phillip de Souza in his grave. Thus our singing seems either incoherent or aggressive.

Which was why, despite myself, I was growing a sneaky affection for these sessions. Someone once wrote one hundred people singing changed the world. We were only around eight. So we could change a bit of it.

Songs resurfaced in my life that, as a rock 'n' roll child, I had not related to for years. Was I really singing aloud 'When I Fall in Love' and 'Some Enchanted Evening'?

I was. And sneakily enjoying it. There was something about our small huddle, in this frozen weather in this tumbledown hall, our brave voices carrying out across the vast dark wastes of the North Sea, a kind of splendid defiance as we stood shivering in our topcoats giving full vent to our lungs.

Being British, not one of us mentioned it.

Afterwards I went subterranean. Religion was beginning to encroach on my life on Holy Island. Inevitable, given that many of the island's active people were involved with it. I was unsure how I felt about this. I had long since abandoned organised religion but if I could sing Nat King Cole, I could go into a chapel.

Each night at 9.30 p.m. a small service was held at the Open Gate's underground chapel, a common practice for all branches of the St Aidan and St Hilda Society. The services were taken from Ray Simpson's book, *Celtic Prayer through the Year.*

The chapel was part nuclear bunker, part Swedish sauna, part place of worship. In one corner a massive wooden cross had been hewn from wood found on the North Shore and dragged across the island by a German called Gert. Gert had cut himself in the process and the cross's splattered blood seemed almost biblical.

The romanticism of dragging materials the width of the island took root in me and would soon flower.

Ross and Jean were there, Chris Holbrook and Derek Pollard, Ray Simpson, a couple more. Today, 26 January, I learnt was St Pauline's Day – the patron saint of widows. I thought of my mother.

And the simple service left me confused. I'd preferred the Holy Island warblers.

That night, with my coal fire still lively, I made a bed on the living-room floor and settled down with book number two.

SATURDAY, 27 JANUARY 2001 – DAY FOURTEEN

Culture Clash – Northumbrian Caribbean

The religious side of Holy Island seemed more than willing to accept me. Not sure if the reverse was true.

And I was – slightly desperately – wanting the indigenous population to accept me. Again, I was less sure about the reverse.

I leapt early from the floor, had breakfast, strode out and was writing at my desk when I first heard the sounds.

They were the sounds of sunny beaches, palm trees, swaying hips, white sands, garlands of flowers, poolside rum cocktails. The sounds came drifting through the grey stone clenched streets of the village. Such were the sounds, I glanced from the window expecting to see native islanders limbo-dancing to the Post Office.

The North Tyneside Steel Band had arrived for that night's concert and were already rehearsing in the village hall. The incongruous sunny sounds, on this island clenched in winter's steely fist, drifted all day long through the streets and even as far as the Manor House garden where I pursued my Herculean task.

I had reached the bottom corner, a place of deep resistance, as if its roots held some dark malevolent secret. I heaved on the fork, making great tearing sounds as up through the soil came large gorgon heads of roots, dragged into the light after decades in the dark.

And as I took my cod-and-chip wages in the bar, I observed Jen Ward and the four generations of her family clustered about.. Father Tom, daughter Jen, grandsons Benjamin and Kieran. I was not a nuclear family devotee. But as I pushed another lump of cod into my mouth, I felt a pang of envy.

The bright weekend weather had brought a few visitors to the island; Americans and French in the bar. I felt envious of them, too, without really knowing why.

The evening was shiver-thin, a clear sky of crystallised stars above the incongruous sight of wrapped and hunched people moving towards the sunshine music from the village hall, my first sight of Holy Island people tempted in numbers from their homes. I had rarely seen more than a handful of residents together. Now there would be one hundred.

Some wore Rasta hats. Some had garlands of flowers. One sported a huge black dreadlock wig. One women had a basket of flowers glued above her headscarf. As if something strange had happened to these people's introspection. Or had I simply misjudged it? Was I trying to simplify human beings?

The 20 young members of the band, playing and swaying in their blue tops, cast an infectious spell over the hall, so that bairns did the congo with grandparents. The Crown and Anchor had laid on spicy Caribbean food, cooked by Kirsty Patterson.

(A quick aside. Only now did I realise there were two Kirstys associated with the pub; behind the bar Kirsty Bevan, in the kitchen Kirsty Patterson. Henceforth the pub would be known in my book as the Sign of Two Kirstys, as the island's penchant for nicknames took a hold of me.)

There was a certain irony in the band's opening number: 'Island in the Sun'.

Several times in my 100 days I encountered occasions which seemed to touch a common island chord. Almost every inhabitant had donated a raffle prize (the proceeds of the evening went to the essential air ambulance rescue service) and, staggeringly, the proceeds, on this tiny island on a freezing January night, reached £1,000, or about £7 per head of the population.

Vicars danced with old ladies, fishermen with children, islanders and incomers mixed freely, competed in the limbo competition. After the band's second long set and the raffle prizes, with matters seemingly winding down, I walked home, made a cup of tea and watched the end of *Match of the Day*.

I was halfway up the stairs, my mind set on bed, when I heard it. The band had begun a third set. The sun had risen again. I walked back down the stairs and pulled on my coat. The hall was again heaving with dancers. And at the end, a custom that took me back to a more innocent age.

'Three cheers for North Tyneside Steel Band!' yelled an islander. Hurrah, hurrah and hurrah.

As Confucius might once have said, you *can* go to the same dance twice.

SUNDAY, 28 JANUARY 2001 – DAY FIFTEEN

Ubiquitous Eddie – Same-Place George

Not that I'd been an intrinsic part of the Caribbean night, you understand. People had said hello, waved, odd bits of chat, but I'd clutched my pint in a peripheral sort of way and often stood with a sheepish grin.

At 10 a.m., remarkably, through the village streets once more came the sounds of the band. After a brief sleep, they were back to more practice. Only a plague of locusts, a tsunami, or a new ice age could prevent this band playing.

I did no digging, no writing, little reading this day. A fair bit of drinking.

First, non-alcoholic, in the Island Oasis Café; ugly as sin on the outside, an intriguing mix of wall hangings, photos and posters inside. It was run by Neil and Cathy Anderson, a cosmopolitan couple who'd provided last night's Caribbean recipes. Outside in the sunlight sat Eddie Douglas – from the supermarket run, remember?

With Eddie I always felt on approval, an island trialist. In nine months the previous year Eddie had collected £2,074 for the air ambulance service. He did this merely by sitting and buttonholing passers-by, who found themselves putting money into his tin because it was much easier than declining. I had never seen anyone decline. I had no idea what might happen, what they might change into. Eddie sat at various village vantage points; some people claimed he could be spotted at more than one simultaneously.

Eddie was the kind of character I could imagine only on Holy Island (supermarket run excepted). To see him walking down Grey Street in Newcastle-upon-Tyne would be as big a surprise as seeing Holy Island castle do the same thing.

And if Eddie seemed ubiquitous on the island, George Ward of the Manor House seemed unipresent (should the word exist), a man whose natural habitat was behind his bar, from where he could reach every shelf, every glass and pump without moving his feet. He pulled drinks here, he held court here, he took bookings here, he spent 20 minutes on the phone to builders here. George, give or take a bit, lived here.

So that on the very rare occasions I saw him emerge from the bar, it was with the realisation – the bar having a raised floor – that he was several inches shorter than imagined.

Nor could I imagine walking into the Manor House to find someone else serving. It would be like going to Santa's Grotto to discover inside the Incredible Hulk.

But, hey, things were to change. The bar would close that day for two weeks of renovations. Where would George go? Where would I go? This was the only bar on the island with any regularity in winter opening. So I'd have no bar to take refuge in, was that it? And I was supposed to be stoical about this?

Maybe it was a reaction to such a sorry situation that led me to drink all afternoon, that kind of hazy freewheeling sense, that delicious drifting into harmless irresponsibility. A session.

For some people this was a way of life. I prefer Hemingway's approach – infrequent but intense.

And the afternoon and evening were hazy. I remember Robert Massey, occasional Holy Island entrepreneur and son of Sue and Clive at the Lindisfarne, inviting me back to tea from the Sign of Two Kirstys, with his girlfriend Charlotte.

I remember him unwisely driving off in his big car to find some steaks (presumably from the Lindisfarne freezer) and pranging the vehicle on the way back. I remember returning to the pub post-steaks, sitting in exactly the same seat and within minutes forgetting I'd ever been away.

I remember walking home at some hour, clambering into bed and thinking what a waste of time and money long drinking sessions were. And the image of a basket of flowers glued on to a headscarf kept coming into mind.

MONDAY, 29 JANUARY 2001 – DAY SIXTEEN

Sloth – Hospitality

As I bent over the toilet bowl and reversed the stomach muscle's normal direction, as tears came to my eyes, a blockage to the nose, as foul-tasting bile forced its way up the throat and the body prepared itself for that horrendous second when the guts heaved their worst and dispelled the foul cocktail of the previous day's semi-digested grub, I found myself lacking a certain enthusiasm for the 84 days ahead.

Holy Island could go hang, but then so could the rest of the universe.

At the afternoon's arts & crafts club in the Heritage Centre I managed the start of a collage before falling asleep. Only one thing appealed on this day, this lifeless, listless, energyless, wasted, useless day. And that was a return to bed. The five women indulged my sloth and carried on making patterns.

I had just returned to my pit, closed my eyes (from which were suspended Olympic weight dumbbells), when a knock came at the door. The rarity of such an event dragged me from the sheets.

A tall thin man stood there, plus a shorter, bright-faced woman.

It was Richard and Mary Binns, who had a holiday cottage in nearby Paradise Row.

'We wondered if you'd care to join us for supper this evening?' asked Richard brightly.

And a man's gotta do, and all that.

I tried not to fall asleep in the pork chop casserole. Their dwelling was called Dove Cottage and had beams made from old ship timbers – see, I was paying attention!

Richard was a retired teacher, Mary owned a small building company in Glasgow. Here's another interesting fact (offered by Mary): Napoleon spent exactly one hundred days on Elba. And another: in the 1940s the locals ran a ballerina off the island (reason unknown).

And here was a photo of the Queen by Paradise Row's outdoor netties on her 1950s visit. No record of her having availed herself.

I thought about two things mainly whilst I enjoyed their hospitality. One – I simply lacked the dedication to become an alcoholic. Even if they sent me to an expensive clinic, I'd be a failure. ('Come on now, Mr Mortimer, we have to drink our 20 units a day if we're to make any real progress. Come along now. It's just a question of will power!') Second, the island was unlikely to attract the kind of flabby complacent second-homers of the Isle of Wight or the Channel Isles. There were no offshore account ruses as per the Isle of Man. No banks at all, actually, nor dentists, doctors, police, cinema, theatre, supermarket, swimming-pool or Spud-U-Like. Those who lived part time here were a different breed. Not that I could ever imagine owning a second home. One's enough for anyone.

At 9.30 p.m. I geared myself up for the journey back home from the Binns'. It was about six seconds. By 10 p.m. I was in bed with a steaming mug of cocoa. I was fit for no one. Even a naked Sigourney Weaver banging on my front door would have been ignored. Maybe.

TUESDAY, 30 JANUARY 2001 – DAY SEVENTEEN

Hanging About for the Dawn – Gothic Light-Show

I woke early, with the post-stupor realisation that someone had actually knocked at my door and invited me for a meal. Such was the invigorating reality of this fact that by 6.30 a.m. I was out padding the deserted streets on a two-mile run.

OK, so the inviters were not native islanders.

I ran the one mile to the castle, no sign of the sun in the pre-dawn sky and only the light of Longstone lighthouse to wink at me. I heard the bumble-bee drone of a small fishing boat heading out to the lobster pots and felt the icing-sugar crunch of frost under my feet. Beyond the half-silhouette of the castle, the sea horizon offered just a hint of light, no more.

I'd planned to run straight home but turned towards the harbour shoreline. Dawn would arrive soon. And no one here to greet it.

For an hour I waited. A flock of unknown birds whirred past like high-speed freckles. Later, in Richard Perry's amazing book, *A Naturalist on Lindisfarne*, I'd discover they were widgeons – and a winter dawn could see flocks of 3,000 cleaving high from the harbour at up to 100 mph.

A shadowy man passed with a dog. I scanned the horizon, the way impatient rock fans scanned the stage for the first view of their inevitably late-arriving hero. I walked about, flapped arms. Behind me the village was merging into light; the windows of the nearby Herring Houses threw back the glowing horizon in molten gold. The upturned herring boats on the shoreline, a monument to the industry's early twentieth-century collapse, defined their hunched shape in the slowly strengthening light.

So where was that blooming sun? I walked to the top of the Heugh, arguing that being 50 ft nearer to a burning globe 83 million miles distant would bring an advantage.

I had, of course, been looking in the wrong spot. Somewhere above the Farne Islands to the south-east came the pierce of a red-hot searchlight. The searchlight escaped from a dark cloud, a single spoke that then multiplied rapidly. The spokes ignited the edges of every cloud, which in turn ignited the sea, and there I was, an apocryphal, biblical scene spread out in front of me.

Later I was back at the school. Joel was away. Molly, Caitlin and me took the art world by storm with a full-blown painting of Blubberloop the Giant and later wandered down to St Cuthbert's beach in search of St Cuthbert's beads, tiny fossilised remains of animals called crinoids, like tiny polo mints.

The beads can be found nowhere else. Nor must they ever be taken from the island. It is said that those who find none, have no heart. Molly found four, Caitlin three. Each donated one to the heartless Mortimer. I shivered. The brilliant dawn of my run had given way to a day of grey cold gloom.

I would spend an entire evening at home, no interruptions. No pubs were open. I lit a fire, made a chicken casserole, wrote, read Richard Perry's book, felt the alcohol continue to drain from my body.

I watched a TV programme on the Congo River, with its vast clouds of migrating birds.

'Ours are as good as that!' I spluttered and realised I was using the possessive.

Something called me back out on to the silent streets at midnight. A moonless night, the village's sparse collection of lamp-posts weakly splashing down their small orange circles; beyond the village confines, the night was gripped tight in a thick black glove.

I walked to Chare Ends, looked out across the dark lonely flats, heard the occasional cry of a bird, saw the smudges of mainland light from Beal up north to Berwick and down south to Seahouses.

Something kept me out there, sent me back on the road to the castle, a solid black curtain of dark.

Until, a remarkable sight. Glimpsed briefly, like a sudden silhouette in a haunting German expressionist film, backlit for one second by the sweeping beam of Longstone Lighthouse, was Lindisfarne castle in all its Gothic glory.

Quickly the night swallowed it again. But wait a moment. The light swept round once more, once more the crag and castle leapt briefly from the dark.

My day had started with the pre-dawn castle and was ending with it displaying for me once more. The island had spoken to me this day, had summoned me twice.

My foothold on Lindisfarne made tiny but important progress.

WEDNESDAY, 31 JANUARY 2001 –
DAY EIGHTEEN

Enter the Stone – Mortimer the Thief

The final day of an endless month: my father's death, my nephew's emergency operation, my exile to Holy Island. Here was something else. My mother was to go into hospital for a hip replacement operation.

And my plan not to leave the island was in tatters. This was my mother, aged 85. In hospital. Frightened. And here was me.

I retreated to the school. Caitlin, Molly and I studied our Blubberloop painting of yesterday. We all agreed. It was crap. We began Mark II.

How many people ever pick up a paintbrush after childhood, except to Dulux the living-room wall? And why was that, exactly?

The new Blubberloop was much improved, in a kind of post-post-modernist deconstructionist kind of way. Maybe I liked the way it expressed the unfathomable alienation of the contemporary urbanite in a techno-violent society. Or did I just like Blubberloop's big belt buckle?

I was now determined to find a stone, to express my time on this island via its natural resources. I could never 'belong' like the indigenous population belonged. Any attempt would be fraudulent. But I could relate to the island in a way none of them had. Just watch me.

Behind the white-painted school, I walked along Tripping Chare path above the western shoreline known as the basin (because it kept emptying and filling up?). The sea was gnawing away at the land here, chewing at the path's rock and mud so at times it all but disappeared and, if you didn't watch your step, so did you.

Below me, a gaggle of schoolchildren was crocodiling its way across the beach. It was low tide, the basin had been emptied, leaving only small rivulets of water. In the distance Dinky cars crossed the causeway; it was a sunny windless day, the mainland bathed in soft light. Cheviot – Northumberland's highest peak – was clearly visible, as was its smaller but more pointy neighbour Hedgehope.

The stillness suggested an unchanging scene, whereas billions of gallons of water were gearing up for what they did twice daily – flood this basin, then empty it. And we humans hadn't quite sussed the reasons why.

I heaved up several large rocks for inspection, finally opting for a longish tablet, grey, a flattish if not even surface the shape of a right-angled triangle, one sharp corner lopped off. Beneath this stone teemed an entire society of bugs, crabs and things that jumped up and down or waved antennae. I waved back. This stone would do.

I staggered with it 20 metres to the landslipped slope, greasy with mud.

I dropped it, then flipped it up and over, up and over. Sometimes it slid back, just as I did on the slippery slope. I grabbed bits of grass, tottered about, heaved the stone. Beneath me the gaggle of schoolchildren watched this strange mud monster's antics with a lump of rock.

At the slope top, with rasping breath, I faced 250 metres of path. I staggered drunkenly in 50 metre bursts. My knees buckled, I resembled a contestant in the World's Strongest Man Pyramid Carrying Heat.

I clunked the stone down by the school wall, arguing it would take a determined thief to nick it.

Are you fed up with me mentioning my Manor House garden plot? No less than I was of digging it. Gardening non-interest had turned to zen concentration and back again to tedium, and the final bit was a horrendous mass of thick weeds, rotting newspapers, sludge and unnameable powders and substances. Almost two weeks I had been about it. Time to move on.

Another Wednesday night. At the Sign of Two Kirstys, the Men's Club would be in session and me a sort of non-speaking member. I had not given up. Soon enough, I argued, they'd be slapping me on the back, laughing at my brilliant jokes and standing another round.

This is how it was. A fierce fire blazed in the grate. The Men's Club were clustered close at the bar, leaving me at the other end, curved away from the blaze. Occasionally one club member would move to a bum-warming stance by the fire, rub the seat of his trousers for a time, then move away. One by one the members did this.

I wanted to do it, too. My bum was cold round the corner and, anyway, I wanted to be part of the ritual. I realised I could as much move into that circle and take up bum-warming stance as I could walk on the moon.

There was progress, though, of a sort. On my second pint, I engaged in conversation Stuart McMurdo, a big genial bearded man who worked on the rigs. I recounted the search for the stone, the struggle up the beach and how the cliffs were subject to landslip, being eaten away.

From behind me came a voice without a tinge of humour. The speaker had his back to me and never once turned.

'That's because some buggers keep stealin' wor stones.'

I walked home soon after, the frost as thick as a pelt. Out of the sky, like in the Monty Python cartoon, a huge accusing finger came down and singled me out. 'Mortimer!' boomed the deep voice. 'You are accused of stealing the very fabric of Holy Island!'

THURSDAY, 1 FEBRUARY 2001 – DAY NINETEEN

Tealess on Lindisfarne – The First Gathering

Holy this island may have been but there were times it seemed particularly godless. Take this day, the start of a new month. We were still deep in winter.

A few hardy visitors ventured across the causeway and a pretty pathetic sight they made too as they drifted round the shuttered village in their anoraks, their faces drawn into that kind of abject resignation the British adopt when they discover not a decent cup of tea is to be had anywhere.

No pubs were open, no cafés, no hotels, not even – on a Thursday afternoon – the Post Office. The castle was shut. Only the Heritage Centre or the Priory offered an open door. The asceticism of Cuthbert lived on.

In the school we put the finishing touches to the Blubberloop painting. Caitlin unearthed old documents and photos. In 1852 there had been 71 children between the ages of birth and four. Now it was four. The island's population at that time had been 553. Now 150. What other place in the UK had suffered such decline?

And, of course, the Manor House garden was still unfinished. I took up the garden fork once more, with as much enthusiasm as Sisyphus rolling the boulder one more futile time up the hill. My pile of discarded weeds was becoming substantial enough to feature on any topographical survey of the island.

This was the day of my party, an occasion which left me strangely nervous, as if somehow it would define my relationship with the island. To combat my nerves I took my stiff hip for a run across the flats. Even at low tide shallow rivers (known as 'goats') persisted. Running through them reminded me of a cowboy film posse splashing through shallow rivers in pursuit of bank robbers. The crime metaphor was extended with the endless bird footprints on the sands in convict tunic pattern.

Out here on these vast flats, alone, total silence, everything seemed to make sense.

This was my party guest list: George and Jen Ward of the Manor House, Ray Simpson of the Society of St Aidan and St Hilda, Jean and Ross Peart of the Open Gate, jazz man Derek Pollard and his aromatherapist partner Chris Holbrook, Mike Burden of the driftwood icons, Anne Burden of painting and arts & crafts, plus school-teacher Caitlin White. Only later did I realise the list contained not one indigenous islander.

And how did they see my party invitation? As some genuine social gesture or merely another chance to gather material for the book? Come to that, how did *I* see it? Not just the party but the entire experience. Had I questioned myself enough on motivation, justification? Not a day passed but that in some way I questioned my being here. But at my core was a stubborn nugget that insisted I should see it through, ride out whatever flak might come my way, write the book and let it speak for itself.

Thus I concluded as I put out some salt 'n' vinegar crisps and stuck the wine and beer in the back yard which, let's face it, was cooler than the fridge. It was the only back yard I knew with a view of two castles.

Only Caitlin was unable to make it. The phenomenon of the rest was them arriving all within 30 seconds of each other, partly due to the small nature of the village, partly because for them 8 p.m. meant just that. No taxis to be got, buses to be missed, traffic jams to be negotiated. At 7.59 p.m. they left their houses and at 8 p.m. they were at mine.

There was no music at the party, no dancing, no illegal substances. I'd devised some games which people took to with differing levels of enthusiasm. Ray Simpson's imitation of Posh Spice was only marginally successful. No one got violently drunk or vomited. No broken glasses. No sex (as far as I could see). George Ward looking slightly at sea away from his bar stamping ground; Jean Peart savouring with increasing relish the chance to do impersonations; Ray Simpson sitting quietly, defended by his giant Celtic cross.

At l a.m., just as they had arrived together, they all left together. I cleared up, washed glasses, emptied the nibble bowls. By which time all the guests would be safely tucked up in bed.

My party had, I admitted, been a slightly manufactured affair. But then, I argued, what party wasn't?

FRIDAY, 2 FEBRUARY 2001 – DAY TWENTY

The Prewar Birdman – Banjo Bill

Ross Peart had lent me a book on the Celtic calendar. The first day of February had been the feast of Brigid, saint of healers, poets and smiths. Brigid had been the sixth-century Abbess of Kildare and after her death an open fire was kept alight by the abbey walls for 100 years, with only females allowed to draw near. This had little to do with Holy Island but I liked it.

More relevant was the calendar quotation from St Augustine. 'That which is called the Christian religion existed among the ancients, and never did not exist from the beginning of the human race until Christ came in the flesh, at which time true religion, which already existed, came to be called Christianity.'

This struck me as conceited tosh. The same kind of dangerous claim to a permanent moral superiority had no doubt at different times been made by Muslim, Hindu, Sikh or whoever, all equally as bogus.

Religion was beginning to occupy my thoughts in a way it rarely did. The Open Gate on this foul morning, which saw me reluctant to leave the warmth and security of my bed, was full of Christians. They talked about God in a way few of us did in pagan Britain.

Why couldn't I talk about God like that? I suspected he didn't exist but I was giving him a lot of thought. Christianity, I realised, was based on the worship of a supreme being. I had only two problems with that. The worship bit and the supreme being bit.

Of more immediate substance than God was my stone, still slouching against the school wall. And in the teeming rain.

'It's shale,' said Ross Peart on inspection. 'You might get away with chiselling it. Or it might just splinter.'

Ross clutched in his hand my shopping list. I was totally dependent on a small group of people for my Berwick supermarket supplies. Making your list in the kitchen, rather than responding to the subtle sales ploys lurking in every supermarket aisle, meant you spent around half as much as you normally did and still rarely went wanting.

I'd now finished the second book given to me by northern writers. This was a rare and valuable volume, *A Naturalist on Lindisfarne* by Richard Perry, an out-of-print collectors' item published in 1946, with the jacket price of 15 shillings (or 75p to you). Children's novelist David Almond was the provider.

This was a time almost out of memory, long before any natural world TV documentaries from David Attenborough or the like, long before we became blasé about being spoon-fed brilliant wildlife documentaries from the world's most exotic spots. Few of us today would read such a closely detailed wildlife book. Modern ones tend to be of the glossy coffee-table variety, big on photos.

Perry wrote vividly of the island's human population but his first love was obviously the 300 species of bird life that annually visit Holy Island. The author would sit whole days, bunkered in the shell of an old car on the North Shore in the depths of winter merely for a quick sighting. No big cash bounty for him from the film-makers; just the satisfaction of seeing and recording in print.

Why so many birds? Five reasons, wrote Perry. The island was halfway house on many flight paths, the most coastal point between Northumberland and Shetland, the mud-flats and inshore waters offering excellent protection, plus bumper feeding. And the Farne Islands were close by.

Each tide, said Perry (quoting fellow naturalist George Bolam), lugworms threw up 4.5m casts and displaced 900 tons of sand and mud. Flocks of up to 12,000 birds (scoter and scaup) had been recorded and even (in 1895) an albatross.

Perry's book, which in a way totally refocused me on the island, was both old-fashioned and modern. He wrote of 'ecology' some 20 years before it entered most people's consciousness or vocabulary. How many people in 1946 were viewing nautical oil pollution with concern? And his fold-out island map emphasised how little, in half a century, the island had changed; both its strength and weakness.

That night I sang again in the village hall with the Holy Island Howlers. The weekly session, the sense of routine, was good for me, made me a part of things. With the Manor House refit, Jen Ward was absent. I was secretly relieved, in case she quizzed me again about what would be in the book. I was a bit scared of Jen Ward.

An old man was on the stage, strumming a banjo, or more strictly a banjolele. There was a twinkle in his eye and a sense of mischief about him that didn't fit our conceptions of old age. 'Something has gone out of them,' said Larkin about the old, and our modern society has left them without a role in life, has shunted them off to dribble their inactive lives away in forgotten nursing homes.

The man was Bill Nelson, 84-year-old father of Lesley Andrew, herself a weekend holiday occupant at Wild Duck Cottage along with husband Roger.

Bill lived near me in Paradise Row and the island's nickname culture soon got to me as I renamed him Banjo Bill. He'd played at the two previous concerts, sang George Formby numbers but also wrote his own. He'd just entered one for the George Formby Song Competition due in Blackpool in the autumn. It was a cheeky thing called 'I Asked Her If She'd Do It And She Did'. I asked him if he'd sing it and he did.

It included such deliciously dotty rhymes as *It was all so very sudden/I was finishing me pudding/And she asked me if I'd do it and I did*. Bill was bright enough anyway but when he sang an extra bulb seemed to light up in him. For reasons I couldn't totally explain, I knew I needed to see a lot of Banjo Bill during my stay.

Culturally the night then changed greatly. I fell in with some of the island's young turks, drank late, was invited back to a house and walked in to see a porn channel playing on a giant screen, a big joint being rolled on a table.

The trouble was, my sex drive still seemed to be wavering on the other side of the causeway. And though I'm partial to a bit of weed now and again, this particular moment was neither now nor again.

SATURDAY, 3 FEBRUARY 2001 – DAY TWENTY-ONE

Job Lots – Holy Island Board Game

Funny about the sex thing. Part of me believed the creative drive and the sexual drive were closely linked, which meant if the latter fizzled out you'd end up staring at a blank piece of paper in your writing sessions.

So I liked the stimulation of a healthy sexual appetite. But I didn't feel that hungry on Holy Island.

There were other distractions. Odd jobs were piling up. I still had to finish the Manor House garden. I also had the painting and haiku on Ray Simpson's bathroom. I'd agreed to help paint the outside window frames at the Island Oasis Café. Now Chris and Derek of the Stables, seemingly oblivious to my horticultural shortcomings, asked for their own garden to be made over.

Another malevolent day. A programme on Radio 4 about Wordsworth contained his advice for writers – get out there and walk. I responded to Bill immediately, pulled on my greatcoat and before you could say 'daffodils' I was wandering lonely as a cloud.

The constant rain had left the island saturated. I walked up Crooked Lonnen, almost impassable with mini-lakes. (I'd already seen three versions of the word 'lonnen'. There was 'lonnin' and 'loning'. Here, on a County Council Rights of Way Notice on a telegraph pole, was a fourth, 'loaning'. I decided later to check the correct spelling. The *OED* has no record of any version.)

Walking due north across the island, Bamburgh and Holy Island castles, clearly visible, seemed remarkably similar, both perched on perpendicular rocks, steep at the front, at the rear descending in a series of right angles. Seen from other perspectives, the castles were totally dissimilar.

Both had been extensively rebuilt in modern times; Holy Island by Edwin Lutyens, Bamburgh by the titled Armstrong family (still in residence). Few people know that Bamburgh was once the capital of England.

I slipped and slid through the mud, a circular route skirting the castle and back. Few visitors this day, though the flatness of the terrain allowed me to plot the progress of all other walkers throughout the entire length of the ramble, like counters in a board game.

I locked on to a woman in a red bobbled hat and tracked her so close that when we finally passed, 45 minutes later, she felt like an old friend.

Most people would claim Holy Island is bridgeless. Which is to forget the humble wooden affair spanning a deep cut at the rear of the castle. In the field back from the castle a flock of sheep (whose overall island numbers exceeded that of humans) jostled round the just-filled circular feeding station like bargain-hunters at the sales counter.

I'd been thinking about Banjo Bill. I called on him. His house, in the small Paradise Row Terrace, had no road nor path to it, just grass. He sat in his kitchen looking like some wild Gothic scientist against a backdrop of glass demi-johns in which he brewed his own wine and beer. The kitchen was cluttered with brewing gear, resembling the back room of a speakeasy during prohibition.

Bill's high regard for George Formby seemed just right. I'd always thought of Formby as a complex character whose silly screen persona and simple-minded image belied his excellent lyrics and melodies. Bill, and Tom Storm from the Manor House, had recently performed 'Mr Woo' in public. And with a combined age of 175.

Several people called on Bill every day. His nature was the antithesis of the slightly dour Holy Island temperament. Bill was the island's official cheerer-upper.

The thermometer was plunging, the wind was rising. My home, the Cuddy House, was on the corner of Fenkle Street and St Cuthbert's Square, and its two external sides meant the cold stone sucked out the heat unless the fires were well stacked. Though fire-lighting was a long process with this grate, it was necessary. Not just for the heat. The pulsing red heart fortified me.

Day Twenty-One and for the first time a sign outside the Ship – MEALS SERVED. I walked in. The Ship was unlike the other Holy Island pubs/hotels. The Lindisfarne bar was small, hidden away; in the Manor House George's close proximity always personalised a visit; the Crown and Anchor, though it welcomed island visitors, exuded the sense of a local. The Ship, on the other hand, had manifestly set out its stall for tourists; the polished wooden floor; brass portholes; framed display of knots; polished ship's wheel; carefully treated rough stone walls, the piped music, open plan bar, the expensively printed menus.

The owners, Peter and Linda Goldsbrough, were retiring to Cyprus. As Peter said, 'From an island totally dependent on tides, to one where they don't exist.'

Cyprus – all that endless sun, sea and sand. Too much.

'So what have you done to deserve 100 days on Holy Island?' he asked me. He himself was obviously ready to leave, and the slight cynicism of the question made me realise how fiercely defensive I could feel about this place, which at other times I wanted to blow out of the water.

I headed home in wind and rain that had ceased to be a laughing matter. I banked up the fire, spread cushions on the living-room floor and stretched out.

SUNDAY, 4 FEBRUARY 2001 –
DAY TWENTY-TWO

Taking the Wafer – The First Cut

Day by day I was sucked into the island a little more. This happened merely by my being there. It happened whether others wanted it or not, whether I wanted it or not.

And my main activity, the early draft of the book, was a thing removed. I showed it to no one nor spoke in detail of it. After each writing session I folded the book away, unseen.

Some days I excused myself from writing for as long as possible. Other days it was my only lifeline. The writing was raw, primitive, unsophisticated. I could discern no pattern.

I awoke to the fire still glowing. I had met an 80-year-old ex-teacher from Edinburgh, Dorothy Walton, who had spent much more time than me on remote islands, including two years on Skye. Dorothy was bright, unpredictable, and had said to me: 'Take communion with me on Sunday.'

Communion? All that Christian cannibalism!

I agreed I'd go to the 10.30 service. I wanted to see the vicar David Adam in action, for one thing. He was another one with a mischievous demeanour and I'd not known any other vicars who were ex-coal miners, or who'd dug the garden stripped to the waist.

He began the service in the draughty thirteenth-century St Mary's Church, as the wind tumbled and rumbled round the ramparts. About 20 brave souls present. No young ones.

Adam was unusual. In his sermon, he pulled faces, grimaced; he laughed out loud on some occasions, injected colour and life into the normal grey monotone of the church sermon.

'A lot of pleasure-seeking in the world,' he said, 'but not much joy.' He spoke of a person with a task but no vision – a drudge. A person with a vision but no task – a dreamer. And one who had both – a prophet. Or, I thought, an artist?

Someone stuck the hymn numbers up like old-fashioned cricket scores. Not everyone knew the tunes. Communion arrived. A slow procession made its way to the sanctuary, including Dorothy. I hung back. After a while, I thought 'What the hell' (if you'll excuse the phrase). I kneeled at the font. David Adam stuck the wafer in my hand. I put it in my mouth where it sucked all the moisture from my tongue. David Adam offered the chalice.

'Drink this, the blood of Christ.'

It tasted like the cheap VP wine we used to get from the offie.

There was a fleeting second. Don't ask me what, but in that fleeting second something got to me.

Later I gave Dorothy tea and biscuits. She was articulate about her religious faith. I tried to be religious about my lack of it and showed her the short piece I had handed out to mourners at my father's funeral.

It read as follows:

> When the sun went down that night, it said goodbye to him on earth. Yet soon he would be the part of that sun, part of that whole great force that claims us, takes us, and builds its own strengths from us, even as we pass from our loved ones. Feel that sun, its goodness and warmth. You are feeling the goodness and warmth that was part of him. This can never die.

And here on Holy Island, attempting to carve poems on to rocks. Was this not all part of the same thing?

Dorothy put the sheet in her pocket without comment.

Weather I had previously shunned, I now went out to seek, as if this act was a confirmation of something. So that when Ross Peart called, invited me, in this ferocious weather, to the exposed cliff tops at Scar Jockey, I pulled on my boots.

We drove to the castle and walked on to the raised exposed path, the site of the former tramway bringing lime from the island's northern quarry to the kilns.

There seemed no way the driving sleet could ever touch land, carried as it was, at high horizontal speed, by the ferocious, unstoppable wind. To walk forward risked death from both hypothermia and from the sleet's thousand cuts. To walk backwards meant to risk falling off the cliff. Thus as we walked we revolved slowly, like chickens on spits.

Somewhere out there in the whirling swirling tumult was the North Sea. You could neither open eyes long enough to spot it, nor properly identify it; the churning grey sea, the grey sky and the grey stabbing sleet were all as one.

A good day for a power cut. It happened at 3 p.m., as many were about to pull the roast from the oven or settle down to Newcastle *v* Southampton on television. It lasted 2½ hours. Locals explained the not infrequent cuts in three ways: (1) swans flying into cables; (2) motorists running into causeway poles; (3) Scottish Power being crap.

I built an ingenious lighthouse contraption of night-lights, saucepans and mirrors, with which I could read the 28 Sunday supplements. As I settled down to test it in the growing gloom, the electric came back on.

Newcastle's Sky game was cancelled. My muddled romanticism wanted Holy

Island to be satellite-free, the same instinct that saw our holiday shots of exotic foreign climes always carefully angled to exclude the local McDonalds.

What dishes there were (none of the pubs had the service) were secreted round the back of buildings.

There were echoes of this instinct that night in the Sign of Two Kirstys. A small huddle of drinkers gathered against the elements, which beyond the walls roared and sobbed and ran havoc over the island, while Kirsty Patterson stoked up the roaring fire. Something basic. Something primeval. At the bar local artist Nick Skinner and community bus driver Hector Douglas were locked in conversation. Their subject? The multi-scanning efficiency of Windows 98.

MONDAY, 5 FEBRUARY 2001 – DAY TWENTY-THREE

The Portage of Gilbert – A Thousand Quid in the Air

The weather was extreme. I needed to be extreme too. In five days time was the second highest tide of the year, 5.3m. I decided to spend it in the causeway refuge box, that slightly precarious hut on stilts which was the last resort by those caught napping, either via misread tide tables or a broken-down vehicle.

No reason for doing this. But the decision left me strangely elated.

A word about my small island. It hasn't always been called Holy Island or even Lindisfarne. In the sixth century the British called it Medcaut, while the Saxons referred to this stretch of coast as Farneland (after which came Lindisfarne). The name could be Celtic. Or Norse. Or Anglo-Saxon. No one knows. It could mean Land of the Fen Dwellers. Or Island of the Pilgrims within the Slake (slack water). Or Land of the Lindis (the freshwater stream that flowed into the slake from the mainland marshes). As I said, no one knows.

But in filthy weather such as this, it was worth thinking of those fourteenth-century unfortunates, who were paid sixpence to stand at Snook End and look out for marauding Scots. You could get invaded two ways, you see. From the mainland or, like the Vikings, from the sea. The Vikings were mean. They invaded when the tide was shut and no one could run away.

Oh, there had been another name too: *insula sacra*.

In this razored cold, myself and the entire school went for a walk, out along Fiddlers Green past St Mary's Church and on to the exposed Heugh, where Molly and Joel skidded over the frozen puddles and leapt from great heights into the unfrozen ones.

Across on the mainland the heavy snow on the Kyloe Hills emphasised the arctic conditions – coast, sea, sky, not a vestige of colour, a monochrome panorama.

On the return journey, the children, Caitlin and I called at the tiny Boiler House Chapel secreted at the back of the United Reform Church, whose wall had a striking mosaic cross made by villagers from pottery fragments found at the local rubbish tip. The chapel shared a feature with the Windmill Theatre. It never closed.

That afternoon, in the middle of a charcoal drawing at the arts & crafts class, the cry went up: 'The air ambulance is coming!'

This was to pick up not the infirm but the £1,000 cheque from the Caribbean evening. A huddle of people were waiting at the West End of Marygate. Unfortunately, the helicopter, a Yellow Squirrel, decided to land in Sanctuary Close. The huddle ran through the village in pursuit.

The helicopter landed in a great whirring of insect wings. Out clambered the crew. Handshakes, photographs with a mock giant cheque, a few exchanged words, then back on board. The bird throbbed back into life, rose, uncertainly at first, hovered, then swept away in a wide arc above the Heugh as we waved it on its way.

That moment – that small huddle of people handing over £1,000 to a service they relied on – symbolised just how unlike most places Holy Island is. And as the helicopter disappeared from sight and sound, and we, the huddle, slowly dissolved, that sense of the island, its independence and simultaneously its interdependence, was never stronger.

I'd named my stone Gilbert and that afternoon dumped it in the back of Caitlin's car, then lugged it through Mike and Anne Burden's house to the garden forge shed, wherein I would do my stuff.

I lugged a stone in and carried a hot water bottle out. The previous two nights the cold had seeped through the walls, the blankets, the sheets and even my skin.

Despite the weather I ran out to the castle and back. The cold was no good for my hip. I knew it was osteo-arthritis. I hated the word 'arthritis'. It suggested the old, the senile, the incontinent, the dysfunctional, the stuff of nightmares.

Just as Dennis Potter had called his cancer Rupert, after the man whose tabloid excesses so coarsened and de-educated Britain, so I would give a name to this hip. A stone called Gilbert. A hip called Arthur.

Chris Holbrook lent me a pocket-sized book, *Millennium Stones* by Richard Kindersley, a sculptor commissioned to create ten giant edifices cut from Caithness stone. These magnificent creations were now positioned in the town with inscriptions from the likes of Goethe, T.S. Eliot, Shakespeare and St Augustine.

I sat up late at night, inspired by this mix of the craftsman, the artist and the natural substance. And thought of little Gilbert.

THURSDAY, 6 FEBRUARY 2001 – DAY TWENTY-FOUR

The Church and Flatulence – Grinding Out a Result

The hot water bottle produced a snugger night's sleep.

Before the stone poem, the bathroom poem.

Ray Simpson had chosen this haiku of mine for the wall, inspired by St Aidan's statue:

Slowly it changes
the stone statue's
smile.

I stood, for the first time, in a vicar's bathroom. Few writers have painted a haiku in one. It was a nondescript affair, sink, shower, loo, all painted in deathly white. At the top was a tiny frosted-glass window.

'My office is the other side,' said Ray. 'If women use the loo, and I'm working, they have to be careful not to fart.'

Ray produced some paint-brushes stiffer than a guardsman on parade. A force 12 would not have disturbed a single bristle.

Paint? He produced a large tin of cheap stuff, colour 'Rocha'. It resembled several gallons of milk into which had been squeezed a single blueberry. The 2.5l tin had cost £4.00, cheaper than lager but with the same spreading quality. Like thin gauze.

I realised never before had I been close to the domestic nitty-gritty of a cleric's life, nor given such aspects much thought, maybe because our priests and vicars were such detached, distant figures, so uninvolved with the nasty realities of life.

I borrowed brushes from Ross Peart at the Open Gate and set to. One hour later the first coat was done. 'Coat' may be overstating it. As I paused to study my handiwork, the visiting veggie van honked its horn outside. I spent £8 on a few veg – expensive but it stopped the money going to the supermarket.

Time for my 'wages'. Ray handed over half a stottie (traditional north-east bread bun). 'Help yourself to cheese and coleslaw,' he said and vaguely waved a hand towards nothing much at all. I dug about in the kitchen and came up with a few bits and bobs.

Half a day in a vicar's bathroom was enough for one session. Plus my master plan to redefine Holy Island in my own image was ready for another stage. Gilbert was waiting.

We urbanites rarely get to grips with raw materials. How often are we closely involved with the natural stuff of the planet? And shouldn't that be the most necessary relationship?

'Please, m'lud. I do chop logs sometimes!'

Is that the best you can come up with?

'Yes, m'lud!'

Pathetic.

Gilbert had dried considerably overnight and lay slumped on its side, cancerous with lumps. Mike Burden lent me protective goggles, mask and a thick apron, and handed me the electric sander. I felt like a real workman.

I turned on the tool, lowering it to the stone's surface. The bad-tempered whine reminded me of the dentist's drill. Sparks flew off the surface on impact, plus a projection of fine dust. The tool's power throbbed in my hands. From Gilbert rose an evocative stench, like something deep in the sea, something dark, secret and brooding. I thought of the book *The Kraken Wakes*.

That pungent stench – I was in touch with the island.

Within ten minutes the shed was thick with dust. I opened the window and door for ventilation as bit by bit the sander flattened down Gilbert's lumps. After an hour I removed the goggles and in the mirror saw my Lone Ranger mask impression.

Despite the mouth mask I had enough dust in the lungs to qualify for an NUM pension and my hands were vibrating like tuning forks.

I liked the muck, the noise, the gear. Gilbert was flattening out nicely. I had no idea what would go on him, word-wise.

But I was doing things. And the Manor House plot, I decided, was finally finished. Or perhaps I could say 'abandoned'. I returned home to find on my doorstep a chilli, courtesy of Jean Peart. That moment was my happiest thus far on the island.

And that evening, en route to the Open Gate, I spotted one of the island's rarest species. Rarer than a red-headed bunting. Rarer than a pine grosbeak. It was moving slowly down the length of Marygate. I stopped and said 'Gosh!'

You simply never saw them, you see. Not native to the island, nor known to visit. The species was depressingly common in cities – but here?

It moved slowly down past the Post Office, turned into Fiddler's Green. I ran in pursuit. It moved through three sides of a square. Prior Lane, Crossgate, back into Marygate. I looked about. No other witnesses. Would the locals believe me?

The rare species finally moved in the direction of the causeway and was gone, picking up speed.

I had spotted my one and only police car seen on Holy Island.

Had there been some major crime? A letter insufficiently stamped? A sweet wrapper dropped in Marygate? Had a motorist pulled away in second gear, contrary to Highway Code instructions? Possibly a shirt had been incorrectly ironed?

How strange that realisation; that despite the island's obvious tensions and conflicts (and I heard of a few punch-ups), the police car looked exactly what it was here – an alien species.

WEDNESDAY, 7 FEBRUARY 2001 – DAY TWENTY-FIVE

More about God – The Magic Castle

Holy Island was tiny. But people could still live on it in total invisibility. Take David Robinson, up there in the castle. I trekked up to see him. In the next 75 days, I saw him only once again and that was at a public meeting.

I'd stayed up late working on the stone poem. I finally went to bed clutching the notebook, knowing sleep would be intermittent and I'd need to work on the *magnum opus*.

Around 6 a.m., on the sixth awaking and draft, I concluded the poem was finished.

I threw it away the next day. Started again.

And before the castle trek, my third book from northern writers, which I'd just finished – *Sacred Roads* by Nicholas Shrady, donated by my novelist and playwright partner, Kitty Fitzgerald.

Each book I related to my own 100-day existence here. No problem with the latest. The author, a Catholic, embarked on six separate pilgrimages, each identified with a world religion; journeys to find the heart of Buddhism, Judaism, Christianity, Hinduism and the Sufi (part of Islam). He journeyed both through the world and his own soul. He was sometimes close to death. He spoke to mystics, read the texts, confronted real holy men and fraudsters. He crossed the globe in search of answers. And found none. The more he searched, the more his faith was tested. In many ways he found the religions, or the pilgrim sites, commercialised, tawdry, exploitative. It was a journey into darkness.

What he had looked for throughout the world, I was probing on a tiny remote island in the North Sea. The difference in scale was immaterial. A universe could be in a grain of sand.

I thought of those thousands of pilgrims trekking their way to seek salvation at some ordained Holy Place. They came on pilgrimage here, too.

Inside me, I felt it was wrong. Travel without expectation.

As I did up to the castle. Property manager David Robinson had agreed to open up and confided a closely guarded method of access. It involved secret handles and locations and I was sworn not to reveal the details, even under threat of severed tongue, pulled out toenails or racked limbs (I was obviously getting into castle mood).

The grey-haired David Robinson was close to retiring but had just been promoted. In his new job he was given a cottage. In his old one he had a castle. His domicile now was in Thropton, Northumberland.

He, his wife Susan and a staff of three were employed by the National Trust to maintain this extraordinary edifice, which was both an essential part of Holy Island (its best known landmark) but also a place apart, where islanders never trod from one year to the next.

His giddily high mullion-windowed lounge felt like the captain's cabin of some great galleon. Only sky was visible through the double-glazing, which, according to David, was useless.

'For heaven's sake, we're stuck 120 feet in the air, three miles out in the North Sea – what use is double-glazing here?'

He was part court jester, part sergeant-major. He bounced me round the castle with a mixture of enthusiasm and discipline.

Its massive oak doors, curved arches, sturdy columns and medieval atmosphere belied its mainly Edwardian fakery, the design of Edwin Lutyens at the start of the twentieth century. It had never really been a castle, more a fortified battlement built by Henry VIII from the stones of the Lindisfarne priory, knocked to bits in the sixteenth century when the king dissolved all the monasteries.

'It's a laughing stock, if you ask me,' said David, showing an alarming disregard for that which he looked after. 'It's not even a fortress. In the Jacobite rebellion in 1715, two men walked up, captured it and ran up the Scottish flag. Fortress? Ha!'

And the castle walls groaned and rumbled at such libellous character assassination.

David bounced me on. The castle consumed him and after a short time he'd built up such a head of steam I suspected that if I'd simply skulked off his narration would have continued.

Into the Ship Room, from whose ceiling was suspended a replica three-masted Dutch merchantman, and whose vast fireplace could have hosted five-a-side games. There was strange Flemish furniture, plus a wind indicator, an unusual wall design/instrument created by McDonald Gill, brother of sculptor Eric. Its painted surface included Northumbrian castles, Holy Island and the defeat of the Spanish Armada, complete with thousands of teeming figures in the style of Breughel.

The strange pink exterior on the castle's wall, he told me, was called harling, a mixture of lime putty, horse and yak hair. Yak hair?

People queued up to get married here; in and out within an hour, several hundred pounds lighter in the pocket.

What did the villagers think of the National Trust?

'I'm not sure they like it.'

What did they think of David Robinson?

'A lot of them think I'm arrogant.'

Could I take his photograph?

'Certainly not.'

He bounced me round for a further two hours in a building which architectural writer Christopher Hussey had said offered 'romance without period'.

We stood on the Upper Battery, familiar from Roman Polanski's 1965 film *Cul-de-Sac*. We looked northwards to the walled garden built by Lutyens' close friend, Gertrude Jekyll. Lutyens had renovated the place mainly to show off to friends. As he'd said to his patron, and the founder of *Country Life* magazine, Edward Hudson, 'I wanted to amuse myself with the place.' Thus from the dilettante indulgences of the well-to-do came great buildings. Of course, he had a head start – the castle's location, perched on top of the 100-ft Beblow Crag, a jutting rock squeezed up from the ground like toothpaste when a core of molten dolerite (whinstone) forced its way through the limestone.

In the long gallery David showed me a strange piece of sixteenth-century Dutch furniture called an aumbrey. It looked too massive ever to have been lugged up here.

'The original flatpack!' said David. 'Long before IKEA – just comes to bits!'

I sensed how the man's slightly prickly enthusiasm would fit uneasily into this small community. I was realising how Holy Island was both highly individual and highly conformist, how a strong sense of community could both nurture and suffocate.

David Robinson perched up here in his castle, looking down on the village he rarely mixed with. His wife had disappeared as soon as she'd given me a cup of tea. But then I was used to Holy Island's army of invisible women.

In the afternoon the second and third coats of paint were applied to Ray Simpson's bathroom wall. On the morrow – the haiku itself.

A small incident that night in the Sign of Two Kirstys. At 10 p.m. a stranger walked in, ordered a pint and took it outside into the strong moonlight.

A hush fell over the bar. Who was he? Why had he gone outside? Was he lying in wait for the unsuspecting?

The man eventually returned the glass, left and was not seen again. And I realised the impact of a total stranger walking into this bar, 10 p.m., mid-week, mid-winter.

Just as I had done.

THURSDAY, 8 FEBRUARY 2001 –
DAY TWENTY~SIX

Short Unsweet

Gilbert proved to be a disaster. Painting the haiku proved impossible. A pox on writing today.

FRIDAY, 9 FEBRUARY 2001 –
DAY TWENTY~SEVEN

A Few Million Gallons and Me

Only now can the truth be revealed about yesterday. The haiku? No suitable brushes to be found. Historic painting delayed. Gilbert? At the first attempt to chisel into the stone, it gave up the ghost. Fell apart. Splintered. Flaked.

I'd heaved Gilbert from the beach, worked two days sanding him down. He proved to be useless, could not hold himself together. I felt like punching him. Except it wasn't his fault. And the only injured party would have been me.

Was the island resisting my attempts? Maybe. I wouldn't give up. Buy brushes. Find another stone. Consult a stonemason. Get decent chisels.

Declare the day a non-event. Go to bed.

And I awoke refreshed, breakfasted on beans on toast. I melted a pat of butter into the beans, something my son Dylan did. The small act made me sad.

It was a clear, sharp day, windless. My day in the refuge box. Tim Parkin had lent me his bike for the three-mile journey along the causeway.

I'd prepared for my stay. I wore three pairs of socks, a thick blue jumper, jacket, large trench-coat, hat, scarf, gloves. I'd made a flask of tea, packed sandwiches, fruit, chocolate. I'd brought four night-lights for illumination (and a bit of warmth). I had binoculars, a newspaper, two books. Ross Peart offered to cycle along with me. I would be totally isolated in this small box for several hours. My mood needed to be calm, settled.

On the bike journey, my trench-coat continually caught in the back wheel. My heavy binoculars case, plus shoulder bag, swung all over the place. Several times my newspaper fell to the ground. The bike's gears constantly slipped and I was forced to stay in low gear. I struggled along, my face growing redder, my temper growing shorter.

'What you need,' said Ross Peart, looking at me quizzically, 'is to adjust better to the pace of this island.'

The fact he was right only made me more irritable. We got within half a mile of the refuge box, the last sand dunes in which I could leave the bike. I had lost the newspaper.

'You don't need a newspaper,' said Ross. 'You were meant to commune with nature today.'

The man was growing more irritatingly truthful by the moment. I dumped the bike, we walked the half mile to the box perched on its four lanky legs. My tensions oozed out onto the vast expanses all around. My face (I estimated) grew less red.

The white-painted box was built on the small, slightly raised 'bridge' section of the causeway, under which ran a permanent channel of water, a main conduit for the incoming tide. The current would swell up, swallow causeway and bridge and be miles wide before you knew it.

Several well-wishers stopped as we walked, including Stuart McMurdo in his Land Rover, who had informed the coastguard the box was to have its first *voluntary* resident.

I climbed the weathered wooden steps for my first acquaintance. Few interior design awards, I suspected. A frugal affair, windows on two sides, a slatted bench in that old-fashioned green, an emergency telephone on the wall.

Graffiti artists had daubed 'THE BOYS FROM HOLLAND', 'HELLO MUM, DAD – DAZ' and other literary gems. There was an official sign which employed strange syntax and misspelling: 'IN EMERGENCY, THIS TELEPHONE CAN ONLY BE USED. CONTAC' (sic).

Several flies, which had failed to realise they were out of season, were banging themselves senseless against the inside of the glass. The only other movable item was a discarded cigarette packet.

The tide still seemed distant, a far off sheen on the sands.

'The biggest tides always take their time at first,' said Stuart McMurdo. 'But then they come.'

Five point three metres. That was three people stood on top of one another. How could the water rise that far? The sands looked dead flat.

To the east a huge flock of Brent geese took to the air. To the north I could see the breaking waves. More sea to the south, a flat, non-wave surface. Sea was approaching sea.

Beneath the bridge the water was swelling. Ross was still with me but as the sea began to flood the causeway he was forced to retreat. I was slowly being isolated. On the mainland the cars had now stopped. I could spot various people watching me. I waved Ross goodbye across the swelling channel. And then only the final few raised yards of the bridge road were still uncovered. I paced my shrinking universe. Soon I would be forced up the refuge box steps.

And then an extraordinary thing happened. Safe-crossing time was now 40 minutes gone but a car set off from the mainland, dropped down into the water and crawled its way through the sea, throwing up frills of foam. It arrived on my tiny oasis of dry land.

'Will I make it?' asked the driver, with a transatlantic accent.

He had no choice. There was no space to turn round. He had to go on. He was disobeying the basic rule – only try to beat the tide when it's an outgoing one.

'You'll have to hurry up,' I said, but then added, 'actually, don't hurry up. Nice and slow.' Panicking into speed at such times was the worst option.

The man crawled off through the flooding tide. I later learned it poured through the gaps in his doors as he drove. Part of me, that terrible part that draws us to look at road accidents, wanted him to stall, wanted to know the consequences. The other part of me won. The car eventually reached dry land, picked up speed and, dripping briny, headed for the village.

As the waters rose, they forced me up the first, the second, then the third step. I watched them swallow the raised plaque on the bridge which read 'Lindisfarne Causeway, 1954'. For no real reason, I calculated this plaque had been swallowed 35,000 times.

The tide rose above the bridge supports. Trapped air inside the joins bubbled to the surface, a sound like boiling cabbage. The sea simmered. The popping bubbles were the only sound as several billion gallons of water slowly flooded the area of a small city. The tide swallowed sand, road, road signs, markers. Its glistening silk spread itself beneath a blue sky in which countless birds wheeled and then screeched in protest at having lost their feeding grounds yet again. To the north, the sea was waiting patiently for its twice daily union with its own.

By this time all land had gone and only the red fruit-gum markers of the road signs were visible. Through my binoculars I could see the small huddle of people and cars on the mainland and wondered if they were aware of me. The unfettered sun was beginning to dip behind the Kyloe Hills, turning the entire basin molten from its angled reflection.

I was totally alone.

One moment later, the emergency phone rang. I hadn't been expecting any calls. A resolute double-glazing salesman? Maybe I'd won a holiday in a prize draw competition! Had I considered new house insurance?

The caller was Stuart Flack, the coastguard from Tynemouth, checking first that there was indeed an idiot spending a voluntary tide in the refuge box and, secondly, that the idiot was safe.

I mapped the tide's slow progress with some chucked-in orange peel. At 3.30 p.m. both tide and peel stopped. The peel bobbed gently. It was as if, for a short time, the universe was holding its breath, the vast basin of water taking stock.

Some moments later, the peel moved again, in the opposite direction. The great natural engine had been put into reverse or, to mix up the metaphor completely, the flooded lungs were now emptying themselves.

This was a quiet, undramatic power. Not a wave to be seen. It was a power that always had, and always would, define this island.

Stranded here, on four spindly legs in the middle of this vast sea, I felt not panic but a sense of well-being. I was relating to this island and its natural elements in my own way, a way that was as legitimate as any.

As a writer, I knew I had to bring something new here, something positive.

Anyone, who did that anywhere, in whatever society or country they found themselves, belonged to that society – for a month, for a year, for 100 days or however long. And they belonged as much as anyone else.

I lit my night-lights, ate a sandwich and fruit, drank some tea. The phone rang again. Was the idiot still OK? The sun had now dipped behind the hills and with the darkness the cold began to seep through my clothing. I warmed my hands on the tiny candle heat, stamped my feet. I was watching the receding tide for the first sign of tarmac on the raised bridge road. It came at 5 p.m. as the waters fell back and slowly spots of sand and mud-flats appeared, gleaming like seal backs. The birds, which throughout high tide had kept up a sad lament from the distant shore, began to return.

At 5.50 p.m., 40 minutes before official crossing time and with the causeway still mainly flooded, a high lorry made its tentative way through the water. I waved as he passed my box. No response. At each end of the flooded causeway cars were beginning to gather, pairs of headlights staring across at one another like some bright-eyed species round a watering-hole.

They were impatient. The tide wasn't.

At 6.30 p.m., by which time my limbs were beginning to stiffen, the first cars ventured across. It was now jet black. I worried about finding my bike in those vast dunes, thought of the freezing uncomfortable ride back with all my gear.

The bridge road was now uncovered, but the waters were still running off the rest of the causeway. On the island side a car flashed its lights. I knew instinctively it was Ross Peart come to save me. I gathered up my goods, blew out the night-lights, left them for the genuinely unfortunate and splashed my way through one hundred yards.

Ross opened the passenger door for me. I was greeted with a delicious wall of heat.

'Get in,' he said. 'Your bike's in the back.' I mentally rewrote my will at that moment. Everything to Ross Peart.

As we drove off, I stared back. The gloom of the night and the vast expanses of the flats had already swallowed the refuge box. For the sea this was just one more tide in thousands. It was one I would never forget.

And the day had been experience. And knowledge. So that now, in the second quarter of my Holy Island exile, I had moved to somewhere else.

After the day's total isolation, the contrast of the Sign of Two Kirstys that night: A darts match against the Black Bull in Etal (on the mainland) which brought boisterous crowds, but also a large group of fresh-faced young Christians on a weekend visit to Marygate House, the large hostel. And Ross Peart, whose Open Gate had booked in the motorist who'd cheated the tide.

'Said he wasn't worried about getting stranded,' Ross told me. 'Said it was a hire car.'

Oh, that was all right then.

SATURDAY, 10 FEBRUARY 2001 – DAY TWENTY-EIGHT

The Bird Man Freezeth – Family Back to Front

The refuge box experience meant a very small part of that tide belonged to me. I wanted to lay part-claim to other aspects of the island. My claims would not debar anyone else's claims. There were no deeds of ownership.

What there was, this Saturday morning, as icy sleet drove against the window encouraged by a wind that would have frozen molten lava in two seconds, was an exceedingly warm bed and the vision in my mind of making tea and hot toast as I drifted in and out of John Peel's *Home Truths*, followed by a spot of supine bed-reading and possibly rising at noon.

The reality was somewhat different. I had unwisely arranged, on a day when I should have arranged nothing, to journey out with Ian Kerr, who, along with another 20 zealots, twice a year walked the 8,000 acres of the Lindisfarne Nature Reserve (stretching from Budle Bay in the south to Goswick Sands in the north), to register numbers of birds present.

I imagined the register.

'Peewits?'

'Twenty-eight, sir!'

'Gannets?"

'Fourteen, sir!'

Ian was a retired 60-year-old journalist. Officially he and his wife Hazel lived in Newcastle but his spiritual home, I suspected, was Holy Island, where they'd spent the majority of weekends in their cottage over the last 30 years.

He was the author of *Lindisfarne Birds*, published by Northumberland and Tyneside Birds Club. This had sold out and he was preparing a second book.

Lindisfarne Birds lovingly detailed every one of the 294 species recorded on the island. Ian could identify each one. Some of his entries were idiosyncratic: 'Red Grouse – extremely rare. One at Ross in 1987 seems to defy explanation.'

I was becoming aware how, on Holy Island, two totally contrasting attitudes to birds lived side by side. The one recorded and observed, the other slaughtered. To islanders there seemed no illogicality.

Only an act of willpower dragged my limbs from bed that morning at 7.30 a.m. By 9.15 a.m., feeling stiff and painful, I was striding out with Ian towards Straight Lonnen path. We did have a third member. Arthur was strongly in evidence this day. I'd tried to dissuade him from coming but more and more he went places with me.

It was a guffie of a day and we faced more than two and a half hours of extreme weather on exposed terrain. In that time we would see (briefly) one other human being and damn few birds, most of whom I concluded had had the sense to stay home and watch *Football Focus*.

Heading towards the Lough and the North Shore, we passed a whole series of waterlogged fields. Ian couldn't remember the island this saturated. Many of the track puddles were frozen and the bitter north-easterly picked up handfuls of sleet and chucked them at us. I had brought my binoculars, which enabled me, with freezing hands, to scan every blade of grass in the bird-free fields.

Eventually we reached the Lough, a glum expanse of reedy freshwater once the island's overall supply. It had a bird hide, similar in shape and size to a Premier League hospitality box, though the comparison ended there. On a cold wooden bench through a propped open window, we scanned the lake.

The hide door opened and another idiot walked in. We grunted hello. Humans were outnumbering birds.

Ian did all his bird work voluntarily, no thought of payment. But as I stamped my feet and mumbled something to the tune of 'Sometimes I wonder why I do this' he replied matter-of-factly 'Because you're getting paid to do it, of course', seemingly unaware of the irony, or indeed of the statement's only partial accuracy.

I heard a sound like noisy bike brakes suddenly applied. A coot, according to Ian, who called them 'bad-tempered birds'. For the next ten minutes he pointed a finger towards the misty reeds and birds I could scarcely see.

'A mallard . . .'

Where, exactly?

'Teals.'

Sorry, I can't quite . . .

'Tufted ducks.'

Maybe you could just . . .

Eventually I did see the tufted ducks, a flotilla of them suddenly disappearing underwater, then popping up like bread from the toaster.

'Birds spend most of their time eating,' said Ian through chattering teeth. 'A migrating bird can lose up to one third of its weight in transit.'

The Migration Diet – why not? They'd tried everything else.

'Some birds travel 2,000 miles from the Arctic,' said Ian. 'And some have made Iceland in 24 hours.' Which compares favourably with Virgin Air, I reckon, given traffic and check-in times.

What drove him to spend so much of his life peering through binoculars at small feathered things?

'I've always liked watching birds and I like to identify what I'm watching.'

The reply was pretty mundane and convinced me that often other people could define what you were doing and why, better than you could yourself. This certainly applies to writers.

'Look – a bar-tailed godwit.'

Bar-tailed godwit. I loved the name.

After the hide we strode out past Emmanuel Head, that distinctive white pyramid. Its official use was as a shipping aid but its presence was so dramatic, so unlikely, I was convinced it marked some past intergalactic landing.

We dropped to the fine sandy expanse of Sandon Bay, where even in high season few island visitors ventured. Ian cracked a joke, which in the conditions, was beyond the call of duty.

He bent down to the calf-high collection of dwarf willow.

'This is the Holy Island forest,' he said.

And very tree-like they were too. OK, it wasn't the kind of joke to make me roll on the floor clutching my stomach from laughter pains. But it was a joke.

And there were few real trees. Odd, emaciated ones huddled close to stone walls or buildings like frozen refugees. Ian spotted a golden plover and a lapwing as we trudged on, past the ruins of Green Shiel – not a savings stamp but a seventh-century Saxon fort believed to signify the island's first settlers. We paused, looked at the remains. Did we both dream of a warm fire at that instant?

On our return walk Ian pointed out a field called locally the Black Forest. This was Holy Island's desertification, where the farmer had abandoned the fight against the creeping advance of sand.

We parted company at midday. Did we shake hands? Or did we just shake? We'd registered few birds. I'd learned little about Ian Kerr. He had learned little about Peter Mortimer. That is the way of it sometimes.

Back home I spent 40 minutes building my open fire high and hot, then stretched out limbs numbed by the cold and stiffness. Only Arthur was happy. As the first vestige of heat seeped through, a knock came at the door. Ross Peart. Did I fancy a bike ride?

Believe it or not, no. I thawed in front of the fire. I snoozed. I finished reading Gordon Honeycombe's Holy Island novel *Dragon under the Hill*, lent to me by Jen Ward. This had been published in 1972 when Honeycombe had been a household name as a television broadcaster. The *Times Literary Supplement* called it 'an impeccable formula, a nicely balanced mixture of detection, slow, but startling revelation and ultimate horror'.

It was nothing of the sort.

I'd been interested to read a novel with a contemporary Holy Island setting. The place so often seemed a victim of its past. Honeycombe's book told of the visit to the island of the Wardlaw family, which unleashed terrible forces bringing dreadful consequences to mother, father and son.

Honeycombe spent a good deal of time on the island – many people still remembered him – but his research sat undigested in the book's stomach and his characters creaked with implausibility, especially the father. The novel bravely tried to combine the island's past and present but the man was not a natural novelist and I wondered: had Honeycombe been a plumber's mate, rather than a TV personality, would the MS ever have got past the publisher's first reader?

That night I made new Holy Island friends, Stuart and Margot Moffitt, who had a cottage in Fenkle Street. Their main home was in Cullercoats, just a few hundred yards from mine, but we needed Holy Island to get to know one another. Maybe it was easier to make friends with Holy Island weekenders. Or maybe they were just kind people. Either way, for the rest of my stay I always felt Stuart and Margot were looking out for me.

That night I walked home from the Sign of Two Kirstys and began shedding clothes like a Chippendale. In the course of two pints, the temperature had risen 15 degrees.

I'd banked up the fire and the living-room was hotter than Kew Gardens' tropical greenhouses.

An interesting phone call from my brother in Rotherham. Did I realise the numerical significance of his daughter's birthday the previous day? The date – 10.02.2001 – was a palindrome. Rare enough for someone's birthday. But there was more. Her name was a palindrome too – Hannah. Blimey.

And when I'd got over that, I thought of my poor old mum in Rotherham, operation pending. And me up here, not spotting birds.

SUNDAY, 11 FEBRUARY 2001 – DAY TWENTY-NINE

The Domestic Rules – The Truth about those Birds

Sometimes I'd wake and think of the whole wide world going on out there and me no part of it. Me locked away on this island for 100 days and did anyone else give a hoot?

Get out of bed, Mortimer.

And run on the sands, a simple act. So self-absorbed was I in the run, I was unaware I was splashing ankle-deep through the water, far from shore and with an incoming tide. In the momentary panic, a book cover flashed through my mind – *29 Days on Holy Island* by Peter Mortimer (drowned).

I veered shorewards, outran the tide.

After the two previous days, the call of the domestic was irresistible. I stripped the bed, washed the sheets, ironed four shirts, vacuumed the living-room. Maybe writers should be encouraged to go on the occasional weekend domestic retreat; concentrate on the ironing away from all those normal distractions of book-writing.

A bath, some yoga, clean duds and my Sunday supplement hour in the Island Oasis Café. The café was bulging with camels: camel prints on the walls, camel paintings (even a Paul Klee), a photo of a camel with its head stuck out a taxi window. Even a camel ceiling hanging.

'Makes a change from Celtic crosses,' said Neil. He and Cathy, I realised, were quite Bohemian, not a dominant Holy Island trait.

Two invitations that night. First, with Chris and Derek at the Stable – shepherd's pie followed by rhubarb crumble and custard, a combination which few great works of art could match for satisfaction – followed by my second Holy Island music night at the house of Beryl Pain, clerk to Holy Island parish council and skilled musician. The agenda for this night was as follows: take along a tape or CD of your choice. Inflict it on others, who will do similar to you. It was the best way I knew of stretching your own musical tastes.

Beryl's night started badly for her. Fifteen devotees were gathered in her living-room. There was also a boudoir grand (a slightly slimmed-down grand piano), which left little room to play tag.

Beryl's CD player then broke down. She repaired to a chair to ponder possibilities and sat on her glasses, which broke. The gathered illuminati included Ian and Helen McGregor, bike-loaner Tim Parkin, Ray Simpson of vicar's bathroom fame, Ross Peart, saviour, plus Chris and Derek. I'd rifled Derek's collection to make my own choice, *All Them Blues* by Elmore James, who knew how to do one thing brilliantly and spent his life doing it.

Try this list for variety: Schubert, Saint-Saens, George Shearing, The Righteous Brothers, Owen Brannigan, Celine Dion, Elmore James, Prokofiev, Roy Orbison, Ella Fitzgerald, Janet Baker – the Eclectic Eleven, plus a few I've forgotten.

I realised a lot of the same faces appeared and reappeared at events. And many more didn't. What did this prove?

Later I was in the Sign of Two Kirstys for a pint. So was bird man Ian Kerr, looking a bit sheepish, if that's not a mixed metaphor.

'It was all a waste of time yesterday,' he confessed. 'It was so bitterly cold none of the other 19 checkers turned out.'

Who's to say what is and isn't a waste of time? And how else would I have got to hear that bad-tempered coot?

MONDAY, 12 FEBRUARY 2001 – DAY THIRTY

Aliens – Not Painting the Haiku

I wasn't used to living alone. I came from a long line of mixed houses. I wasn't used to bars of soap, tubes of toothpaste and toilet rolls lasting so long. I wasn't used to things staying where I put them. If I left a slice of apple pie in the fridge back home, it was with the realisation it would probably be snaffled when I looked again. Though I washed the dishes regularly, I grew accustomed to the sink mysteriously filling with dirty ones.

I'd been alone now for 30 days. And I was due visitors from the mainland, a couple I'd never even met, a planned brief visit, but part of me must have hungered for the external. I ended up asking them to stay the night. And they agreed.

They were Nigel and Adrienne Shipton from Newark, who'd contacted me just before I left. They'd read my book *Broke through Britain* and wondered if they could call en route to Scotland. They wanted to put one of my wilder notions into practice. I'll be on Holy Island, I said. But call anyway.

I was nervous, like a prisoner waiting for a rare visit. They arrived with Lotte, a gigantic dog attaching itself so closely to Nigel that he could draw a response merely by raising an eyebrow.

We chatted politely for an hour or so and as they prepared to leave with the tide I told them I was off to paint a haiku – but why not stay? Make themselves at home?

There was no sign of Ray Simpson, nor of the paint-brushes he'd promised. Delayed haiku delayed longer. My alternative plan was to drink several glasses of wine at Banjo Bill's.

'The first glass might not do the trick,' said Bill, producing his own vintage. 'But the second will.' As indeed did the third and fourth.

It did the trick for Jean Peart, too, who'd been away several days on her native Merseyside. An island return always threw her, that emotional turmoil only appreciated by those who were long-term on the island and totally indiscernible by the casual visitor of a few days.

It was also indiscernible in the countless books and documentaries about Holy Island, all of which 'bought into' the accepted Holy Island package, creating an image much more than a reality. Maybe, as someone said, we couldn't handle too much reality.

A person felt constantly 'on trial' here, always observed, always judged. Hard to pinpoint this exactly, except the smallness and tightness of the society brought a pressure-cooker effect, walking on eggshells. One of my responses was over-compensation, trying excessively to be 'nice' to everyone. Probably misjudged and later, my confidence higher, I'd be more cavalier.

Another visitor to Bill's was the Dutchman Harm, who turned up daily. A word about Harm. He'd moored here some years ago in his yacht, liked the place and never left, his craft now propped up, unused, above the harbour. He'd brought his wife Magda to the island (would you welcome, please, yet one more member of the Holy Island invisible female army!), they had a little girl, Marina, and Magda was pregnant again. Harm (pronounced Har-um) was said to be a homeopath. He had a distinctive wild look, eyes that bore right through you, an insistent voice, strong features, a shock of hair. His controversial presence had already seen him barred from one island pub. My imagination conjured up for him all manner of secret exotic lives, a fantasy fuelled by his seeming reluctance to be in my presence.

On this day he beat a hasty retreat on spotting me in Bill's kitchen. Another time, in the street, I'd mentioned popping round to see him some time and he'd looked askance.

If I felt knocked back by the rejection it at least afforded me a dreadful pun, as I realised that for the rest of my 100 days I would simply need to stay out of Harm's way.

By the time I left Banjo Bill's, I was squiffy. And Nigel and Adrienne were waiting patiently in the Cuddy House.

'I bought a bottle of wine,' said Nigel. I cooked an intoxicated beef casserole (me, not the beef) and that night we three trundled round to the Open Gate to watch with Ross and Jean a video of the BBC documentary *An Island in Time* made by Max Whitby.

The programme stuck various time-delay cameras round the island, capturing the changing seasons. Farmers were interviewed, fishermen, clergy, sheep-shearers, visitors. It was a beautifully made film, atmospherically shot.

But why was it not the island I knew?

Partly the subconscious desire of documentary and film-makers to perpetuate an image by now fortressed against almost any attack. Partly because the island did not reveal itself to you by publicly talking to people. I know. I talked to a lot of people. That was journalism. And journalism about Holy Island was a dawdle.

That night I slept in the small room. I liked the idea of two other people (plus a nervous pooch) sleeping in my cottage. But things were going through my head. What of my stone poem? What of my mother? What of the 70 days to come?

TUESDAY, 13 FEBRUARY 2001 – DAY THIRTY-ONE

Haiku and Horse-Play

For the first time in my opening month on the island the weather had settled to a fine spell. Beyond this small place, across the causeway, a world was getting on with its madnesses, its excesses, its beauties and its celebrations.

I read of yachtswoman Ellen MacArthur's 93-day single-handed round-the-world navigation. Almost the same length exile as me.

I had the novelty of making breakfast for three. People getting up in the Cuddy House, the sound of brushed teeth in the bathroom, padding feet upstairs. All this was strange to me.

Nigel and Adrienne left me a gift of food and I waved them off, one month since I had waved Kitty off. The island's flowers and buds would now be in the first stages of stirring. I was such an urbanite, I could pass the whole cycle of spring without noticing an opening bud. For a poet, this was disgraceful. The days were lengthening, each day the poor old sun dragging itself a little higher from its bed. The lambing season was close.

And my boiler suit arrived from Cullercoats. I pulled it on, stood in front of the mirror. A noble son of toil. Except my writer's hands were a give-away.

The closure of the Manor House had left me with little contact with George and Jen Ward. Would they still ask to see the proofs of my book? And did Jen's straight talking hide a general island unease at my presence? Was I, in fact, not welcome here? And did it matter? Of course.

The answer was to find a new stone. And complete the bathroom haiku. The latter took one hour. I was no calligrapher and gloss paint looked unkindly on errant brushstrokes. But my muse kept my hand steady and Ray Simpson was so delighted with the outcome he cooked me a large, if somewhat misshapen, fry-up.

My first poem was *in situ*.

I had laid siege, culturally, to this island.

Later, in search of a replacement stone, I headed down Jenny Bell Lane towards St Cuthbert's beach and passed, in a field, a large horse. The horse, I later learned, was named Najana. I spent 15 minutes stroking her. Nothing is quite like the presence of a large horse; those sad liquid eyes, that huge head given to total calm or sudden wild tosses, that sense (and nothing in between) of either the dreamlike or the nervously hyper. The heat of a nearby horse. Sometimes at traffic lights a large bus pulled alongside my bike, the pulse of its engine reminding me of just that.

I whispered in Najana's ear.

'I'm going to ride you.'

There was no reply. That was OK.

Along the low soily cliff by St Cuthbert's a family of fulmars, nested in rabbit holes, saw me off with a wide-beaked call of 'Ah-ah-ah-ah!'. Around me, like some ruined city, were tons of large rocks and boulders. But no suitable sandstone.

Along at Chare Ends the island was simultaneously shrinking and expanding, a JCB shovelling away the sand's insidious progress across the causeway, while in the basin the land retreated as the sea chewed away at the cliff.

The road from Chare Ends to the village had a wooden shelter taken by all visitors as a bus-stop. I suspected it was no such thing. No houses, for one thing. Hardly any buses, for another. The shelter, I realised, had been built specifically for this moment in this day, to allow me to sit and take in the great sweep of the estuary, the mainland hills, the sky, and plot the progress of the slowly spinning bright coin that was the sun.

It had also been built in celebration of Holy Island's culture, which dictated that wherever you pause for two seconds, someone you knew would come and speak to you.

With me it was Ross Peart, glistening like a seal after his mainland bike ride. Two minutes later, a brace of nuns walked past. Ross knew them and we fell into conversation.

Nuns did not fit easily into my religious, or anti-religious, philosophising and very soon I realised these two had the power, quite painlessly, to undermine me.

Nuns occupy a strange position in our pagan consciousness. On film, they sing or fly. Monty Python lampooned them. It is considered a hoot for American actors to make a film disguised as them. Nuns, who are much more serious than most of us, are rarely taken seriously. They are the butt of several sexual jokes, mainly from repressed males.

These nuns were called Sylvia and Linda, sisters of the Jesus Way. Ross had asked them to look after the (now closed) Castle View Hotel, whose owner, John Collins, was semi-paralysed in Newcastle General Hospital after a horrendous loft fall.

I quizzed them. Where was the order's home? The Wirral, Cheshire. How many? Six nuns. How funded? Voluntary donations. Did it offer the outside world anything? Yes, retreat facilities. How many came in a year? 1,600. Did they pay? Voluntary donations again. What kept the order alive? Faith.

Faith. That small word. What did it mean to most of the UK population?

I quizzed the nuns further. How did they acquire their eight-bedroom premises? They built them themselves. What, nuns on dumper trucks? More or less, yes. How long did it take? Five years. A house and a chapel. What had decided them to build?

One day they had opened the bible at random. It was Isaiah 65, which read: 'And they shall build houses, and they shall inhabit them, and they shall enjoy the work of their hands.'

You mean, that was it, that decided it?

Yes.

In that small shelter the sun shone on their faces and reflected back innocence. I gathered wood on the way home, their image and words still in my mind. They had a calm, peaceful, non-evangelical strength. They seemed not to be concerned either about my moral improvement, nor to profit from, nor put to rights, the world.

Linda, the younger, was 30 and had an attractive fresh face. I realised my instinct to flirt with attractive women was useless here. As they later told me, they considered themselves brides of Christ. I floundered at this. They did not.

People were beginning to knock more at my door. On this day, Christinne Holbrook. Would I like to come to the next book club meeting? The book was Hemingway's *The Old Man and The Sea*, which I hadn't looked at in 30 years, but seemed somehow just right.

Rumours that the Lindisfarne would reopen that night proved groundless and for the third week the island, during the week, was virtually publess.

I noticed, before retiring, a large streak of blue gloss paint on my cheek – an errant brush stroke from the haiku painting. It must have been clearly visible to Ray Simpson, Ross Peart, two nuns and Christinne Holbrook. And how come no one had said a word?

WEDNESDAY, 14 FEBRUARY 2001 – DAY THIRTY-TWO

On Death, and all that Horse Sense

Valentine's Day. I awaited the sackful of mail. A redirected insurance company circular popped through the letterbox. Later I did get one card.

I had been on the island 32 days – almost one third of my stay. It was a place of no traffic lights, no ice cream vans, no roundabouts, no nose-to-tail cars, no supermarkets, no banks, no trains, no taxis, no department stores, one brief police car, no doctors, no dentists, no nurses, no traffic wardens, no motorways, no security cameras, no cinemas, no theatre, no commuters, no jukeboxes, no one-armed bandits, no wide-screen television, no McDonalds.

I had been the antithesis of the traveller. The world flew round in jumbo jets, whizzed across continents, booked foreign holidays, went to endless conferences and on business trips. My own universe was tiny. I could travel barely one mile in any direction without a change.

South brought me to the harbour rapidly. East was one mile then the castle and the cliffs. North offered the footpaths over the island to the North Shore – just over a mile. West was the biggest distance, curving three miles along the shell road, over the main causeway and the (increasingly) mythical mainland beyond.

I was writing daily, one-dimensional tentative stuff. I was unsure of either my response to the island, or it to me, and regularly wanted to hurl the writing to the ever-constant wind.

Faith. I thought of the nuns.

My own faith had to be in the creative process, that ultimately it would not let me down. But the writing was jottings, journalese.

I told myself becoming a writer had changed my life, had given me a direction and security previously lacking. Had given me meaning in a world often without meaning. Faith.

I'd read Ray Simpson's pre-publication MS *Before We Say Goodbye*, about our preparations for death (our own and others). It gave comfort to the believers but to those of us for whom 'Trust in the Lord' was a comfortless maxim it gave little. I couldn't see our life on earth as some dress rehearsal, a warm-up before the real race.

For me, promising the benefits of the after-life was little different to the promises an insurance company makes of the delights of delay deferred, if only you'll hand over your loot. The best way to face death unafraid was to leave something of value behind on earth. A lot of religion was fear. Think of Pascal's wager: if you believe in God and he doesn't exist – nothing lost. If you don't believe in God and he does exist, you risk all sorts come the final day.

That was just another insurance policy.

In my muddled way, I knew I wanted something different, a spirituality as against religion, an acknowledgement of the great mysteries of life without all this endless adoration of some aloof supreme being.

Time for breakfast porridge.

The sustained spell of good weather led me to conclude winter had done its worst. In fact, it had hardly got out of bed.

Something took me back to Najana, the horse. Twenty years previously, when I was a journalist, I'd ridden a massive 17.2 hand show-jumper called Trojan across the country from Cumbria to the north-east coast. I'd been a novice but had convinced the owners otherwise. The journey almost killed me. I broke every piece of equipment, sank with Trojan in a swamp and ended my eight days in the saddle swathed in a giant protective nappy. But I'd made it and learnt how to ride a horse, the final miles done at a full gallop in celebration. Humans fused with horses in a unique way. With no other animal would we share that intimacy of spreading our groins across their backs and clinging tight.

Najana flared her nostrils. How like female genitalia they were. And how little I'd thought of such things on the island.

'I *am* going to ride you,' I repeated in her flicking ear.

A call at the Open Gate led me once more to the brace of nuns. Each lived on spending money of £15 per week. They knitted their own clothes. They had quietness, humility. Truly exotic creatures.

The Lindisfarne reopened that evening. Sue and Clive Massey returned from their Gran Canaria trip. All those thousands of miles. And me still here. They had suntans, too.

Behind the bar was mini-bus driver Hector Douglas. Various couples were in for romantic meals. Perfume and aftershave wafted in the air.

Two well-spoken couples from Durham University quizzed the bearded Hector. He was able to impress their wide-eyed curiosity in a way I suspected he'd impressed many before them. He had been the last Holy Islander born on the island to two Holy Island parents.

'Gosh – really?'

He'd been one of the final lifeboat crew before it was disbanded way back in the 1960s.

'Golly!'

And see that giant lobster on the wall? He'd caught that.

'No!'

Hector had an impish sense of humour. They were eating out of his hand. Time to vary the diet. The students asked about two tall needle thingies just off the harbour. (They were the Beacons, navigation aids.)

'Cuthbert's buried under one,' said Hector, 'and Aidan under the other.'

And not the flicker of a smile on his face.

Later one of the students, his RP accent somewhat distinctive in this setting, said: 'A lot of religious people on the island, I shouldn't wonder?'

'Oh aye,' replied Hector. 'And there's a saying here: the nearer the pulpit, the bigger the rogue.'

These few words encapsulated a lot of the island tensions. Lindisfarne – a place of retreat and tranquillity. Put your ear to the ground and you could hear the rumbles.

THURSDAY, 15 FEBRUARY 2001 – DAY THIRTY-THREE

A Plethora of Cabbages – Gardens Are Go

If there were no God, who could have moved that ironing board? I'd left it in one place. It was now in another. A small frisson of panic as I awoke.

My imagination ran to poltergeists, ghosts, demonic possession, burglars, aliens. Until I realised Nigel and Adrienne had stayed in this room and probably ironed a shirt.

Day Thirty-Three saw me in sombre mood. I'd been reading the latest book from a northern author. The poet S.J. Litherland had given me Annie Proulx's short stories, *Close Range*. Proulx had won the Pulitzer, National Book Award and other accolades for her work, notably the novel *The Shipping News* (which I hadn't read).

I read five of the stories and could read no more. They depressed me enormously. Tales of dismembered feet, babies hurled from bridges, the awful revenge wreaked on flashing retards – my state of mind was too fragile for such things. I slumped away from each story in a state of dejection and after five I could stomach no more.

The decision to abandon a book can bring enormous relief, as if some onerous 'duty' has been cast off. I picked up Hemingway's short novel and within the first few pages felt he was my mate.

I had never owned a garden. And I had never planted a cabbage. Now I was staring at 40 fledglings. My final act in the Manor House garden (and the hotel was due to reopen the next day) was to plant the cabbages and order them to grow.

They were, as yet, little more than tiny green flags housed in a kind of ice-tray container. Their sheer vulnerability created in me a protective instinct as I pressed each in turn into its small dug-out hole. Their final, fluttering serried ranks gave me great satisfaction and was to lead to my first, I imagine only, cabbage poem.

After which I was booked to tackle the garden at the Retreat, second island property of Chris Holbrook and Derek Pollard. Tending the garden of a holiday cottage somehow wasn't quite the same.

'Ten pounds a session and your food,' said Derek. This brought a certain commercialism to my labours, which thus far had been fired by a muddled Utopian sense.

And the garden was vastly overgrown, so much so that I expected to find a princess who'd been sleeping 100 years. Compared to the Manor House it was small, enclosed by fencing and accessed only through the house, which increased the claustrophobia. In theory, the estuary could be glimpsed through the fencing. In practice, the neighbours' drying sheet blocked the view.

I pruned the bushes and ferns. I lit a fire in the dustbin which (a) directed all its smoke towards the drying sheet and then (b) choked itself to death from oxygen lack.

The garden drooped its sad and excessive tendrils over its weed-choked paths. For two hours I hacked away but the garden still looked as hang-dog as at the start. I was knee deep in clipped branches which had nowhere to go. At the same time this garden was hemmed in tight, next door's bedrooms were peering over the fence.

I left this garden to look at another. Gertrude Jekyll's walled garden (and walled gardens were a Northumberland speciality) was across a waterlogged field from the castle and had been created for Edwin Lutyens at the same time as the castle's renaissance.

It was not open to the public till Easter. In February, every vestige of colour seemed sucked from it. On three sides the walls were eight feet high but facing the castle the wall was only four feet, allowing the castle viewer to see directly in but diluting the sense of secrecy.

The weathered gate was locked. Inside was a single seat, what looked like a fountain, a small tucked-away shed. I stared at that shed and thought of Bill and Ben. Thinking of the Flowerpot Men returned me to the greatest state of innocence I knew.

On return I heard the single bell of St Mary's Church toll out for evensong. Something about that bell, its simple repetitive note, a sound that spread a protective and unifying net across the island and all its inhabitants. Trouble was, as soon as the bell ceased, so too did the net.

FRIDAY, 16 FEBRUARY 2001 –
DAY THIRTY-FOUR

Horse Mail – To the Manor Reborn

News from Rotherham. My mother's hip replacement operation had caused complications. She would need a second operation. At the age of 85.

Guilt flooded me like the tide flooded the estuary. Father dead. Mother stricken. Me on an island.

I had to visit her. Soon.

Meantime, I'd been thinking about the horse. I decided on a plan and sent the following letter to Najana's owners, Mary and Ralph Wilson, whom I'd never met.

> Feb 16, 2001 – Straight from the Horse's Mouth
>
> Dear Mary & Ralph,
>
> There's this writer bloke, see, and he's been calling down the field a few times, and we've chatted on. He's doing this book called *100 Days on Holy Island* and he says he'd like nothing more than being up there and riding me on the island. Well, I said, no problem, but I'd need to check it out with Mary and Ralph.
>
> Over to you, then. See what you think. I've never been in a book. He's staying at the Cuddy House in St Cuthbert's Square and I'm including his phone number. Oh – his name is Peter Mortimer.
>
> Ride on!
>
> Najana
>
> P.S. Is that how you spell my name?

I called my present scene of labours the Garden of Great Sorrow, a faintly biblical ring. After two more hours of pruning, I decided to try another fire to save me vanishing under the cuttings. The neighbour peered over the fence.

'No fires, please,' she said. 'I've got the washing out.'

'I'll light the fire when you haven't, then,' I said.

'I wash every day,' she replied.

My sense of imprisonment grew. I dug. I pruned. The pile of unburnable cuttings grew to the background noise of a rumbling washing machine.

An hour later the same neighbour poked the same head over the fence.

'My washing's in now,' she said. Again I tried to light a bin fire, leaving room for ventilation. It spluttered and died. I tried to bag the cuttings in some black bags which proved no thicker than a wisp of smoke, with even the flimsiest twig poking its digit through. I made the bags two-ply, left the sharpest prunings alone, bagged the grass and weeds.

The Garden of Great Sorrow had found several ways to irritate me. The garden fork, painted in a cunning camouflage of brown and green, rendered itself invisible and unfindable whenever laid down. The green clothes line strung right across was equally indistinct and on several occasions proved a highly effective garrotte.

I worked all day, digging, pruning, bagging. Not a vestige of growth remained in the deep dark soil. Suddenly I was proud of my labours.

On my way out through the house I met up with Derek Pollard.

'Cleared it,' I said.

'You haven't pulled the crocuses up, have you?' he asked.

'The what?'

We walked back to look at the soil. It was dark, moist, weed-free. And crocus-free.

'Ah,' said Derek, in a masterly understatement.

I had murdered his flowers. At a rate of £10 per session plus food.

Something Banjo Bill said later stayed with me. He was talking of his daughter Lesley, who along with husband Roger spent many weekends in their Wild Duck Cottage island home. It was a long trek from Oxford and Lesley was keen to settle permanently on the island.

'I tell her not to rush. The island is magic to her right now, as a visitor. That's not the same if you live here. That magic isn't here.'

Banjo Bill knew this. Jean Peart knew this. Deep down, everyone on this island knew this. But it was not a truth universally acknowledged. The sustaining of the island's 'image', the perpetuation of the spiritual idyll, came often from the outside, the visitors, the media, but the islanders were silently complicit in such sustaining, so that the unreality of this image continued.

Such things were still in my head that night at the grand reopening of the Manor House. Both Jen and George looked truly knackered, having worked almost round the clock on the alterations and decorations. My fears that the bar itself would suffer interior designer blight were unfounded. It seemed little changed. Behind the bar George had more space, a fact he accentuated by staring at us through binoculars.

A man I'd not previously seen sat next to me at the bar.

'All right for some,' he said. 'A three-month skive.'

'Actually,' I said. 'I'm here to write a book.'

'Yeah, that's what I said,' he added. 'A three-month skive.'

He'd got me wrong. He'd got the island wrong. And he'd probably got himself wrong. I took a cue from Derek Pollard. Instead of telling him go boil his head, I took a quiet sip from my pint.

SATURDAY, 17 FEBRUARY 2001 –
DAY THIRTY-FIVE

Equine Rejection – The Day of the Stone

The day dawned bright and warm but it made no difference. I had resolved not to rise till I'd finished *The Old Man and The Sea*, a book in the long US tradition (not known much in UK literature) of the individual pitched against terrible natural forces: Melville's *Moby Dick*, Jack London's *To Light a Fire*, even Peter Benchley's *Jaws*.

Hemingway's novella touched a chord. Both for its ever-present sea metaphor (just like this island) and for its old man (called Santiago – not many people know that). I'd befriended two older men on this island: Banjo Bill's house was a haven, a friendly port, a place of succour, while Jimmy 'Clinker' Brigham unfussily gave me advice and information when I needed it.

Both men helped dilute the sense of unease, the sense of not 'belonging', the artificiality of me being here, and some dark unspoken fear that my time here at any day might implode, might run into the sand, might run out of momentum.

A wedding that day in the Catholic church. And spotted in the village streets the sort of large wedding hats not often seen on the island. Plus a large man in a kilt.

Plus a setback. And a piece of good fortune. I'd decided on a long walk and near Chare Ends I heard galloping hooves. Racing across the sands was my mate Najana and, up top, owner Mary Wilson, riding side-saddle. I flagged them down.

'I'm Peter Mortimer,' I said. 'I'm the person who delivered Najana's note to you.'

Mary Wilson seemed to loom incredibly high in the saddle, accentuating a sense of dominance as she stared down at me. I felt like some petty criminal in the dock under the stony stare of the magistrate. Mary's words reinforced this feeling.

'We couldn't possibly let an inexperienced rider on her,' she said.

'Oh,' I said, realising even then my cause was lost. 'Well, I have ridden a horse before and she seemed placid and —'

'Placid?' Mary spoke the word with incredulity. 'Oh no, she'd run away with you. Does it with everyone. She'd dump you.'

I was already dumped. By Mary. She stared down at me. Najana, who I half-expected to come to my rescue, or put in a word on my behalf, showed absolutely no sign of support. As if we'd never spent that time together! As if she'd never sent that letter! As if we were not buddies! A few moments later, rider and horse were gone and I was left at the roadside like a silly little schoolboy shown up for his stupid prank. There had been no mention of the letter. Holy Islanders had more serious things to do than respond to daft letters. That was obvious. To everyone except me.

Glumly, I left the road and walked the footpath past the old golf course. I wanted to tell the rabbits that the world was just too serious for me but there were no rabbits. Their holes had turned the terrain into a Swiss cheese but where were the bunnies? The endless rain had drowned them in their burrows, said some.

I strode out to Coves Bay on the far shore, stood on the craggy cliff top, felt my stomach lurch then scampered down to the beach below.

And just as the island had not long before knocked me back, now it lifted me. For there, near high-water mark, waiting for me, just as it had waited patiently for centuries, even millennia, was my stone.

It was perhaps one metre in height, shaped slightly like a kidney. It looked like sandstone and when I took a sharp piece of rock and tested it for carving it felt like it too. I clasped it and heaved. I was able to lift it but only just. It was solid, unflaky. I moved it up the beach with a series of flip-overs, found a spot for it above high-water mark, alongside a bush that resembled a giant porcupine.

I found a six-foot-long piece of driftwood, dug a hole and planted it alongside the stone as a marker. I packed the hole tight with sand and grass, pressed some small supporting rocks at the top.

I had my stone. But ironically, on this tiny island of confinement, my problem now was distance, how to transport stone across the rough, hilly, often flooded terrain, a journey of two miles or more. The challenge excited me, made me feel in touch.

I walked the return journey, plotting the most accessible route up and down the sandy dunes, round expanses of water, along muddy paths. It would take me half a day and I'd need to borrow Mike Burden's barrow.

I'd need to wait too – give this saturated island time to dry out.

I was excited. I passed the smaller of the two public car parks on return, noted how it was crammed full this day with 200 cars. I felt superior to all these car-owners, felt I had a right to be on this island more than them. What did these mere trippers know? Them and their anoraks and their flasks and their cameras.

And I realised, with a flutter of panic, I was responding just like an islander.

Something was compelling me on this island to go to church. In Britain, generally, churches sit in our cities like great rotting teeth. We walk past them, round them, never glance at them, even less consider entering them, except for a wedding or a funeral where our ill-fitting suits symbolise our misplacement.

They had little part in my life. I had no idea why I was making a conscious effort on Holy Island to enter their doors. I didn't find the experience revelatory, a sudden conversion seemed unlikely, but here I was again, in Barry Hutchinson's United Reform Church for his STAR session – 'Saturday Night's All Right' (whose acronym was, in fact, SNAR).

The church was a bright spacious airy hall, informal, pewless, featuring a semi-circle of chairs inside which was a proggy mat decorated with a Celtic cross. No altar, no finery, just three candles lit in the name of the father, the saviour, and spirit.

There was a slightly happy-clappy feel to the sung hymns, on CD operated by Barry with a remote control. He'd recently lost his mother-in-law and both he and Beryl Pain (council clerk, musician, broken glasses) addressed bereavement, the physical and emotional pain. I couldn't relate any of their well-meant observations to my father. By the service end my feet were chilled.

Back in Barry and Hazel Hutchinson's house, Beryl Pain asked me 'So what are you writing about today?' and I attempted another piece of jocularity which rebounded on me.

'Any minute now,' I said, 'I'll be writing about you lot.'

There was a silence. Then someone said 'That's why we haven't invited you round' and another added 'We have no idea what you might put in your book.'

I felt awkward and later sat with a pint in the Sign of Two Kirstys. I was branded. Just as it was often impossible to get beyond the image of this island, so it was impossible for people to get beyond the image of me, as writer. I was a mortal, too.

A man I didn't know approached my table.

'I'll give you a good story for that book of yours,' he began but I held up my hand to stop him.

'Not interested,' I said. 'Just want to drink my pint.'

The man pulled up short, gave me a look to suggest 'Well, there's gratitude for you!' and walked away, no doubt to impart that-there writer's ungrateful nature to others.

SUNDAY, 18 FEBRUARY 2001 – DAY THIRTY-SIX

Short Unsweet

All of which affected me much more than I could have imagined. I woke that morning, a sense of being chained to the book. I wanted nothing more to do with it. I hated the book, hated writing it.

MONDAY, 19 FEBRUARY 2001 – DAY THIRTY-SEVEN

Bad Crab Karma – A Spat with an Islander

There were several reasons I slept fitfully. Falling out with the book but also the prospect, come the very early morning, of heading into the great wastes of the North Sea in a fishing boat. I seemed to be awake all night, witnessing the digital clock's change to 3 a.m., 4 a.m., 5.15 a.m. – time to get up.

Not a vestige of light in the sky as I rose and dressed. While washing I switched on the radio, heard that medley known to every British fisherman, Fritz Spiegl's 'UK Theme', played prior to the day's first shipping forecast.

Its tones took me straight back to 1986 when I'd sailed and worked on six North Shields fishing boats over a six-month period and written the book, *The Last of the Hunters*. This was my first real foray into that sea since then and, for the first time, I would be sailing on a lobster boat.

I had on my boiler suit, thick fishermen's socks, wellies and an unlikely Afghan hat. I met Richard Ward (son of Jen and George) and we trudged down through the inky blackness to the Ouse. Richard was decked in bright orange waterproofs. On the quay we met up with the other crew member, Sean Brigham.

In a tiny boat we phut-phutted out to their 35-ft vessel, the *Mona M*, by which time just the very faintest brushstroke of light was behind Lindisfarne castle.

The diesel engine throbbed into life, a spotlight flooded the deck and we headed out into the limitless black. Alongside us were the three other lobster boats of the Holy Island fleets (no trawlers on the island), though we would soon all go our separate ways.

Sean and Richard had left three boxes of velvet crabs stashed underwater overnight, marked with a buoy. We pulled them up. Crab-buyers called to the island once a week. Lobsters – the aristocrats – warranted a daily visit from the purchasers. The wooden fish boxes of my memory had given way to the more durable (but also more slippery) plastic variety. Under the netting the crabs were packed as tight as – well, sardines.

The *Mona M* was wildly overpowered with an 82-hp engine (fitted two years previously) which, when opened up, gave the distinct impression the craft would soon take to the skies.

While Sean headed the boat to our first pick-up, on deck Richard was busy slicing up £20 of horse mackerel – the bait to lure the crustaceans to their doom.

In the day we'd be picking up, emptying, rebaiting and dropping again 200 pots in six separate 'fleets' at various points offshore – we would virtually circle the island.

As we steamed out, the castle's bulk began to emerge from the slowly lightening sky. To our stern were the red and green navigation lights high on the Heugh.

Like most fishing boats, the *Mona M* had an open deck, though the wide wheelhouse did give the working area some protection against the elements. Ralph Wilson's boat, *The Talisman*, was still to our port. To the stern, a scavenging cloud of gulls stayed close. They would, though, get less bounty than with a trawler – no fish guts tossed overboard on a lobster boat. The gulls knew the pickings were few and knew they had to be quick. Any live fish caught in the pots were tossed overboard. Once in the sea, the race was on – could they dive quicker than the gulls?

Sean, with his broad solid build, was a native islander. Richard was the only 'incomer' fisherman on the island, often not an easy state of affairs. He'd come here 17 years previously when his parents Jen and George had taken over the Manor House. The two men had bought their boat from Jimmy Brigham (Clinker), Sean's uncle. They were contrasting characters – Richard talkative, jokey, Sean more introspective and given to little verbal communication at sea.

They operated – quite literally – a tight ship. During our five hours at sea there were no tea-break, no snacks, constant work, few words exchanged, their working methods by now honed almost to perfection.

We picked up our first pot at Bridy Hole off the distinctive white beacon of Emmanuel Head (look out for aliens). Sean's responsibility was the wheelhouse, the navigation, finding then dropping again the pots. Richard took charge of the deck. Once the boat was stationary, both worked the deck.

Sean cut the engine in 30 ft of water, ran the marker buoy rope over the motorised winch and up came the first pot. We had three different prey. Lobster – the best prize – which fetched £6 per pound. Small velvet crabs weighed in at £50 per box and the large brown crabs at £25 per box. Much of the day's catch would go to the wholesaler's, though I knew there was a healthy (if unofficial) trade direct to the island hotels. In summer especially, visitors had a seemingly limitless appetite for Holy Island crab sandwiches.

This was cottage industry in many respects. Richard and Sean made their own pots from wood, tubular alloy and netting. Inside each arched, netted pot swung a suspended stone for ballast. This could not always prevent whole fleets of pots shifting along the sea floor.

Into each pot went two pieces of hooked bait and as each pot came up from the sea Sean checked for occupancy. White fish were tossed back into the sea, lobsters tossed into one box, velvet crabs a second, brown crabs a third.

It was then Richard's job to rebait the empty pot and relace the netted entrance. This he did with the blurred-hand speed of a card-sharp, seemingly lacing from thin air. He then picked up the pot and gavotted with it across the deck to form a pile on the ship's stern, or washboard.

So synchronised were the two men's movements that within ten minutes the pots were emptied, baited, laced and stacked, and we were under way to the new site chosen by Sean.

Meantime, the haul. The jet-black lobsters (they turn pink when boiled) gleamed like coal. Their waved giant claws reminded me of a conductor's baton. Their armour was layered and curved at the edge in Samurai style. Their small eyes were extra-terrestrial.

Over each large claw Richard pulled a thick rubber band to prevent mutilations in the box's closed confines. There seemed something ignoble about these remarkable creatures being rendered inoperative via an office accessory.

Velvet crabs were plentiful and were tossed into their box by Sean casually, like stones into a bucket. For a few seconds each crab would gavotte frantically (more frantically than Richard) across the carapaces of their compatriots below them. They too would soon lessen their movements and before long more frantic crabs would land on top of them. Thus layers of crabs built up; the deeper they went, the less active they were.

Crabs and lobsters were sophisticated enough to survive both in the water (indefinitely) and out of the water (for several hours) and they returned to shore alive.

For some reason, humans consider it the height of culinary sophistication to boil a lobster alive in front of restaurant diners' eyes.

Crabs already dead were tossed back into the sea, also lobsters measuring less than the required 8.7 cm from eye socket to first joint. The tool used to measure reminded me of a tailor measuring up for a suit – do tailors still do that anywhere?

As Sean recast the pots, the line whiplashed out into the sea. It had been expertly folded to ensure tangle-free, hyper-fast release. At the end of each line was the marker buoy and flag, and the pots' position was recorded by Sean both hi-tech (a sophisticated satellite navigator) and lo-tech (a dog-eared notebook). The navigator was Sean's pride and joy and seemed capable of offering all the information anyone could ever need, the next Grand National winner apart. The wheelhouse also boasted an echo sounder and radar, a trio of sophisticated electronic pieces which sat alongside the dishevelled clutter elsewhere in the wheelhouse, a jumble of clothing, old stained mugs and odd scattered items, the most incongruous of which was an ashtray, a piece of domesticity fitting strangely into this wind-blown, untamed scenario.

Some crabs flipped themselves over to reveal the soft underbelly. Sean and Richard turned them back and administered a sharp tap on the shell, as if in admonishment. A few had the audacity to crawl from the confines of the box and clatter to the deck in the misguided belief they had attained freedom.

By now the sky was full of light. We dropped the baited pots and opened the throttle towards the second fleet. The boat rose and dipped into the growing swell which sent waves smashing against the wheelhouse window with the impact of hurled gravel. I caught Sean giving me a sideways glance.

'Rough, eh?' I shouted.

'Nah,' he shouted back.

The seas off Emmanuel Head, the island's most easterly point, were often this rough. We steered past Ness End. Both crew were virtually silent, contrasting with the incessant babble on the boat's open radio channel. I remembered this from my North Shields fishing days. The main subject matter hadn't much changed, nor the style of delivery. In language bluer than a police light, the different boats were lamenting the terrible state of that particular day's fishing. Just occasionally Sean would chip in, usually with one, perhaps two syllables: 'Aye' or 'Mebbes'.

'In summer,' said Richard, 'when the seas are warmer, the crabs and lobsters are livelier and we pull in twice as many pots.'

I wondered where, on the cramped deck, they would put the catch.

Which on this day was one dozen lobsters, three boxes of velvet crabs, plus a few brown crabs – total worth about £250. From this came two men's daily wage, the fuel, the bait, boat depreciation. Pots had to be made. Some vacuous marketing consultant, quoting £400 per day for his or her useless labours, would find the occupation something of a mystery. And a risk of drowning thrown in – whereas the main risk to a marketing consultant was a burnt lip from over-zealous application to a hot cappuccino.

By mid-morning the sun shone down on us. Both Lindisfarne and Bamburgh castles were in view, plus the Farne Islands, plus two ranges of hills on the mainland.

Here's a guide on how to pick up crustaceans. Lobsters: simply hold like a cigar along the main body-length. Crabs: in no way attempt to hold like a cigar. Pick up by one leg to remain nip-free. Do it swiftly and boldly.

We steamed in a long arc round the island and towards Snook Point, picking up, rebaiting and dropping six fleets of pots. Sean's aim was to drop the pots on a rocky floor but there were no guarantees he would find one.

The crustaceans had been dragged up from their deep, sunless terrain and crammed tight into boxes. They were humiliated, doomed, and I wondered whether, during this squashed imprisonment, they suffered more or less than the hunted deer or fox.

By midday we were steaming home. Sean threw overboard any redundant bait, eagerly gobbled up by the assembled ranks of eider ducks, the males black and white, the females speckled brown. These were also known as Cuddy Ducks, after their supposed allegiance to St Cuthbert.

The bait sank quickly. The ducks dived down after it. They could dive 20 ft from a standing (or sitting) surface start, more than most birds could dive from the air. They vanished for what seemed infinity, then finally popped up like corks, usually with the bait in beak.

We brought the catch ashore, labelled it and locked it away in a container for collection by the purchaser.

Land-lubbers often romanticise fishermen's lives. In truth the work is hard, unrelenting, dangerous, dirty and often tedious. At sea fishermen are mainly silent and communicate without language. Their lives have little to do with most of our twenty-first-century lives, our sophisticated urbanisation. Most people have little clue what happens on a fishing boat beyond the general activity of catching fish. Fishermen disappear beyond the horizon, beyond our consciousness. It is this removal from the familiar that sees fishermen gather together on land, in a pub, or elsewhere, talking constantly about fishing. What they failed to do at sea, they did incessantly on land, a kind of bonding, an affirmation, a way of putting themselves apart. Fishing is different. Which does not make it romantic.

As Sean's pick-up dropped me off at the Cuddy House, he said, 'Take some crabs home with you,' and shoved a plastic bag in my hand. 'Just boil them for 20 minutes.' And the vehicle drove off.

It was only when I removed the crabs, placed them on the kitchen work surface and saw their enormous claws reaching up in supplication that the full implication struck home. These were living creatures. Which I was expected to kill. What choice did I have? Put them back? Their home was out there somewhere, one mile from shore. Give them away? This would merely transfer the location of execution.

Millions of creatures and animals were slaughtered every day – humans, too. Here I was, anguishing over a brace of crabs. Except you could read of endless deaths. But needed to see only one.

Something of that morning's experience, something of fishing's inevitable brutality, had stayed with me, as if here I was about to square the circle, as if I were destined to perform this act of murder to resolve the day.

The two crabs interlocked their claws, as if seeking safety in numbers. Their live presence filled the kitchen and though I turned my back on them it made little difference.

Crabs and lobsters were normally dropped into boiling water. I'd read that the more 'humane' way was to place them in cold water, slowly brought to the boil. This way, they fall asleep and death was relatively painless. Had someone asked the crabs about this? Else how did they know?

I found the largest pans in the house and filled them with cold water. I placed the incredibly animate creatures one into each pan, where their clattering noise was intolerable.

The clattering classes.

I turned on the electric plates and searched for pan lids. One lid was stainless steel, which conveniently hid from view the sight of the slowly murdered crab. The other lid was glass and the crab died in full view. Nor was I simply able to walk away for 20 minutes.

Electric cookers have a pathological dislike of anything that simmers. They allow either (a) furious boiling or (b) bubble-free hot water. Thus the pans boiled over; froth and scum hissed on to the cooker top. I opened the kitchen door to release the nauseous smell. For 20 uncomfortable minutes I boiled my two crabs before pouring the water away. I removed each pink hot crab with a tea-towel, placed them on the draining board and shot out of the house.

But if I was looking for relief elsewhere, it was not to be found. I walked into the Post Office for my newspaper and came up against the first head-on spat thus far. Day to day, I'd felt various simmering hostilities. Now it came into the open.

The background was as follows. The previous day someone had driven up and parked right up against my front door NO PARKING sign. A sign at the village entrance requested visitors use the car parks and not drive into the village. Thinking I would do my bit for the island's conservation, I shouted after the driver who was disappearing into the gloom. Would they mind using the village car park?

Only when the figure turned did I realise it was Malcolm Patterson, village postmaster and a Fenkle Street neighbour of a few doors down.

'Sorry, Malcolm!' I shouted after him. 'I didn't realise it was you.' He turned away without speaking. Something about his body language forewarned me trouble was ahead.

Malcolm was at the counter. The atmosphere was like walking into an ice-box. As he handed over the paper without making eye contact, he said: 'You're on this island five minutes and already you're telling people where to park.'

'Sorry,' I said, 'I thought you were a visitor and —'

'So what if I had been a visitor?' he cut in coldly. 'Visitors bring money. Visitors are our livelihood.'

A few more icy words were exchanged, after which I took my leave. Only later did I get the full context of all this. The island was split into two schools of thought; those who thought the village was best served by keeping cars out and those who felt trade improved by letting cars in. Malcolm Patterson was of the latter school and I had involuntarily trodden on, and disturbed, the hornets' nest. And the thin skin of peaceful co-existence had been broken.

All this may seem small beer to you, if you live in a large conurbation with a mainly anonymous population. In this tiny, self-enclosed community even the smallest ripple caused ructions. The Post Office was a focal point. The Pattersons were one of the island's longest-established families. By that evening, the whole island would be aware of this conflict.

At such moments you felt out of your depth. The island became a totally unpleasant place where you had little desire to linger, certainly not for another 63 days. I fantasised about the whispers going the round of these small stone streets. That writer fellow, coming here, bossing people about. Not one of us.

Back home, it was the crabs' turn. As I cracked open one shell, a sharp edge cut my finger and out gushed the blood of guilt. I wrapped kitchen roll around the wound and there came a knock at my front door.

I knew it was the vigilantes. They had come to run me off the island. Like that ballerina back in the 1940s. I picked up a crab claw.

It was Christinne Holbrook, picking up her copy of the Hemingway book. Over a cup of tea, I blurted out the whole story.

'A lot of people come to this island for the spiritual side,' she said. 'But with the spiritual, there is always the opposite, the darker side at work, too. Spend any time here and you come across this darker side. Just as you have.'

That evening, in the village hall, the Holy Island Howlers were put through their paces by Jen Ward. Was it my imagination or did I sense some unease here too, a slightly less joyous feel to our warblings? My bandaged finger pulsed.

My mind was far away from 'Tea for Two'. It was filled with the nauseous smell of boiling crabs and the stern sight of the postmaster's face.

TUESDAY, 20 FEBRUARY 2001 – DAY THIRTY-EIGHT

Comfort of Solitude – The Refuge of Books

Solitude was a state human beings both craved and dreaded in equal measure. On this day I craved it, a fervent desire to remove myself from human interaction.

I strode out along the causeway, headed into the sand dunes, explored little-known island relics and ruins, made my way to the North Shore, a place of such utter loneliness and space as to satisfy even the most ardent recluse.

At low tide the sand was limitless, the sea heard but not seen, somewhere beyond the horizon; this was a lonely dreamlike place whose vast flat surfaces housed various large objects seemingly tossed here by giants.

One gnarled tree trunk, spindly branches jutting out, resembled a huge preying insect making its scabrous way across the sands. I photographed it – and it is now the front cover of this book. Other huge pieces of wood leaned this way and that, curved or angular, cast on to this desolate landscape like objects in a Tanguy painting.

Islanders were occupying my thoughts. They were simultaneously prying and uninterested, so that while hardly a native islander quizzed me directly on my task here I sensed they all knew about it.

Holy Islanders were well accustomed to the outside world – documentary-makers, journalists and the like – being interested in *them*. They sat back and waited for the next documentary team or feature writer to arrive and, in wide-eyed admiration, ask their questions, shoot their footage. The world came to Holy Island. Holy Island felt little need to return the compliment. This made it, at the same time, both famous and remote in the extreme.

Nothing of note happened on my long walk, for which I was extremely grateful. The solitude left me equipped to reacquaint myself with humanity.

That evening was the monthly meeting of the Good Read Club. I'd felt an affinity with Hemingway while reading *The Old Man and The Sea*; the lean, no-nonsense but vivid prose style.

In the old man I recognised a painful necessity to go out and face this ordeal alone. The same ambivalence had brought me here, to this island.

Some of the group found the book tragic. I found it optimistic but then I needed to. Whatever else, the old man had caught the big fish. The rest was not of his doing.

We are never totally in charge of our own fate. But if we simply sit back and let that fate roll over us, we are pathetic creatures.

I couldn't control what Holy Island had up its sleeve for me. But I could get myself ready for it.

WEDNESDAY, 21 FEBRUARY 2001 – DAY THIRTY-NINE

Stone Safari – Ubiquitous Eddie

I am a voracious reader of newspapers. I do too much of it, need to balance it out more with books. I often look in the least likely sections. Like today, on the agricultural pages and passing almost unnoticed: an outbreak of foot-and-mouth had been confirmed after a routine inspection of pigs at the Cheale Meats abattoir in Little Warley, near Brentwood, in Essex.

And after *The Old Man and The Sea*, the Middle-Aged Man and The Stone, aka the Holy Island Heave, aka the Barrow Boy Strikes Back, aka the Portage of the Potential Poem Purveyor.

This was a proper Holy Island task and one, probably, unique in the island's history. Who else would lug a stone over the island, carve a poem on it and plant it?

For some days I'd been writing and rewriting the simple poem, looking for the kind of uncluttered lucidity and strong resonance I believe the best poetry contains. Such a combination is always difficult. It is artistic obfuscation that is a dawdle – and our lives are surrounded by it.

I wanted the poem to have some reference to stone, to its origins in the sea, some human reference, some sense of the links I made between the animate and the inanimate. But poets trying to define their poetry should usually keep quiet, so here's the poem instead.

Out of the sea
a heartbeat
of stone

One last point. My son Dylan's name in Welsh meant 'up from the sea', so there was another little link. Completing a poem could act as a restorative, even a mini-poem, and in total contrast to the previous morning I awoke at 5.30 a.m., long before the dawn, my first impulse to race across the island to where my find lay waiting.

I resisted. Tackling the sand dunes, the sudden flooded craters, in jet black was bonkers. I read in bed till 6.15, had tea and scones (courtesy of Jean Peart), fiddled on till 7 a.m., then climbed into my boiler suit and clattered the Burden barrow through village streets totally deserted save for road sweeper Arthur Shell (who'd been doing that same job for so long, some said he'd swept up behind the Vikings).

The Burden barrow, like all barrows, had a split personality and was totally incapable of sticking to one intended direction. It would turn this way and that without warning or logic, so that when we headed out of the village and along Straight Lonnen the barrow made a mockery of that name.

It was still dark but just the slightest hint of pink, like the smear of a blusher sampler, was visible behind the castle as the sky became a dull grey.

Trolley and man came to terms with one another as we headed through the dunes, skirted round the flooded craters, up and over steep hillocks, avoiding rabbit holes and sand traps. The going became heavier and I had to remind myself the trolley was thus far unladen.

Down through the marram grass we made a circuitous way to the east end of Sandon Bay, with Emmanuel Head's white tip just visible as we dropped to the beach and headed west.

A sudden urbanite fear – what if stone was gone?

Stone wasn't gone. Nor the totem, which I replanted to make more secure, wanting it to stay as a permanent marker.

I could barely lift stone, the weight of a small man. I wrestled it on to the barrow, rueing my lack of securing rope, then wheeled the barrow up the steep slope of soft sand. By the top I was puffing like a marathon-runner.

Wheeling the barrow the conventional way was impossible; it simply sank into the sand, the rabbit holes or the thick mud. I devised two other methods. Pull the barrow by walking backwards or walk forwards dragging it behind me.

I needed to pause every few yards, partly because I was knackered, partly to check the route ahead.

Some dunes were too high or too sandy. Others led down to the dead-end of flooded craters. Thick mud was no-go. Often I had to cover large distances to gain a few yards. Three times stone slid off the barrow and needed wrestling back into position.

At the summit of several dunes, I tried the ruse of tipping stone up and over, hoping it would continue thus to the base. Invariably it simply landed with a dull thud and had to be tipped again.

We struggled on until a gap in the dunes revealed the public footpath sign at the north end of Straight Lonnen. The land was flattening to pasture and one mile ahead I could see the huddle of the village.

This task was strenuous but gave me a deep satisfaction. It was part of my own statement on this island. En route I lay several times in the grass, stone and barrow alongside. We were a trinity, holy or otherwise.

At these moments, it seemed stone was alive and willing me on.

The barrow's small wheels squeaked in complaint at the great weight and though our homeward route was initially different from our outward one, the two now met. I noticed our second set of tramlines was three times as deep as the first.

Straight Lonnen, still partially flooded, led through farmer Jimmy Patterson's land. He was outside his barn.

'You sure that's sandstone?' he asked.

'Course it is,' I replied with more confidence than I felt.

'You'll soon find out,' he said.

I trundled the barrow through the village, up Fenkle Street to the Burdens' domicile, the White House. I propped stone up in the shed, went home to a late breakfast then lowered my weary limbs into the bath. At 1 p.m. I lay on the bed, pink and smelling like a baby, and allowed myself the decadence of an early afternoon one-hour kip.

And awoke to the news – otter spotted on island!

The otter-spotter was Jean Hadley from Leamington Spa. Otters were virtually unheard of. I tracked her down. Was she certain?

'I'd know an otter anywhere!' she said, a claim I'd be hard pushed to emulate. 'And anyway,' she continued, 'what are you doing on this island?'

She listened to my explanation, nodded.

'Islanders are very wary people,' she said. 'This is an island race and we ourselves are wary. The smaller the island, the more wary the people.'

I thought of Holy Islanders' wariness of incomers. Thought of Great Britain, its knee-jerk reaction to asylum-seekers, prejudices happily fanned by the tabloids. Thought of the otter.

Later, at Jean and Ross Peart's Open Gate, I watched the video version of Magnus Magnusson's one-hour documentary *Cradle Island*, shot in the early 1980s. I spotted younger versions of many residents talking to camera, often lamenting that things were not what they used to be. But of course, as Mr Punch said, they never were.

I found myself increasingly dissatisfied with island documentaries, found the gap between their perceptions and my realities growing so that, without any conceit, and allowing for Magnusson's long-term association with the place, I felt I 'knew' this island in a way they either did not, or chose not to.

I walked home, Malcolm Patterson's car was parked right across my front door. But my thoughts were with stone and its journey across the island. As if it were a landmark day or some such.

THURSDAY, 22 FEBRUARY 2001 – DAY FORTY

Writer's Cramp – Island Diction

I awoke at 2 a.m., cold as death, body and bones chilled right through. I rose, filled a hot water bottle, drank hot tea, but it was a coldness neither the bottle nor the tea could combat.

It was the coldness brought on by the death of a father, a coldness reinforced by the murder of two crabs. I turned on the electric fire and spent the rest of the night in a cold discomfort nothing could dispel.

My thoughts were on my 85-year-old mother awaiting her second operation in that Rotherham hospital, and my 16-year-old son Dylan, these months of his growing I would never know. And my partner Kitty, the vacuum of her absence.

Eventually I rose, washed, breakfasted and wrote in my diary, 'Day Forty'. Suddenly I felt fatigued by the task of writing 1,000 words every day.

I walked up to the Heugh, stared across at the mainland. It was like looking at a memory, a half-forgotten world, an echo of what once had been familiar but was now removed, as if those three miles of water traversed an entire universe.

And I knew why almost everyone who lived on this island needed to leave it at least once a week. The island's physicality had a strange effect; that vastness of space, the limitless skies that ran to flat horizons; yet alongside this vastness, a claustrophobia.

I thought of a fly trapped under a glass. Horizons that stretched forever but able only to move the same small distance, day after day.

A word about the Heugh. The word is impossible to pronounce but I will try to help. Take it syllable by syllable, slowly. Firstly, say 'hee'. Practice that a bit. Follow it by 'yer'. After a few times, run them together. Finally 'uff'. On its own, then with 'yer' then with 'hee' also. Bit by bit the syllables will run into another naturally. In time you may find you can say it even without thinking. This is the moment to walk into the bar of the Sign of Two Kirstys and casually mention the word in conversation, where you may well get offered a crisp.

A midday meal invitation to the schoolhouse, lasagne and white wine with teacher Caitlin White and her mainland friend from Alnwick, Lizzy Sharp. I realised I was staring at Lizzy like a recent convert to non-smoking stares at someone happily puffing away. It was knowing she was soon to return to that mythical mainland.

A small piece of Holy island news. Caitlin White and fisherman Sean Brigham were now an item.

FRIDAY, 23 FEBRUARY 2001 – DAY FORTY-ONE

A Shadow Looms – Howling On

An exclusion zone had been placed round a pig-rearing unit at Burnside Farm, Heddon-on-the-Wall, Northumberland. This was little more than one hour's drive from Holy Island.

The foot-and-mouth outbreak had now made the front pages. A government spokesman was quoted as saying they were fairly confident the outbreak could be confined to one case.

Foot-and-mouth was almost a haunted phrase in the UK. The outbreak 25 years previously had wiped out vast swathes of the country's livestock. To read this shocking news was like watching some spectre rise from a grave. Any animal of cloven hoof was vulnerable. And the disease had the power to spread with terrifying speed.

Meanwhile I had been thinking of stone and the poem. I rang the Kelso Tool Company in the Borders, explained to owner Bill Douglas my 100 days, my need to chisel.

'I'll send you the special tungsten chisel,' said Bill. 'Any experience of this kind of thing?'

None.

He advised me go into the graveyard, look at the gravestones.

'Though most of the modern ones are done with a ten-minute, sand-blasted stencil. Customers still think they're getting a hand-crafted job. But the art of chiselling is very therapeutic,' he said. 'In London they have chiselling courses for stressed businessmen.'

Stress could be relieved by anything that wasn't your norm. Doctors could build a brick wall to relieve stress, while brickies might paint a picture and artists dig a hole.

I had a soft spot for ironing.

Bill Douglas also sent me some photocopied articles on the art of sculpting on stone.

A special tungsten chisel . . . already I was feeling like a craftsman.

Through my door came a leaflet. 'Six Talks on Faith' by the island's religious big cheeses were to be given at the Heritage Centre around the time of Lent.

I was quite interested in faith. Mine. And other people's. I'd go to them all.

The weather had turned cold, a fierce wind had whipped up. Out along the causeway a car pulled up. Inside was Ross Peart and two nuns, Linda (who I already knew) and Florence (who I didn't). I thought of the faith lectures, wondered if for any of the speakers the faith would be as powerfully simple as for these nuns.

The wind-wrinkled sea was running over the causeway as I walked home, while out in the flooding basin the same wind was scrawling its signature time across the water surface.

That night the Holy Island Howlers met for more rehearsals. Something seemed to have happened. The sessions had become ragged, semi-shapeless. The Manor House, still undergoing a great deal of room decoration, took Jen Ward away. There was some rumbling from the troops. Mark and Mary Fleeson, who ran the Burning Light shop, brought along some comic sketch material which they handed out.

Would I perform this small duologue with Jean Peart? I didn't much like it, nor Jean, and suggested a two-voice comic poem of my own instead. Jean and I arranged our own rehearsals and worked hard making it stage-ready.

I sensed conflict in the air. Potentially corrosive.

One curio in the somewhat tumbledown village hall was the display of photographs from the island's Keep-Fit Pantomimes held in the 1970s and '80s. Various principal boys were in the photos, slapping thighs of generous measure. There were giants, witches, cows, ugly sisters and simpletons. What there wasn't, in any of the many characters portrayed, was one single male. The pantos had died out. And instead of all those women strutting their stuff in public, we now had the Holy Island invisible female army.

I mentioned the Howlers' coming concert that night on the phone to a mainland friend.

'Let's get this straight,' she said. 'You'll be up on that stage singing songs from West End musicals?' She roared with laughter. I didn't see the joke for a few moments.

I was a man who lauded the likes of Capt. Beefheart's 'Trout Mask Replica', who'd collected works by Pere Ubu and Faust as part of my alternative education. I had insisted visitors listened to the likes of West Coast weirdos The Residents. And now I was preparing to sing Lloyd Webber. Ha!

I put down the phone and stared at the receiver. I walked round the house, arguing fiercely with myself and whistling defiantly 'Love Changes Everything'.

And in the Sign of Two Kirstys that night, all talk was of foot-and-mouth and the threat to the island livestock and livelihood. It was strange to hear such earnest talk interspersed with the word 'guffie'.

SATURDAY, 24 FEBRUARY 2001 – DAY FORTY-TWO

Island Snappers – An Island Transformed

Talking of stress relief and therapy, I could find domesticity tremendously beneficial. For the bored housewife, it was no doubt hell. For the writer pummelling the typewriter each day, the changing of bedsheets, the vacuuming of carpets, the cleaning down of work surfaces could work wonders. I set to.

The weather forecast was bad but I looked out on to a clear blue sky. What was the problem?

I wanted to visit the world's smallest art gallery. That was my description, for I can envisage no rival to Nick Skinner's tiny centre. Nick was an ex-policeman who'd retired to the island and now did a lively trade selling prints of his Holy Island paintings – well-crafted, if conventional, views. Nick had the Castle Gate Gallery.

A door opened off the main street and allowed you into a very small 'cupboard'. On all three walls were displayed Nick's paintings. To view the entire collection required only small movements of the neck and eyeballs. There was a bell to ring should you require a purchase or more information.

Ring this bell and a panel opened in one of the walls and there was Nick Skinner's head as he eyeballed you. It was possible, assuming they had not overeaten previously, for three people to share the gallery at the same time. There was no curator.

I returned to finish the vacuuming. The Cuddy House was more personal than most holiday cottages, mainly because it hadn't been planned for letting. Only the death of Wendy Harman's husband, Frank, had forced her to leave the island and family photos (including ones of Frank), plus Wendy's own island paintings, were liberally sprinkled round the rooms.

Up till now I'd done all my writing in the living-room on the beautiful inlay desk. But I was on the move, taking advantage of the morning sunshine to work on the kitchen table, to the barely audible hum of the fridge. And I'd move again, to write on the fitted unit in my bedroom, as if somehow I needed to prove my mobility on this small island.

This was a day for island painters and photographers. I paid a second visit to the Heritage Centre's exhibition of island photographs by islanders.

Pursuing these painters and photographers was, I realised, an antidote. My daily visits to the Post Office for the newspaper were non-pleasant affairs, the transaction between Malcom Patterson and me conducted in a sullen silence. I (and no doubt he) was mightily relieved to find someone else behind the counter occasionally.

I needed the island's creative side.

Much of the photo exhibition got no further than the subject matter of the castle. I wanted to use some of the photos in my book and looked for less predictable subjects. I chose only one with the castle as main feature, by the ex-warden of the nature reserve David O'Connor, where the foreground was piled deep in snow (snow was rare on the island).

I liked George Walker's wide-angle photo of Snook House and Tower (seen by few visitors) and he also had a magnificent dawn over the Farne Islands, where we would not have been surprised to see a white-bearded old man appearing in the blood-tinged clouds.

Enid Riley's skyscape was in total contrast, a huge serenity of blues and greys that seemed to drench the island in a dreamlike state.

A photo also from ace charity collector Eddie Douglas, which captured both a fine sky and the silhouette of a gaunt arthritic Holy Island hawthorn bush.

Soon after, life imitated art. I had been reading at home for 30 minutes when I looked up from the book and saw the outside view totally changed. Snow was thick on the ground and drifting through the air like the fall-out from a feather pillow fight. A car was driving slowly up the street through the virgin snow, leaving thick black tracks in its wake. Incongruously, on the car's roof were strapped a pair of surfboards.

Seemingly, in the blink of an eye, the island had been blanketed in snow.

And my first unpredictable thought was that this severe weather would do for the foot-and-mouth. In fact, it thrived on it.

It seemed almost simultaneous to the snow that I developed a deep racking cough. I am not normally given to coughs but this one shook and convulsed my frame, made me feel like a sick old man. I banked up the fire, drew closer, heard the tuneless whistling down its chimney. The temperature had plummeted, the day outside bulged tight with snow. I trudged through the village, up the Heugh and stared over at the mainland which shimmered in a pale white luminescence against the grey sky. And I thought of stone, propped up in that cold garden shed.

The poem I carved would outlast me, whatever its quality. This was what all artists craved. Our grab at immortality was through our work.

Through the seasons and years and decades and centuries, this poem, if none other of mine, would be intact, on display. Long after spats over parking, long after foot-and-mouth.

Foot-and-mouth. Lambing grew near on the island. Already travel restrictions were being imposed on the mainland. Soon possibly here.

The mainland television scenes seemed to belong to another age, as if we should be watching black and white. They belonged to a time of whooping cough, London pea-soupers, rickets and ration books.

Huge piles of burning animal carcasses whose dark plumes of bitter smoke blotted out the sun. Men poured disinfectant over hay roughly scattered across tracks and paths.

Was this the twenty-first century of the internet, the hi-tech society? What was going on?

SUNDAY, 25 FEBRUARY 2001 – DAY FORTY-THREE

Shanty Town – Asylum Seekers – The Macho Men

That night, to combat the external severity, I banked my coal fire up high and made my bed up on the living-room floor, as the rest of the house retreated before the plummeting temperatures.

The next morning, for the first time, I set to writing without poking even my nose outdoors.

This daily routine of writing, the application, moving the nib across the page, gave me some small affinity with Eadfrith and the island monks in their mammoth seventh-century task of inscribing the Lindisfarne Gospels.

Their labours had produced what many saw as the greatest artistic creation to come from the Dark Ages, a dismal and terrifying time where to create something of great beauty was a defiant act of the greatest heroism. The Gospels had been inspired by St Cuthbert, himself inspired by God.

I could claim no similar inspiration. But the religious did not have a patent on such dedication. At the start of the twenty-first century, for whatever reason, my daily task was to take up the pen and respond to the island around me. This was all I knew.

My cough had taken a vice-like grip. It convulsed me. I was eating well, plenty of exercise and fresh air, no illegal substances. Daily yoga. As some wag might have put it – that explains it. Tactics – to take to your bed or get out and do something. The puritan in me, the ascetic, the drive of the work ethic (which I tried to disguise in an attempt to be 'laid-back' but never quite could), took me out the front door, striding out to Castle Point and the lime kilns.

There was something about these deep gaping holes that haunted me. A metal fence was the only obstacle. Climb this and you were on the lip of the six silent black orifices, circular shafts for an industry which had thrived till the start of the twentieth century. Ingenuity had been needed to construct such deep kilns on a mainly flat island. The kilns were behind the castle and had been connected to the lime quarry by a small railway whose track remains were still visible. Walk down the steep hill and you could gain access to the kiln bottoms, stare up at the lofted circle of sky above. No access for fat people, though – entry was through a narrow aperture.

And beyond, on a flat, featureless and inhospitable peninsula, someone had built a miniature Long Meg or Castle Rig, 14 stones in a circle.

There was a part of this island, probably the least photographed, least famous, least 'beautiful', that I visited times over. It was a place tourists skirted. If they happened upon it, they hurried past with scarce a look. As far as I knew, the place had no name but I had given it one – Shanty Town.

Tourist board brochures would fail to mention it. Documentary-makers did not point their cameras at it. There was little of the aesthetic about this tumble-down spot. It was a shambles of clapped-out shacks, cast-off boat wheels, upturned herring boats used for storage, skips, indeterminate bulky substances under flapping blue plastic sheets, ropes, buoy markers, palettes, barrows, fish boxes, a rock hopper, rusting anchors and chains.

The grass was long and untended, the track puddled and muddied. Some of the fragile huts were tacked with tarpaulin. One had a notice-board in peeling blue paint with the title Northumberland Sea Fisheries Committee. Its mucky glass looked not to have contained any notices for a century.

Rusting window frames were scattered about, a brimful rain barrel was under a drainpipe. There was an air of desolation, neglect. Shanty Town hid itself away at the base of the Heugh, near the start of the pier.

Many of the island males retreated to this ramshackle corner. Much of their work revolved around these huts but I felt there was more, felt that here was a place that was unburdened with the Holy Island image, a place they could retreat to and not give a fig about living in the cradle of Christianity.

I had another planned tactic – drown the cough. Unlikely to succeed but a pleasant enough process, so I drifted round the island drinking holes on this bitterly cold day.

Emerging from the Ship, I heard the bolts pulled shut behind me. It was early afternoon and out in Marygate was a forlorn group of three adults and a baby. They had missed the tide and now faced five hours on the freezing island. Was there anywhere they could go?

By this time, the island had closed down. Only the Sign of Two Kirstys open. No children allowed except in one of those empty, cold back rooms the British keep specially to punish those who dare try for a drink of alcohol while accompanied by infants.

I led the asylum-seekers back to my own house, plonked them down in front of the banked-up fire, told them I still had two hours' drinking to do and left them to it. On return they were stretched out half-snoozing in front of the telly.

I cooked beans on toast for all. I was slightly woozy but remembered the father was Portuguese, the mother a teacher, the baby ten months. I remember little about the second woman. They lived 60 miles south in Chester-le-Street and left at 7 p.m.

Later that night I returned to the same pub, knowing some of the inmates would never have left. Half-slumped at the bar was fisherman Sean Brigham. Behind the bar Kirsty Bevan was eyeing him critically.

'You need a cup of coffee,' she said and returned a few minutes later with a steaming mug which she plonked in front of him. Sean sipped it with obvious relish as its revival qualities seeped into him.

A roar of derision arose from Sean's drinking mates gathered round a near table.

'He's drinking bloody coffee, look – Sean's a big softie.'

Sean winced and tried to disappear into the mug. I thought about the crosses we males have to bear.

Still the temperature fell. And I was coughing up phlegm. I took to my bed with a hot water bottle, sat propped up with a steaming mug of cocoa. Macho man, or what?

MONDAY, 26 FEBRUARY 2001 – DAY FORTY-FOUR

Bed-Bound

Thick snow drifted past the window in that silence only snow could know. I had planned on the next day to journey down to Rotherham to see my poor mother. But the snow may well have been the wrong kind for Railtrack, who I suspected would need to cancel trains.

It lay in the street thicker than a lord's ermine robe. I got out of bed with all the enthusiasm of a slug, slurped down the cornflakes while listening to Radio 4's new book of the week, Stanley Stewart's *In the Empire of Ghenghis Khan*, a horseback journey across spectacular Mongolia.

Trapped and consumptive on my tiny snow-bound island, it was the book I did not want to hear.

'I know this kind of book,' I told the trannie. 'In a few pages he'll be sat with ethnic natives in a primitive hut, eating a local stew that has a sheep's eye in it.'

He was, too.

I was cheesed off with travel writers eating sheep's eyes. Cheesed off with these people swanning round the world and getting paid for it.

Course, I was just jealous. And sick.

I'd planned this day to begin the task of stone. I donned the boiler suit and in the Burden shed lugged stone up on to a work bench position. I was scratching and scribbling at stone's surface and I was coughing and shivering while I was doing it.

Half an hour passed before the realisation that this was a total waste of time and all I was good for on this day was coughing.

I left that cold shed. I trudged back through the ever-thickening snow to the Cuddy House. I returned to the bed I had not long left.

And I closed the chapter of Monday, 26 February.

TUESDAY, 27 FEBRUARY 2001 – DAY FORTY-FIVE

Call of the Wild – Staying Put

There was simply no chance of making Rotherham that day. I had slept off the ill health but there were worse things to worry about.

I awoke to find the winking red eye of my digital clock blinded. My watch told me it was 5 a.m. I tried the light switch. Nothing. A power cut.

Outside the winds were hurling blizzards of snow against the window. The worst weather in a decade was unleashing itself against the island. And we had hardly any defences.

A power cut here meant no lighting, no cooking, no heating – all powered by electricity. I switched on the battery radio. Southern Scotland and northern England were in the grip of an arctic spell, with all traffic in chaos. And foot-and-mouth was spreading rapidly.

Attempts to phone for any rail information were met with a recorded message of 'all lines busy' and a suggestion to try the website. Presumably on a computer powered by rubber bands.

I attempted to phone Berwick railway station. It is now as impossible to phone individual stations as it is individual banks and police stations, all of whom have fortressed themselves inside call centre technology. I phoned my sister-in-law in Rotherham, asked her to look at the web. The news was no trains between Edinburgh and London.

The entire island was without electricity. As were 20,000 homes on the mainland. I did at least have an open fire so I lit it, waiting for its flickering strength to grow before I struggled through to the dark, ice-cold Post Office, complete with soaking floor. Stuart McMurdo drove up in his Land Rover, armed with the batch of daily papers left at the nearest mainland garage. This was as far as he'd been able to get on his planned Newcastle trip for daily radiotherapy treatment for his bowel cancer.

All over the island food was thawing in deep freezes, storage heaters were cooling, people were rooting through drawers for candles. More than at any time in recent years, I felt at the mercy of the elements.

The alarming newspaper headlines on foot-and-mouth only heightened this sense.

And suddenly our grip on this planet seemed exactly what it is – fragile, precarious. All our sophisticated technology, our advanced civilisation. With one tiny virus, one night of extreme weather, we were floored.

The wind whistled round my unlit house. Snow swirled against its walls. And throughout the country, piercing the blinding snow, dark plumes of smoke were rising from the pyres of burning cattle.

I looked with some affection at my small portable typewriter. All the Apple Macs, the Microsofts, the IBMs – useless. But I could still type.

I managed to boil a pan of water on the coal stove top, made a pot of tea and filled a flask.

The island had battened itself down. Not a soul to be seen in the white-piled streets. Dusk would come soon. Then dark. There would be no street lights, no welcome lights in windows. No illuminated entrance to the Manor House. TV screens would be dark, computers inert. No hot water would flow from taps. Radiators would be as cold as death.

And no news as to when power would be restored.

I rang my mother, who had been expecting me that day. It was a poor line but I could hear her sobbing, hear her repeated question, 'When are you coming, Peter? When are you coming?'

I stumbled round the house. I was a prisoner of the weather and of my own conscience. Confinement crowded me in. I cursed everything: the elements, the fates, the world in general.

I sat down, tried to focus my thoughts on something outside myself. What of foot-and-mouth, its effect on the island? I rang council chairman Ian McGregor. Thus far, he said, there were no restrictions on island footpaths or walks.

Outside the wind moaned its cold loneliness. Only three items worked in the house. My watch, the battery radio and the phone. None would keep me warm or fed. And suddenly, whatever the elements, I wanted to be outside the confinements of the house.

I plunged through the deep snow of Fenkle Street. George Ward had valiantly kept open the Manor House and offered hot soup heated on the Aga. Jen gave me some invaluable candles, while a couple from Lincoln sat in the bar and stared out at the white wilderness. They'd sneaked round the police A1 roadblocks to make it via the coastal route. But now what?

I called at Banjo Bill's. Eighty-four years old, alone, and heating water on a Primus. I shared a cup of tea and, in the fading light, returned home. Word now was of a cut lasting at least 24 hours.

I was unable to stay in, ventured out to a north-east wind of such ferocity that the snow travelled horizontally. It clung to the sides of all walls and trees like lichen. The castle road at Glebe was flooded for more than 30 metres and for the first time in most people's memory the Rocket Field was under water.

Down by the Ouse, the wind's ferocity was ladling great scoops of water into the reclining boat's rotting hulk. In Shanty Town a lone fisherman, so heavily swathed as to be anonymous, was (incredibly) busy with his pots.

Next to the Priory, Sanctuary Close was also flooded and the burglar alarm at the Priory Museum, triggered by the cuts, fought to be heard against the whining wind.

I called on Chris and Derek at the Stables. Human company at such times was as warming as the open fire. The house had a portable gas heater; several giant flickering candles gave a defiant sense of warmth and welcome. Derek, recently returned from Brussels with a bad cold (good timing), offered Belgian biscuits and tea.

And asked me – how about a pancake party?

One was to be held that evening at the Burdens' White House. Not in spite of, but because of the extremes. Already, said Derek, it was the longest power cut ever known to the island.

I looked forward to that pancake party more than I've looked forward to anything since a feverish childhood Christmas Eve sleep knowing morning would bring a pair of Stanley Matthews Netbuster boots in my stocking.

Back home, I took up the pen and wrote by candlelight. I felt like Dr Zhivago. I managed to cook mince and tatties on the stove top and kept the fire banked up while the other rooms fought an increasingly futile battle against the cold.

Darkness loped in. It took possession of the village as easily as a war commander when the opposition army had fled. No resistance. We urbanites normally gave darkness no more thought than was needed to flick the light switch, draw the curtains or turn on the headlights. We banished darkness as if banishing it were natural.

Darkness did not mind. It was patient. It was unperturbed at this banishment. Darkness knew its day would return. No matter it was rejected for decades, centuries, millennia. Darkness was natural. Our created light was not. Which meant, in the end, there could be only one victor. Ultimately, darkness could not be denied.

I moved round the house and on entering each room noted how my hand moved involuntarily to the light switch.

We were a valiant, small group gathered at the Burden house. Mike and Anne, myself, Chris and Derek and Banjo Bill Nelson.

A hot fire in the grate, the room's flickering, candlelit atmosphere, Primus-cooked pancakes with such delicious additions as banana liqueur or brandy and sugar. Everyone had produced at least one bottle of wine and there was little doubt it would all be drunk.

As indeed we might be.

And there was something in that gathering, some sense of unity against powers greater than us, so that we slipped gently into a slightly inebriated sense of bonhomie and togetherness, so that we knew the world was dark, cold, inhospitable, but that there was some redemption in that togetherness, that celebration, in all the imperfections and inadequacies of our fellow humans.

So that we stayed together till 11 p.m. and were all reluctant to leave. Out in the streets I walked the short distance with Banjo Bill and noticed how the cold went fiercely for his chest.

The cricketer Don Bradman had died that day. And Banjo Bill had once met him over a billiards table in Leeds.

My fire was still banked high. The room was too hot to sleep in, my normal bedroom too cold. I opted for the small room, which picked up much of the living-room heat, and as I lay in bed the pancake bonhomie dissipated. I realised that at such times, previously, I would have rung my parents, joked on about the adversities. But my father was dead. My mother was sobbing in a Rotherham hospital.

I tried to sleep. Several times strange noises from the roof suggested some creature crawling over it. Each movement was followed a few seconds later by a crashing sound.

The roof was slowly releasing its huge banks of snow. I gleaned some small comfort from this. Without justification, as it transpired.

WEDNESDAY, 28 FEBRUARY 2001 – DAY FORTY-SIX

Matters Worsen – A Narrowing of my World

There was a depressing inevitability about waking at 7 a.m. to find the digital clock still unblinking, the light switch redundant.

The power cut had lasted 27 hours. How much longer?

I turned on the trannie. Here was a velvet-voiced PR man for Scottish Power. His message was as follows: by that lunchtime a repair plan programme would be about to be put into operation. And for such weasel words, such nonsensical stone-walling, the geezer was probably paid £60,000 p.a.

Still no trains from Edinburgh to Newcastle. I formulated a plan. I would somehow make my way to Newcastle and catch a train from there.

But when the fates combine, they employ no half-measures.

A radio newsflash told of a bad accident near Selby. A Land Rover had plunged off a bridge into the track of a train, which had hit another train travelling in the opposite direction. All services between Doncaster and Newcastle were cancelled.

Worse news on the foot-and-mouth. All Lindisfarne footpaths were to be closed. My main route across the island was gone.

There's this character in Edgar Allan Poe's story *The Pit and the Pendulum* who feels the walls, ceiling and floor of his small cell slowly move in on him, his world shrinking and threatening to crush him.

The story came to mind as I moved down the chilly stairs, revived the fire. My house was growing colder. My wailing mother in Rotherham was beyond reach. I could not walk across Holy Island.

And suddenly I was sick of the place. I felt locked in battle with its negative energy. The island seemed to mock me.

'Why aren't you with your sick mother? With your neglected son?'

'Who asked you to come here anyway? The island is telling you. Leave. Leave. Leave.'

I knew somehow I had to see my mother. From the window I could see Stuart McMurdo's parked Land Rover. If he were able to get me to Newcastle, I could hire a car.

And return? Impossible in one day. But to return the next day still meant spending part of each of those 100 days on the island. And what alternative was there?

Stuart was now able to get through. He could take me down one day. Bring me back the next.

It was now 32 hours without power. Power cuts, Selby rail crash, foot-and-mouth, worst weather in a decade. Armageddon. And at Berwick railway station, my ordered ticket, waiting patiently.

In Marygate, Ray Simpson took me under his wing. He was looking after the Open Gate during Ross and Jean's week absence and on the gas stove rustled up a meal.

'You don't look happy,' he said.

'I just want to be off this place,' I replied.

'People need to,' he said. 'Mind, Cuthbert and Aidan never left the island.' He plonked a fish-cake on my plate. 'They were both dead by 40, though.'

Somehow I had failed to notice that this was the first day of Lent. In this I was identical to 99 per cent of the population. Lent passed by in the UK with barely a tremor. Who observed it? How many people had even a clue as to its relevance or meaning? I wrote a small poem:

Miss Otis
failed to notice
as Lent
came and went.

Four o'clock. No electricity for 36 hours.

School-teacher Caitlin White called round. I stuck a saucepan of water on the stove and we watched it for two hours as it failed to boil, as if even the fire's energies were giving out. Eventually we settled for tepid tea the colour of mushroom soup. I rang my partner Kitty in Newcastle, who booked for me a 2.4l Ford Mondeo. This was the kind of gas-guzzling, high-powered macho monster I felt normally belonged to men with penis problems but I wanted something that might get me through the bad weather.

People keep going in adversity but the initial defiant energy bursts are hard to sustain. As the island prepared for its second cold, dark night, a sense of isolation drew in. Again I needed to get out of the house and walked to the Castle View Hotel.

Maybe I needed people with a strong faith. The nuns Linda and Florence were still looking after the place as owner John Collins remained in intensive care following his loft fall.

A closed-down hotel drips with sadness and melancholy; from the empty menu board outside the main door to the sauce bottles standing to attention in the dining-room, and in the self-serve breakfast area, the tupperware boxes in which the cereals waited patiently for guests who would never arrive.

Marmalade cruets and cutlery were still on duty, still to be stood down. This ghost of a hotel did, however, still have 200 guests who needed daily feeding – the array of plants up the stairs and along the hallways. The white-painted building had one of the finest island views, across farmland to the castle, and only two nuns to enjoy it.

There was something strange here; on a closed-down island, in a dead hotel, two nuns huddled round the Aga and offered me a KitKat. They'd spent a freezing night in these cold rooms. And not a hint of bitterness from either of them.

Fierce snow had set in again. I left the hotel and with turned-up collar walked down to Shanty Town. Despite the weather, Sean Brigham was busy fiddling on.

'Nice weather for writing books,' he said. I kept walking, not knowing what else to do. I walked out to the near end of Straight Lonnen where farmer Robert Brigham, whose land the path intersected, already had up the NO ENTRY signs for walkers. The path also ran past the land of the island's second farmer, Jimmy Patterson.

Jimmy was out on the lane. I chatted to him about the outbreak.

'You must be pig-sick,' I said and wondered why he fixed me with such a strange look, till I realised I had said the forbidden word.

I also realised that, had the restrictions come much earlier, getting stone across the island would have proved impossible. I walked on. I didn't want to go back to that house where darkness was taking up residence. The food in my freezer was ruined and only later did I realise I could have removed it and stuck it outside in the snow.

And though I wanted to walk, I couldn't leave the house totally helpless before the dark. I returned home, lit night-lights in every room, felt better.

Thick snow creaked underfoot. Many of the village houses were hunched in total darkness. In some windows candles flickered. Candles made friends of shadows, brought them to life, whereas electric light either banished them or sterilised them. The Manor House was still bravely open, odd shadowy figures hunched over candlelit tables. I walked down Jenny Bell Lane and stared across at the mainland. This could have been some deserted country. No light from Seahouses, the fishing village a few miles south. Nothing from Beadnell. Nothing at all, save the very occasional swish of a car's headlights on some lonely country road.

Bamburgh, Goswick, Berwick – all dark, dead. For several moments I stood and stared at this black landmass. Only the single bright finger of the Longstone Lighthouse moved its optimistic way round 360 degrees.

And on my return walk even the Manor House had given up the ghost, closed its doors.

We were primitives, we were primevals, huddled round our small naked flames. Darkness pressed onto our backs, and onto our consciousness. This was Lindisfarne brought back to its roots, its history, its centuries of huddled survival, its flickering light in the long, long dark.

It was as if these power cuts had come as a reminder of the island's harsh history and its darker forces, forces that were beyond the comprehension of the tourist board, forces which I now believed Gordon Honeycombe had tried – albeit unsuccessfully – to tap into with his novel, *Dragon under the Hill*.

These forces had now manifested themselves, a reminder of their power. I stood silently in the village street. Only the occasional flickering window candle challenged the dark.

And the island, the real island, the essence of the island, which would not be toyed with or played with or indulged, seemed to swallow me down, then spit me out, as if testing me.

And the test left me the most desolate, the most removed, I could have felt.

THURSDAY, 1 MARCH 2001 – DAY FORTY-SEVEN

Stranger in a Strange Land

More snow was impossible. Yet more snow arrived. The angry sky hurled it down throughout the night. Outside the front door, my two black rubbish bags became huge white monstrosities.

I walked ankle deep in the snow to Stuart McMurdo's house. Five times a week Stuart drove the 120-mile round trip to Newcastle for his bowel cancer radiotherapy treatment. This lasted ten minutes. He'd had to give up his oil-rig work. His future was uncertain.

Never once did I hear him bemoan his fate.

And I was to leave the island. A strange elation took hold. An escape, albeit brief, from the severities. And my mother, who I had not seen since my father's funeral, was waiting.

The island was totally white, the causeway and flats splintered with ice. Our first few A1 miles were hazardous and there was some light relief over Stuart's tale of Debbie Luke (mother of Molly in the school) snatching triumph from adversity – rather than chuck out her deteriorating freezer food, she'd thrown a barbecue. Guests munching burgers in a howling blizzard.

Everyone had their own hardship story about the power cuts. My own cooking attempts the previous day had been mixed. A half-cooked pork chop on the stove top, accompanied by frozen peas that refused to boil and resembled grapeshot when eaten.

And suddenly we were in Newcastle. I was out of the Land Rover and in the teeming city centre. After 47 days on the island, there was traffic, crowds, noise, the strong smell of petrol. There were big shops, traffic lights, honking horns.

If all this was disorientating, so was my brief meeting with Kitty and her dog Polly before I drove the monstrously big motor south from Newcastle. The first few miles were in a snowstorm, the car slipping and sliding, a sort of rhumba dance exit from the city.

What a posh car. It had a posh fragrance. I'd once walked through first-class on a big plane – it had smelt like that. Posh.

En route I listened to Radio 3 and Shostakovich's 14th Symphony, 'The Choral'. This was the Russian composer's penultimate work written as an old man in 1969, living in a Soviet nursing home, racked with pain. The work was a defiance; strange haunting music including orchestrated death poems from Lorca and Apollinaire. Death had been staring the composer in the face, inflicting its lingering miseries on him. He'd stared right back at it and written his symphony.

Just as soon enough my mother was staring back at me from her hospital bed. She was a small shrivelled figure. No one had replaced her teeth that day, leaving a sunken mouth similar to that of my father when I'd seen him in the morgue. I replaced them for her.

A drip was attached to her wrist. From under the bedsheet a tube ran out to a waste bag. Her hand, whose veins stood up like old tree roots, was shaking. She asked me to rub cream on her foot pressure sore. An expressionless nurse came in and without looking at or speaking to my mother adjusted the drip. The brusqueness of the act caused my mother to wince.

The window looked out across a bare space to another hospital wing of brutalised architecture. No greenery softened that scene. I brushed her hair, which was like dry white straw. I gave her a ginger biscuit.

'Soon I'll be dead,' said my mother in a faltering voice. 'Then I won't be any bother to anyone.'

I thought of Shostakovich, some creative life force driving him on to battle pain and old age and write his symphony. Did anything drive my mother on?

She was sobbing gently.

'I keep thinking your father will walk in.'

I took her frail hand, felt her brow. I felt useless. She was Irish farming stock, had grown up a Catholic, long since lapsed. I'd been brought up Catholic, too, and even now wondered if I was free of its guilt and its repressions. Even now, tugging at my coat as I indulged certain harmless pleasures, it was there. Catholicism.

My brother Alex was away. My nephew Matthew was out of hospital, still weak but convalescing. My sister-in-law Helen gave me a hot meal, warm room, hot shower, central heating. I sprawled about in this luxury, knew its nature was transient.

On television was the film about Ellen MacArthur's single-handed round the world journey in the yacht *Kingfisher*. She was 24.

I suddenly realised how, for most people, this was the golden age of non-responsibility. We were grown up, independent. Most of us were yet to have children. Most of our parents were still fit and strong. We needed neither looking after nor to look after others.

How brief was this honeymoon between our own adolescence and then our responsibilities to our children, and more and more to our ageing parents. And how little we appreciated it at the time.

I lay in the soft warm bed. Would Holy Island drain me or energise me? It seemed even stranger, more remote and isolated from here.

What did the island want from me? Why had it asked me to come?

FRIDAY, 2 MARCH 2001 – DAY FORTY-EIGHT

Few Reasons to be Cheerful

Helen cooked me a huge hot breakfast. I was cocooned in this safe warm environment, far from the cold, dark, blizzard-lashed island.

I called again to see my mother. During the hip replacement operation, they'd broken her femur. The hip had become infected and was being treated with antibiotics. I asked to see the relevant doctor. He had a charming bedside manner, was ultra-polite, but could tell me nothing about her length of hospital stay, healing time and so on.

Everything had gone for my mother. The house, sold to pay for the nursing home. Most of the furniture and possessions – gone. Her husband, dead. Her health, failing. Her universe had come down to this hospital bed, this trembling hand struggling to lift a spoonful of Weetabix.

Times over on this brief morning visit, she asked me the same questions. Was Helen bringing her soap? Was Alex still away? And then, unexpectedly, before I left, she said, 'Write your book, don't worry about me.'

The two were inseparable.

I didn't know when I would see her again. I needed her to smile for me, cajoled her till a weak smile forced its way through, just like that sun forcing its way through the appalling weather.

I walked down the endless hospital corridors, unconcerned if people could see the tears on my cheeks. I knew there would be tears on my mother's cheeks too.

The big fast macho car whizzed me back to Tyneside and past the Angel of the North at Gateshead.

'Fill me full of hope, Angel,' I said. Because that was the angel's function.

Another desperately short meeting with Kitty and Polly, then Stuart McMurdo and I were trekking to the far north where, unbelievably, snow was falling even harder, so that the A1 south of Holy Island was blocked.

We needed a high detour through Belford. As we dropped down again the island stretched itself out to the east, white and ghostly, like something from a morgue.

Over the causeway, which seemed to seal itself behind us, pushing us towards the island where another seven weeks awaited. And where good and bad news awaited, too.

The power cut was over. But a letter from Jen Ward cancelled the Holy Island Players (the Howlers) concert, putting lack of rehearsal time as the reason. Also cancelled was the Monday arts & crafts club, a regular refuge for me and a rare chance for all-female company.

There was a sense of things unravelling, of the extreme cold forcing apart the atoms that made up this small society.

And far from being a restorative, my mainland visit proved disruptive, disturbing, left me unrooted.

News came through from Tyneside, where my son Dylan was in a play of mine. He'd failed to turn up for a performance. I felt him drifting from me, our lack of contact ripping the fabric of our relationship. As if my real life were all drifting away. And for what?

I tried to think positive. Good things had come from the long black-out. Islanders had sought out the old and the vulnerable and helped them. Pubs had acted as meeting places, both for material and mental support. This small community had also shown its strengths, had reached out to protect its own, as it always would, no matter what feuds, what bickering was rife.

Sometimes I wanted to lie back, allow its warm embrace to surround me, aware at the same time of the risk of suffocation.

SATURDAY, 3 MARCH 2001 – DAY FORTY-NINE

The Shrinking World

Or maybe suffocation was never a risk. Certain agendas were always on the table, if rarely addressed. Thus some islanders' concerns as to what I would write. Thus postmaster Malcolm Patterson's hostility at my seeming interference in island affairs.

Others felt disgruntled at me, too. As I would eventually learn.

That night, temperatures in the borders were recorded at 20 below. I had slept fitfully. My big heavy Civil Defence coat, which I'd worn on and off since 1967, I threw over the bed. I moved the hot water bottle round a permanent circuitous route to spread its heat. Mercury plummeted to new depths, the cold clenched its fist so tight it cracked its own knuckles.

There was a terrifying sense to this cold, for it seemed to go hand in hand with snow that simply refused to stop falling. So that it would fall and fall and fall, slowly burying us all, and that would be that.

Old people shrivelled at firesides. Youngsters whooped with glee to sledge down the Heugh. And as the weather took hold, so too did that second, more serious adversary, foot-and-mouth.

All island footpaths now had NO ENTRY signs. The dunes were also out of bounds. My universe, small enough to start with, shrank even further and I contemplated the prospect of the next 51 days spent walking up and down the main street.

The sequence of events had thrown my routine. I had fallen behind with my island books. I also realised my front step was the only village one still to be uncleared. Was I being paranoid or would this have been noted in the appropriate places? I set to with shovel and brush.

My insecurity had led me to arrange another party, due the next day. This was my 50/50 party and making arrangements gave me the perfect excuse not to write.

All afternoon I made up party games, hoping there would be enough guests to play them.

Remember the Dutchman Harm, who preferred to give me a wide berth? In the next 24 hours I was to feel a strange affinity with him.

It started on this day. He was standing at the main village crossroads. It being

Saturday, a few visitors were coming to the island. As they passed Harm, he would shout, 'We have foot-and-mouth in the country – all visitors should be kept off the island!' He was making the same insistent views heard that night in the Ship. Harm was shouting himself into trouble.

I doubt any of this would have been evident to the new owners of the Ship, Frank and Pauline Gregory from Burnley, who'd jumped at the chance of buying the pub/hotel.

Here, on their opening night, Frank was waxing philosophical behind the bar.

'When that tide closes,' he said, in a distinctive Lancashire brogue, 'there's just this beautiful feeling of peace and tranquillity on this island.'

Of course, he had only just arrived.

I left the Ship, and though my first thought was for another drink, my rasping cough and aching limbs reminded me that I'd been feeling dog-rough for the best part of a week. This was almost unheard of for the hardy Mortimer constitution. But there was no denying it. I made my timid way home and went straight to bed.

SUNDAY, 4 MARCH 2001 – DAY FIFTY

The Trapped Sea – The Tidal Party

My instinct on waking was to roll over, pull the sheets above my head and remain there for about three centuries.

First, though, I would need to stagger from the bed and Blu-Tack a note to the front door: '50/50 PARTY CANCELLED. BUGGER OFF.'

I engaged in a full coughing symphony. This comprised four movements and brought into action every part of my tired old body. The cough was the only part of this body with any energy and seemed oblivious to the rest of me feeling knackered.

We had now had a full week of ice and snow, a week in which the temperature had stubbornly refused to reach freezing point. The island, I told myself, was slowly draining me of energy. It had waged a war of attrition against this nosy upstart of a writer.

Or was this all in the fevered imagination of someone suffering an excess of coughing and snowing?

And hadn't I arranged this very party to gauge whether I could lay claim to the title Mr Popularity or deserve the acronym HIR (Holy Island Reject)?

These thoughts stirred me to more positive action. Plan A would now be to rest in bed till 10 a.m., recover my strength, rise and prepare the house for the onslaught of guests.

I willed myself for the next 90 minutes to re-energise and at 10 a.m. I rose, washed, dressed, vacuumed and cleared the house. I put out bowls of nuts and crisps, arranged the rooms into party mode. I hummed aloud, dragging my spirits up by the scruff of the neck. My mood improved.

And improved even more with a knock from my Cullercoats/Holy Island neighbour Stuart Moffitt. Did I want to drive out on to the causeway to witness the extreme sights produced by these conditions?

We drove off with his daughters Jenny and Helen on this bitter-cold ice-blue morning, parking the car near my erstwhile home, the refuge box.

Cold could be a drag but also a small miracle. As here. The light was extraordinary, shimmering like some living entity against the huge reflecting flats. And spread before us was the largest expanse of frozen sea you are ever likely to see in the UK.

In these extreme temperatures, nature did what humankind could never do. It trapped the tide. The incoming water made its thin and silky way across thousands of acres of flat sand. It was normally an unstoppable force. But for the last few days it had been heading into an ambush.

The tide, unknowingly, simply spread itself too thin to combat the extreme cold. It pushed onwards, rather like Napoleon's army towards Moscow. Doomed. Its resistance to the freezing air weakened. The water surface began to splinter into ice.

Eventually the tide would turn and run back to the safety of the deep, unfreezable sea. But for some it was too late. It was trapped, frozen *in situ*. Miles and miles of it.

And so the next tide would come and push this ice on and the process would continue. With the temperature unmoving, more and more ice pushed on, banking up like those 2p pieces rolled down chutes in amusement arcades. It banked up on the causeway where council bulldozers had to shift it. It had been known to bank up to the height of a man.

This huge skating rink stretched south down to Fenham Flats and north up towards Goswick. In the distance the layered lines of snow and ice looked like breaking waves captured in a deep freeze.

We were looking at nature defeating nature.

And on this bright, clear, vivid white sea and icescape, with a backdrop of frozen hills, on this day was spotted (though not by me) a black swan. I imagined its great beating black wings silhouetted against the shimmering white.

The effect of this whole spectacle was to make me forget all ailments. Driving back through the village, we were stopped at the Marygate crossroads by Eddie Douglas. Nothing in particular. It happened to everybody. A bit of chat, then on. Halfway through the chat, his air ambulance collecting tin might mysteriously appear. And you'd fallen for another sucker punch.

My 50/50 party mimicked the tides. One wave arrived at 12.30, then receded late afternoon. A second wave arrived early evening and stayed till midnight. My party thus lasted 12 hours, during which time I engaged in some serious coughing.

ROLL CALL

First Wave – Stuart and Margo Moffitt (bearing cheeses), teacher Caitlin White (bearing Mediterranean snacks), Mike and Anne Burden, Chris Holbrook and Derek Pollard, council chairman Ian McGregor (all bearing booze).

Second Wave – Jean and Ross Peart, Robert Massey, son of Lindisfarne owners Sue and Clive, Lesley and Roger Anderson of Wild Duck Cottage (all bearing booze), Banjo Bill Nelson (bearing booze and banjolele).

Notable absentees – Jen and George Ward of the Manor House, Ray Simpson.

Verdict – Ah, fellow humans! My heart bleeds for you!

MONDAY, 5 MARCH 2001 – DAY FIFTY-ONE

Rumour Factory – All you Mead is Love

As you do, I lay in bed running through the events of the party. No sex or drugs or rock 'n' roll. Lots of crisps. Lots of guests having to imitate famous people. No hassle.

A knock at the door. Who was the least likely island inhabitant to knock at my door?

Harm.

It was he.

He looked wild-eyed, dishevelled. So little change there.

'Peter,' he said (and I felt strangely affectionate towards him, hearing him say my name for the first time), 'have you been spreading rumours about me not wanting people on the island?'

Harm had been given a roasting by various islanders for his views, though it had not been me spreading rumours, more a case of him making the utterances loud and public. I told him this.

'OK,' he said and nodded his head. He looked strangely sad. As I shut the door, I heard the voice of another islander raised against him in the street. Harm was berated long and loudly.

Suddenly I felt sorry for him. He was an outsider, something of an eccentric, one against whom invective was always likely to be unleashed. On this small island ran a strong conformist streak, a protective instinct that could see ranks close rapidly against anything seen as errant.

Harm's outpourings – which had some logic behind them – threatened the island's economic survival. And running beneath the surface of the hostile reaction he attracted was the unspoken, only half-understood criticism that he didn't 'belong'.

Harm had already been banned from one pub. Now he found himself banned from the Post Office.

He could have survived in a big city with little problem. But this wasn't a big city.

Living on this island wasn't always easy. I met several people who worked here but had chosen to up sticks and live on the mainland. Lyndsey Hackett was one such, the 38-year-old owner of the Lindisfarne Mead factory, or St Aidan's Winery. He'd inherited the business from his father but had moved his home some years back to Berwick-upon-Tweed, nine miles up the coast.

I didn't fancy indulging in much alcohol on this day but thought I might go and visit some. Hence I found myself inside the premises of the island's largest employer.

It wasn't Whitbread's Brewery. It did not churn out endless barrels to be sped to an ever-thirsty nation. Distilling took place four times a year and took ten days each time.

I'd never given mead that much thought. You neither, I wouldn't wonder.

I'd never walked into a public house with the ejaculation, 'Ah, landlord! A glass of your best mead, if I may be so bold!' Who has? But somebody drinks the stuff. A million quid a year's worth, just from this distillery, the largest of six in the UK.

Mead seems removed from the prevailing alcohol culture in the UK, which sees millions spent on advertising booze as a sexy attractive lifestyle for the young and beautiful, whereas it causes more violence, broken homes and crime than any other drug. The nihilistic drink culture of our repressed, sullen society astonishes many foreigners, for whom a night out could be something pleasant, rather than a desperate journey for the dubious delights of oblivion.

I should know. I'd been rat-arsed often enough. But I was beginning to look on it as just a bit tedious. Contrary to several comedians' portrayals, drunks are usually boring.

Kingsley Amis invented the only honest alcohol advert – which of course was never used. 'Drink Beer – It Makes You Drunk'.

Mead seems to be the only alcoholic drink totally removed from the 'image culture' of the ad men. Examine a bottle of Lindisfarne Mead and note its medieval script, its old-fashioned design, its seeming lack of interest in suggesting street-cred.

Mead is wine and honey (plus a few secret herbs) and has been produced on the island for half a century, though some say the island's first monks made the initial batches.

In those 50 years they've produced only three different brochures. The company spends virtually nothing on advertising and despite the 'Celtic boom' exports nothing.

Lyndsey Hackett welcomes thousands of visitors a year to the premises. A look at the tasteful leaflet might suggest something other than the box-like functionalism, the pebble-dashed monstrosity that is the distillery, attempting to skulk behind other buildings, and erected in the virtually planning control-free decade of the 1960s.

The dozen or so employees included only one island resident, Sheila Wilson, who had been stirring the fudge (a by-product) for 36 years.

'Islanders don't really like regular work,' said Lyndsey. 'They prefer a bit of this, a bit of that.' So the employees worked flexi-time to combat the tides.

The distillery gift shop ironically stocked the island's biggest range of groceries and was the only island place to buy the famous Craster kippers.

So was he interested in some slick advertising make-over, some high-powered campaign to make mead the got-to-have drink of the moment? No, he wasn't. He was all right, was Lyndsey.

Did he have children who might inherit the business begun by his father?

'I have two sons and one daughter. One of the sons is interested.'

How old was he?

'Eleven.'

That afternoon I sat on the top of the Heugh and looked down on St Cuthbert's Island. This was cut off for at least seven hours each tide and offered about as much shelter as a mountain top. St Cuthbert would spend days and weeks there in contemplation.

In the second half of my 100 days I should do a bit of that too. Just because it was there.

That night, the Russian satellite Mir was in the south-west sky for a brief two minutes at 7.30 p.m., and what better place to view it on this cloudless night than the light-pollution-free heavens of Holy Island? I took myself up Sanctuary Close and the clear sky had such an intensity of moonlight that for the first time ever I had to shield my eyes against lunar light.

I spotted Mir through the binoculars, arcing its brilliant parabola across the night sky. Its red and white light spluttered like a sparkler. I stood in the silent empty dark of the sanctuary, my feet rooted to Holy Island soil, tracking the satellite's great restless journey round the earth that was biding its time till it pulled it back to destruction.

How free the satellite was. And how imprisoned in its arc. In that silent moment I empathised with Mir on its great isolated journey. Its faint spluttering light seemed to be the light of humanity, vulnerable, beautiful, erratic, breathtaking in its journey potential, yet ultimately doomed.

That satellite shone for everyone. A great feeling of solitude took hold. This was not loneliness. I felt linked to every other human on the planet yet knew, ultimately, each one of us was alone.

I followed Mir's arc to the horizon, watched it fall and splutter out of sight.

I decided I would raise a glass to Mir.

Except I couldn't. Not one of the four island pubs was open. Foot-and-mouth. No trade.

TUESDAY, 6 MARCH 2001 – DAY FIFTY-TWO

The Screw Tightens – The Folk of Faith

Sunshine poked its head round a cloud, spluttered 'can't stop!' and was gone again. The sky returned to a dull grey and the piles of snow, momentarily alarmed, settled back into their street-corner huddles, their stretched-out reclining on roofs.

I noticed how my clothes were becoming darker, more functional, my bright colours more and more confined to the wardrobe.

I had with me few of my own possessions. At home, like all of us, I owned too much. No car, no dishwasher, but still too much. The vast majority of items I'd left at home and never once missed them. What were they for?

This eternal cold was taking its toll. My friend Banjo Bill had been taken off the island to Ashington Infirmary with an infected chest.

Also taking its toll was foot-and-mouth, slowly eating into the island's economy. At lunchtime in the Manor House George Ward told me he'd lost a party of Norwegian vicars, which may have sounded like a Monty Python sketch but was more serious. A joint full-week booking with the Lindisfarne for 50 from Newcastle Royal Grammar School had been cancelled too.

The island was closing itself in. On this day Sanctuary Close had an exclusion notice attached. This caused some dissent. Livestock was rarely kept there and the closure meant the two-minute walk to the Heugh now became a 20-minute diversion.

Foot-and-mouth had never crossed the causeway to the island. But as the mainland crisis deepened, and lambing grew closer, there was even talk the island might be closed altogether.

Tourism was by far the biggest earner, and though the season was some distance away, so too, everyone believed, was the end of the foot-and-mouth crisis.

I wasn't certain if this was the best or worst time to hear the first talk on faith at the Heritage Centre that night. Fourteen people turned up to hear Kate Tristran, former warden of Marygate House, and present curate of Holy Island. Fourteen may sound a small audience. Percentage-wise, if the same proportion turned up for an event on Tyneside the audience would be 100,000.

And as was the way with such things, the audience contained no native islanders.

Part of my experience here was, I began to realise, coming to terms or otherwise with religion. This was a slow, changing process, whose end product I was uncertain of. All I could do was look and listen.

Kate Tristran was 70 years of age and possessed a formidable gentility. She was humorous, self-aware, both critical of and at ease with herself and comfortable with an audience. As an Oxford student she'd had a moment of epiphany and gone off to study theology at Durham. Her and 200 blokes (no female vicars then). Another 'moment' had told her, 22 years ago, to leave her comfortable academic life and come to Holy Island.

Christianity, she said, was her liberation. She was energetic and enthusiastic, assets which, despite my huge doubts on matters religious, were a perfect antidote to the island's growing gloom.

This gloom transferred itself later into the bar of the Lindisfarne Hotel where Clive and Sue Massey stood surveying the empty tables and chairs. The previous night's takings had been £2.00 (if they'd stayed open later, I could have doubled that). Tonight was little better.

I drank quickly, eager to help.

The island seemed to be closing itself down, wrapping itself up in protection against the times to come.

WEDNESDAY, 7 MARCH 2001 – DAY FIFTY-THREE

The Bead Game – AGM Red Mist

The soul, the bones, the whole body and spirit longed for sunshine to lighten us. Monday had offered a vestige. Tuesday, none. And on this cold grey Wednesday, to replace the snow a freezing grey rain set in as temperatures plummeted once more.

The island was starved. Of everything. At the school, Caitlin was in low spirits. Even the sight of snowdrops in the yard failed to lift her. Joel and Molly spent playtime searching for rabbits – not many schools where this was possible.

We decided to write a communal story. Molly was proud of her bead collection. Joel wanted his favourite rockpools mentioned. Here's what we came up with.

'THE LOST BEADS'

One day, on Holy Island, no one could find any St Cuthbert beads. They looked at Jenny Bell's Well, at Chare Ends, in the sand dunes and all around St Cuthbert's Island (where they were normally to be found). But there was none.

Everyone was really sad because the beads were lovely, like jewels, and finding them made the islanders happy. The fishermen looked, the farmers, the publicans, the vicars, and they even sent a telegram to the Queen – but it was no good.

Everyone met in the village hall to see what could be done.

'Let's look with a magnifying glass,' said one, but that didn't work.

'Let's look with binoculars,' said another, but that didn't work either.

'Why not try a telescope?' suggested a third, but that didn't work either.

'We could sift through the sand with a soup spoon,' said a fourth, so they tried that, but again no success.

'Why not ask Joel and Molly?' asked someone else. Joel and Molly knew all about the beads. But where were they?

'I bet they're playing in Joel's favourite place,' said someone. This was the rockpools and when they looked for them – there they were! Everyone in the village wanted to know if Joel and Molly could help them find the beads.

'Yes,' said Joel and Molly, 'but we don't think you're all in the right mood. You have to feel good about one another before you can find the beads.'

So the farmers decided not to think nasty things about the fishermen, and the publicans not to feel bad about the vicars and so on and so on. And when they'd got rid of all the nasty negative thoughts about one another, Joel and Molly said, 'Right. Now, let's all look together.'

So they did. And all the places where they hadn't been able to find the beads, they now could find them! Some of the beads they found were star-shaped, some had a hole in the middle.

And everyone was amazed and took the beads home and put them on the mantelpiece.

After that, they knew exactly what to do when they wanted to find any more beads. And when they couldn't find them, they knew what was wrong.

The island was so pleased with Joel and Molly that they were appointed as the Official Guardians of the Holy Island St Cuthbert's Beads to ensure all the found beads stayed on the island, which was where they belonged.

By Molly, Joel, Caitlin and Pete.

Now, dear readers, I tell not a lie – the moment we finished this story, the sun came out! This was so exciting I rushed to get Tim Parkin's bike from the Palace Field barn and cycled as far as the causeway bridge.

I stood at the edge of my universe, thought of my night-lights in the nearby refuge box. Under the raised bridge road a torrent of brown water was hurtling its way back to the North Sea as the flats emptied themselves. Three hundred yards from the causeway was one of the pedestrian refuge boxes on the Pilgrim's Way.

Something drove me to examine it. Twice I ventured out into the water, only for it to lap over my welly tops. Only on the third attempt had the waters receded enough.

Walkers got a less palatial refuge than motorists. No roof. No bench. The rough wooden ladder was vertical and the whole affair resembled a primitive machine-gun tower.

A metal plaque announced the box had been built by the Community Task Force of the Manpower Services Commission and opened on 14 Sept. 1987 by John Selwyn Gummer, of daughter and beefburger fame.

I decided to inspect the box's interior. This took up a good 20 seconds. By the time I descended the ladder the flooded area I had walked through was now simply muddy sand, an unpleasant experience akin (I imagine) to walking through a treacle pudding.

Alongside my parked bike was a parked car. Inside were two gadgies in peaked caps and faces as polished as a Worcester Permain. In broad Northumbrian one leant from the window and asked, 'Are yee a painter 'n' decorator?'

I was wearing my paint-splattered boiler suit.

'Actually,' I replied, 'I'm a writer.'

They stared at me without conviction and told me they were from Bowsend. 'That's near Ancroft,' they said. 'Yoos ivvor hord of Ancroft, hev ye?'

'Not only have I heard of it,' I replied, 'for many years a travel article of mine was framed on the wall of the public house there, The Lamb.'

They looked slightly surprised at this. I pushed my advantage home.

'Of course, The Lamb is closed now – you'll know that.'

They looked me up and down again without replying. Eventually one said, 'Aye, well – ah suppose ye'v got the hair of a writer.'

I waved them goodbye and cycled back to the village, happy to have established some credentials.

That evening was the AGM of the Holy Island Development Trust. Following the philosophy that I nosed my way into every single meeting on the island unless physically barred, I made my way along the street.

AGMs were, in my experience, the most tedious of meetings, a mechanical ticking off of formalities, a re-election of the same dumb clucks in the absence of anyone else mustering the energy to stand and the eventual relief-filled repairing to the bar. Thus democracy.

For a while it seemed the same dull format would be followed. Minutes and motions were hurried through in the packed rear room. 'Matters arising?' People stared at the floor. 'Those against?' Not a murmur.

Until 'Any Other Business'. Foot-and-mouth was mentioned and the policy of restricting vehicular access to the village. The effect was explosive and immediate – a firework dropped into a petrol tanker. Within seconds people were on their feet. One trust member and one audience member pointed folded agendas at one another and shouted. They were like two battleships training their guns.

More and more people were joining in, raised voices, red faces, shortened tempers. Something had been unleashed. The village's smouldering volcano had erupted. The festering sore had burst its scab. These were the same shark-infested waters (steady with those metaphors, Mortimer) I'd been cavorting in when I'd asked postmaster Malcolm Patterson to move his car that fateful Sunday. The two opposing armies poured on to the plain, closed ranks.

One army believed the village should be kept free of all visitors' cars. The other army believed this damaged trade.

Rene Richardson of the Heritage Centre turned on her heel and walked out in disgust. Chairman Ian McGregor struggled to keep order.

The uproar lasted several minutes. Eventually a peace about as fragile as those brokered at Camp David was established. None of these people right now, I realised, would have a snowball's chance in hell of finding a single St Cuthbert bead.

The meeting closed uneasily. Beneath the surface, something rumbled. And the following Friday was the meeting of the Parish Council. I wondered: did we need to bring our own weapons or would they be provided?

It was in the context of this battle royal that I watched, the same night, a video of Holy Island's programme in the Channel 4 series *Paradise Found*. Celebrities were invited to spend a retreat somewhere and discover the effect.

This 'celeb' was the mainly forgotten actress Shirley Anne Field. Her Holy Island week was under the guidance of Andy Raine, Christian dancer from the island's Catholic church (and Joel's dad). We heard the two of them in conversation, saw her in all the island's well-known religious sites, heard her thoughts. At the programme's end she revealed how much enlightenment this spiritual place had brought her.

It wasn't Andy Raine's fault, nor particularly Shirley Anne Field's, that the programme was such a sham. After all, a gel's got to get what publicity she can in that game. And to have confessed to no enlightenment would have meant no programme transmitted.

The programme took on board and greedily indulged every Holy Island stereotype to create its artificial conclusion.

They should have filmed the AGM at the Heritage Centre. Now that would have been enlightenment.

THURSDAY, 8 MARCH 2001 – DAY FIFTY-FOUR

Silence of the Lambs – Bread Cast upon the Water

The uproar at the AGM had made me feel good. So it wasn't just me that people shouted at. The more upset they'd got, the calmer I'd felt.

I'd finished the latest book from northern writers – given me by novelist and playwright Julia Darling. This was in line for worst title of the year, *The Lost Salt Gift of Blood* by Alistair Macleod (no, no, not Maclean).

I'd read nothing of Macleod's but noticed later he'd been given a major international award and can only hope he survives it.

The book's short stories revolved round the remote Nova Scotia fishing community in little-known Cape Breton, so the social and cultural similarities with Holy Island were obvious.

Macleod could take as long to write one story as I might to write this entire book, his every word polished like a gem. The events in the stories were simple but profound, with an almost mythical resonance that in the best way made the stories haunted.

The death of a fisherman swept overboard is seen through the eyes of his young son with shocking effect but not a shred of sentimentality. It left me in tears, not the cheesy Hollywood variety, but real ones. One story has what could be a panto plot – a farmer forced to sell his favourite beast to the knackers' yard – yet Macleod invests it with almost unbearable sadness and power, again through the eyes of a child.

All the stories are seen through children's eyes; a vividness, purity and power adults are no longer capable of. And no, not like a Walt Disney film.

In fact, the greatest compliment to these stories is that they will never be filmed. Bad books make good movies and no amount of hi-tech nor millions of dollars could recreate the painfully and richly layered textures of this one writer's imagination. Read 'em!

I wanted to be close to the lambing. At this strange time, especially. Farmers had a reputation for grumpiness. How would Jimmy Patterson react to me? An added piquancy was his relationship to the postmaster Malcolm. Brother.

But there was no problem. Come and look anytime, said Jimmy with a total grump-free air. His Beblow Farm had 270 acres and 400 heavily pregnant sheep, breeds whose names were mainly unknown to me: texel, mule, beltex and – more familiar – Suffolk.

One thing I learnt fast – new lambs were rapidly introduced to the world's harsh realities. Males were immediately castrated and both sexes were spray-painted for identification.

The castrator-in-chief was Jimmy's 31-year-old son Martin. The instrument in question resembled a large nutcracker (sorry about that). It was slipped up over the lamb's tail, one snip and the job was done. The lamb needed to lie down afterwards but then so would I.

At least lambs, unlike calves, got a brief spell of time with mum before being whisked away in June for the mint sauce treatment. Often, said Jimmy, they were still suckling at the time.

On the lane that led up to both Jimmy's farm and that of Robert and Janice Brigham was laid disinfected straw, plus large NO ENTRY signs. My work clothes had been on the island eight weeks, so posed no threat. Both farms were owned by Lord and Lady Crossman and both were small, non-industrialised settlements where livestock at least had the chance of discovering what grass and sunlight were.

Jimmy's barn was 80 ft x 60 ft, the lambs and sheep housed in clean, dry, sweet-smelling straw, no overcrowding, no signs of stress. Each time I entered the serenity of this barn my main desire was simply to lie down with the lambs.

On a day such as this – it had turned to blue sky, gentle sunshine, a light breeze and that special vivid light unique to Holy Island – striding out across the open fields could make tales of farmers' despair seem ridiculously remote.

'Come and see the lambing in the middle of the night in a howling gale,' said Jimmy. All right. I would.

The farm had a fantastic backdrop across the fields – the rising magnificence of Lindisfarne castle. Jimmy looked surprised when I waxed lyrical about it.

'Don't suppose we tend to notice it any more,' he said.

I'd come for the freneticism of lambing. Here we were, Jimmy, Martin and me, swinging on the gate and chatting on. The only busy bee was Jimmy's wife, Margaret. In an example of that diversification of labour that saw many Holy Islanders doing a bit of this, a bit of that, she was boiling up a vat of crabs.

But like Jimmy said, at lambing time you never knew: a few quiet hours, then you could be off – whoosh – a 23-hour day.

I'd never closely studied a ewe and newborn lamb. The mum was waddly and pudding plump, the infant as skinny as a pipe-cleaner, legs wobbling like a 1950s rock singer. Mum's bass-baritone bleat contrasted sharply with the baby's falsetto.

Martin spotted an imminent birth up in the fields. Don't ask me how. We were off. By the time we arrived the first lamb was already born. Martin helped the delivery of the second, as slippery as an orange pip, as yellow as turmeric. A new lamb attempting to balance on its ridiculously long and thin legs resembled an apprentice stilt-walker.

The long and empty road to Holy Island – Day One.

George Ward behind the bar at Manor House.

Digging for victory – early days on the Manor House plot.

Coffee break – teacher Caitlin White
in Joel and Molly's café.

Jimmy 'Clinker' Brigham – one
of my island mentors.

'Banjo Bill' – 85-year-old
banjolele player Bill Nelson.
His demi-johns of wine mature
nicely in the background.

Ray Simpson and his bathroom haiku.

Fundraiser extraordinaire –
the ubiquitous Eddie Douglas.

With poet Andrew Waterhouse.

Ross Peart on his daily bike ride.

Holy Island Parish Council
Chairman and local activist
Ian McGregor.

Jean Peart in the garden of the Open Gate guest house.

Here comes the tide – waiting to be stranded in the refuge box.

Net profits – Richard Ward and Sean Brigham making new lobster pots.

'In the midst of death . . .' – in the shadow of foot-and-mouth, farmer Jimmy Patterson checks a new lamb.

Jimmy Middlemiss after securing the stone outside the Cuddy House.

View from the refuge – three feet
beneath the poles lies the causeway.

Striding to my first tide for Cuthbert – whose
island is across the rapidly filling channel.

Me and son Dylan on
his birthday visit.

After 100 days, Kitty
and Polly return!

An unusual view of the well-photographed castle – snow is not common on the island – except for Peter Mortimer's 100 days.
(Copyright: David O'Connor)

'A Brooding Calm.'
(Copyright: Enid C. Riley)

Lobster pots.
(Copyright: Jill Turner)

The little-known Snook House and Tower at the west end of the island.
(Copyright: George Walker)

As the lamb struggled, the mother licked it down. Martin picked up the brace of newborn and carried them upside down by one leg, a lamb in each hand, like a gamekeeper carrying dead pheasant. The theory was that mother would follow on and they'd all end up in the protective pen. Occasionally, though, sheep showed a hint of rebellion and independence. This mum showed no sign of being easily manipulated and stood her ground.

Martin boxed clever and totally outfoxed her (I really must watch out for these mixed metaphors). He laid each lamb in turn on the grass, ten metres apart. Their pathetic abandoned bleating was too much even for an independent-minded, free-thinking mother. As she walked up to each offspring, Martin picked it up and carried it a further ten metres ahead of the other lamb, similarly bleating, which mum now also approached. Bit by bit, lambs and mother were safely in the pen, and to reward the ewe for her compliance Martin stuck his hand deep inside her to check no shy bairns were still up there. Ewes had normally one or two lambs but sometimes three.

Consider the lucrative nature of rearing lambs. After four months they'd go off to Wooler Marker in Northumberland and fetch a price of £30–£40. After all that time on full board.

I'd often wondered about shepherd's crooks. Purely decorative? Not at all. Martin yanked the ewes up by their back feet and did a similar 'lost baby' check.

There was something about a newborn lamb. It was almost a walking (or wobbling) cliché, a conduit over the centuries for all manner of sickly sentimental tosh from writers and painters. But there was still something about this thin vulnerable creature tottering its way to stability, bewildered by the world, licked and protected by its mum.

I'd enjoyed my first contact with the sheep. Animals could be easier than humans. But then that was known by all those eccentric old ladies who retreated from the world to surround themselves with cats. Trouble was, sooner or later, we had to deal with the humans, too.

I'd enjoyed the farm. Its welcome spaciousness, plus Jimmy Patterson's seemingly unconditional acceptance of my presence put me at ease. I was never totally at ease on Holy Island, though. It was the nature of the experience that a certain tension and anxiety would surround it.

That afternoon I returned the *Paradise Found* video to Anne Phillipson on Fiddler's Green. Despite the fact that a couple of weeks ago I'd 'smoked' her drying sheets, she gave me a newly baked loaf, still delicious with aroma. I was tempted there and then to tear it to bits and devour it.

Instead I stuck it in a plastic bag and took it with me on a spiritual experience. I was en route to two hours' reading at the little-known prayer holes in the Heugh's cliffside.

These small recesses could be reached only via a rocky hazardous path virtually invisible from all points. The prayer holes faced across the estuary to the great fireball of the sun dipping down towards the mainland hills; the sea was 25 metres below, lapping and sucking at the rocky shore. You were in total privacy, secreted in your little prayer hole, bum cushioned with grass, a magnificent panoramic sweep in front of you.

I had come not to pray but to read. Maybe it was this misuse that led to the calamity. I moved the plastic bag at my feet and from it rolled Anne Phillipson's gorgeously crunchy newly baked loaf. My memory now is of the faintest whiff of that crustiness as, seemingly in slow motion, with me impossible to prevent it, the loaf rolled out of the bag, bounced down across a rock, then all the way down to the sea below – the sound of one loaf falling.

The bread bobbed below me in the water. It continued to bob there for the next hour. Visible. Out of reach.

Luckily the book I was reading was a Buddhist one. Buddhism taught us to remember all possessions were transitory, passing items.

Possessions, I told myself, were not to be coveted or jealously guarded. Here was a dictum, I further told myself, that could be learnt worldwide and hence lessen the occurrence of wars and conflicts. My mind was firmly resolved on this.

So why was I so pissed off to see that bloody lost loaf bobbing in the sea?

I'd even planned my evening meal round it. Soup with fresh crunchy bread, followed by tuna and tomato sandwiches made with freshly cut slices of yummy crunchy bread, followed by a nice piece of cheese, accompanied by fresh crunchy bread on which I'd liberally smear raspberry jam. And perhaps, as a climax, an extra slice of fresh crusty bread with half an inch of butter.

As it was, I had bangers and mash.

In the village that afternoon I bumped into poet Andrew Waterhouse and his partner, singer Stella Davies, who were holidaying for a few days on the island, though Andrew's residency at the Woodhorn Colliery Museum in Northumberland also involved him with the Lindisfarne Gospels (a computerised version of which the museum housed).

I'd missed the company of fellow writers. I'd never met either of them before and Stella disarmed me with the information that she was from a long line of nudists, though exactly where the line stood she didn't say.

Drinking with them that night afforded me the luxury of talking about the island to disinterested people. Much of the time was spent roaring with laughter. I needed regularly to roar with laughter. It put things into perspective. Not giggling, not tittering, not laughter that was dismissive or sarcastic, but that kind of explosive celebration of the great absurdities of life. When I laugh with people I like to get a glimpse of the roof of their mouth. Then I know we're roaring with laughter.

And how could I have possibly known, on that most attractive of nights, which both fortified and enervated me, that within a few months this young talented poet would take his own life?

FRIDAY, 9 MARCH 2001 – DAY FIFTY-FIVE

Points of Order – The Flaming Ducks

A knock at the door and there, beaming at me, were my mum and dad. I invited them in, sat them down, gave them tea and biscuits.

This pleasant dream dissipated as I awoke to a colder reality. Ten minutes later, a real knock at the door – Ross Peart. He bore a piece of paper with the printed words: 'Cast your bread upon the surface of the water, for you will find it after many days' – Ecclesiastes, Chapter 11, Verse 1.

Obviously the bread in those days was a deal less porous.

I was nervous this day. Two reasons. The next day would bring the visit of my 16-year-old son Dylan with his mother, Mo. This was the longest I'd ever gone without seeing him. Second, that very evening was the occasion of the annual Duck Supper, an almost mythical male event to which, against the odds, and with the help of George Ward, I'd wangled an invitation, unsure just as to what I was entering.

More restrictions on the island. The planned ceremony for a new St Cuthbert statue was cancelled. Also cancelled was the Good Friday pilgrimage across the sands by thousands of cross-bearing Christians.

Banjo Bill was still in hospital. And just where were these tungsten chisels? Stone sat in its shed, neglected.

An island under siege. The crisis invigorated the democratic process, so that the Parish Council meeting (previous attendance of public, three) now saw an audience of 15 crammed into the small, panelled reading room. Strangely enough, I was amongst them.

This burgeoning of interest and the sense of anticipation threatened totally to destroy the ennui which usually held together the fabric of such meetings. Questions came thick and fast. Where could people walk and not walk? And why? Why was the road to the castle – a public highway – closed? Why did the Northumbrian Tourist Board website claim the entire island was closed? And would it be better if it were?

Islanders were confused, not a little frightened. Under the cover of my great-coat, anxious not be seen in the act, I jotted down a few notes.

At the last minute, in the absence of Ian McGregor, Sue Massey of the Lindisfarne had agreed to chair the meeting. Here was a quirk of Holy Island life.

At the very moment she was cooking more than four dozen ducks, she was called upon to abandon her post and further the democratic process.

What if the ducks caught fire?

Actually, they did. Luckily they were saved, though 'saved' might not have been the verb chosen by the ducks.

The meeting was able to resolve little. Against most questions I'd jotted 'TBI' – to be investigated.

It would have taken more than foot-and-mouth to see off the Duck Supper. This strange ritual was begun 30 years previously with a group of island wild-fowlers in the now defunct Iron Rails public house. Each fowler had to shoot and bring along his own duck; the venue laid on vegetables and pudding.

The small informal gathering grew yearly and was now hosted by the Lindisfarne Hotel for more than 50 eager males (there had seemed no attempt to invade the ranks by females, who perhaps couldn't see the point). Not all the guests were native islanders but, me apart, they all had close associations with the island's wild-fowling culture. One came from as far distant as Stratford-upon-Avon.

The requirement that you brought your own duck was still in place. As a man who had never picked up a firearm, I threw myself upon George Ward's mercy and my duck was provided via a circuitous route.

Here was the 2001 Duck Supper roll-call: 42 widgeons, 12 mallards (slightly frowned upon due to the required increased oven space) and a solitary teal. All to be gobbled down by a group of mainly corpulent males dressed, as the phrase used to have it, in 'Sunday best'.

The men first gathered in the small Lindisfarne bar before being summoned to the dining-room. I was, of course, a total impostor but be assured – *I had brought my duck*!

Special guests were on the top table, other seating seemingly pot-luck. The non-islander opposite me, I learned, was on a lifetime island shooting ban, having mistakenly potted a protected red-breasted merganser. His indignation seethed across the table throughout the meal.

The only females on view were the waitresses, one of whom had a macabre link to the occasion: 20 years previously her brother had died in a punt-gun accident, punt-gunning being the by now rare (and some might claim unsporting) method of blunderbussing up to 90 birds at one time with scatter-shot.

Seven of the original Duck Supper members were still present. Soup, main course, trifle, coffee, one free bottle of wine per table of four, and, even allowing for bringing your own duck, a cost of only £7 – hardly enough for a bread roll in the Mirabel or such like.

All-male gatherings weren't my ideal night out. A lot of one-upmanship, sense of competition and not being inclined to fantasise what any of the assembled were like in bed took away much of the fun.

Many were fundamentalist smokers. And there seemed an unwritten requirement to get drunk. But at least getting drunk on Holy Island could be less fraught than on the mainland. Your front door was always close. No Plod to haul you out of the gutter and chuck you in a cell, and on occasions such as this everyone else would be far too drunk to mug you.

In the dining-room I was sat next to Harm the Dutchman, for whom the Lindisfarne was still among the unbanned premises. Harm smoked as if his health might suffer for every moment a cigarette was not between his lips. Smoke seemed to envelop him the way ectoplasm could surround a medium. To his credit he didn't smoke at the table but nipped outside for the occasional fag. Like after every mouthful. Like everyone else here, Harm loved to shoot off guns at flying furry things.

In swept the waitresses with the 55 ducks, which took 5 hours to cook, 15 minutes to eat. My widgeon resembled a small armoured vehicle. Its flesh was dark and mysterious and I found myself wondering who had shot it.

Or maybe I was just a wimp, a buffoon likely to walk the streets with a SAVE THE CRAB or SAVE THE DUCK banner.

The highlight of the Duck Supper each year is the main speaker.

Ex-game warden David O'Connor spoke first, briefly, then over to Clive Massey of the Lindisfarne, who seemed to be suffering post-duck traumas before handing over to the star turn, Colin Mole. 'Moley' had been guest speaker for six years and it was hard to see anyone else taking on the role. The ex-landlord of the Sign of Two Kirstys, he was now a salesman living in Berwick-upon-Tweed.

Each year, Moley would select certain island individuals and subject them to outrageous insults. These were usually as tasteless as they were comic – their imagined sexual peculiarities, their wives' or girlfriends' frequent infidelities. The cruder and greater the insult the more the diners cheered and hooted, and the more the insultee beamed. To be insulted by Moley at the Duck Supper was something of a status symbol. Imagine my delight, then, when the man trained his guns on me.

By coincidence, I'd known Moley a quarter-century earlier and he recalled the occasions with the required amount of Mortimer degradation, also highlighting my state of being follicly-challenged.

I noticed a few disgruntled looks from islanders and one remarked to me later: 'Ye bugger – it took me years coming to the Duck Supper before I got insulted.'

Among those thunderously applauding Moley's speech – an applause which shook the heavy table cutlery – was the Holy Island vicar, David Adam, one of the few God Squad to venture into this territory.

I thought of my island cultural evenings – books, music – and of this tiny island's extraordinary contrasts.

Later I heard another remark: 'The Duck Supper is like the Masons gone wrong.' There was the same defensive herd instinct but (to defend it) no real secret agenda.

Post-meal, the gathering retired back to the bar, soon wedged thick with baccy smoke. Some serious drinking began. I noticed fisherman Richard Ward, smartly dressed in blazer, tie, collar and what people used to call slacks, was looking at me through eyes like arrow slits.

There was something fiercely working class (despite the presence of the vicar and one QC) about these trussed-up males. The middle classes had long since abandoned themselves to leisure wear or even scruffy chic. There was also something almost primitive about the gathering itself, the intensity of the occasion.

Soon after midnight, Moley made his excuses and left, while others made no excuses and stayed. By 1.30 a.m., full of duck and bitter and with my throat rasping like two sheets of rubbed together sandpaper, I walked home with Stuart Moffitt.

We were, I felt, both observers to the ritual and in some ways I was uneasy about this. I could never throw myself into the Duck Supper the way (for several hours yet) some of the diehards would. I had little inclination for that all-male gradual slipping into unconsciousness.

None of which could explain why just a small part of me felt excluded.

I climbed into bed at 2.30 a.m. and started counting 55 flying – or was it dying – ducks.

SATURDAY, 10 MARCH 2001 – DAY FIFTY-SIX

How Not to Arrive on the Island – A Silent Mother

For an entire week we had enjoyed uninterrupted electricity. Surely, I thought, this could not last and it didn't. At 7.15 a.m. the supply went off.

At 9 a.m. I cursed loudly at the inconvenience. This frightened Scottish Power so much they immediately restored it.

Everything I had worn to the Duck Supper stank like a stale ashtray. I bunged all my clothes in the washing machine and shampooed my thinning locks. I was unsure just how to wash out my lungs.

The Duck Supper would have kept anthropologists busy for weeks. It lived on in my consciousness but also in those same lungs. I was rasping like an asthmatic and any deep-breath intake produced a sound like Pan-pipes.

Jimmy Brigham had told me of a fine piece of sandstone on St Cuthbert's beach. I walked down, took note of its position, also its layered 'flaky' look which would probably preclude chiselling. Plus which my chisels had not arrived.

By the time I got back to the Cuddy House, they had. I picked them up, fondled them; more elegant, more aesthetic than your common-or-garden chisel. More cerebral entirely.

Post Duck Supper gossip – fisherman Tommy Douglas seen making his uncertain way home from the Lindisfarne at 6 a.m. A 10 a.m. sighting of Robert Massey the worse for wear.

Today was the visit of my son Dylan and his mum, Mo. How would I react after 56 days? How would they? I was like a nervous caged beast, pacing anxiously.

They were due before the 1.15 p.m. tide which was a high one. At 1.25 they rang from their mobile.

'The causeway's covered,' said Mo. 'It looks pretty high.'

There was a kind of recklessness to what followed. Both from my own advice and Mo's acting upon it.

'You should be OK,' I said. 'Only just past crossing time.'

'Lots of cars here,' said Mo. 'No one else is going over.'

'You'll be OK,' I repeated. The tide was 5.3 metres, one of the biggest. And because, to island inhabitants, driving slowly through a covered causeway slowly became self-evident, I failed to mention it to Mo.

This is what Mo did. She pointed her car at the flooded causeway, put her foot down and drove at 40 mph.

According to Ross Peart, who was out at Snook End watching the tide, the sight was of eight-foot-high walls of curved spray rising up each side of the careering vehicle. According to Mo, the experience was sheer terror. The wipers were on high speed but she could see nothing through the torrent. She kept the wheel straight, gritted her teeth and kept going. The normal outcome of which would have been a flooded exhaust, drenched plugs and points, and a stalling car. After which the tide would have carried it away, and possibly Mo and Dylan with it.

Somehow the car made it through. It arrived at the Cuddy House plastered in mud, seaweed and detritus, and within seconds all three of us were given to the semi-delirious laughter which a narrow avoidance of a catastrophe normally brings in its wake.

There was a delayed shock effect for Mo. A few hours later she lost her voice and never found it again before leaving. She remains one of the few people to whisper her way through a Holy Island weekend.

Dylan seemed to have grown five inches. I looked at him in wonder, like he was someone just beamed up to the transporter room. The world I'd left behind and my present world collided.

And, of course, for Mo and Dylan this was a small and pleasant break on a delightful island. They carried none of my baggage. I realised this soon enough as we walked out along the Heugh in the gentle afternoon sunshine and returned via

St Mary's churchyard, for it was here, directly on top of a grave, that their dog Jess vomited a mixture of Pedigree Chum, bile and slime.

To Mo and Dylan it was an unfortunate accident. To someone who – possibly in paranoia – believed he was under constant observation and judgement, it was something more. I stared at this slimy putrescence desecrating the island dead, stared across at the various large houses which overlooked the graveyard, stared up into the sky for a possible dirigible, scanned the cemetery bushes for hidden witnesses.

The vomit's consistency made it impossible to gather up. I found myself praying for rain and scattered a few pathetically camouflaging bits of grass over the top.

As we walked on, Mo commented: 'How peaceful it is. How calm and tranquil.' Aaaah.

The incident stayed with me. That night, Mo whispered her appreciation of the Manor House food and Dylan took full, if illegal, advantage of his dad treating him to a few seventeenth-birthday celebration pints.

Lots of my island friends were also dining out. A few looked puzzled to have previously seen me on the island with one female (Kitty) and now another. But we sophisticated urbanites were like that.

Just as I tackled the pudding, I noticed a few spots of rain splattering the window. Rejoice! Dog vomit, farewell!

SUNDAY, 11 MARCH 2001 – DAY FIFTY-SEVEN

The Sadness of Toast – Concerning Pub Doors

While Mo and Dylan were on the island I pretended to be on holiday, attempted to see Lindisfarne just as another brief visitor might. It was no longer possible. The days behind me and the days still before me would not be denied. The detached, hedonistic perspective was not an option. It was a strange task I was about, not a divertissement.

I was wrapped round with Holy Island's tentacles.

And we had worsening foot-and-mouth; Britain, the leper of Europe, tourist trade threatening to collapse. Dog vomit in the churchyard.

On the island, the North Shore was now inaccessible, Sandon Bay, Coves Haven, Emmanuel Head, the sand dunes. Forty-three days still to go. And nowhere to go.

Dylan had slept downstairs in front of the fire. Like father, like son. My breakfast egg delighted in having two mates alongside in the frying pan and for once I was freed of that inevitable sadness that accompanies cooking for one.

We drove out that morning to Snook End. An islander stopped and barked chastisement for Jess being off the lead. I imagined in the Mortimer Book of Misdeeds, another entry.

I was already feeling the sadness of Mo and Dylan's impending departure and knew my tendency for melancholia.

It had been a brief glimpse into my other, more usual, life. Now finished. I watched them drive off, returned to the silent and empty living-room and felt a great sadness to see the remnant of toast on Dylan's plate and the smear of Mo's fried egg. I ate the toast, like some strange act of communion.

The morning's bright sky had turned to rain. I hurried to the churchyard, relieved to find the overnight downpour had all but obliterated Jess's churchyard chuck-up.

A phone call to a friend brought the knowledge that my fellow Tyneside writer David Almond had just left on a reading tour of America. I rarely felt envious but did at that moment, thinking of him freewheeling across the great wide highways of the States and me here forgotten, imprisoned.

I felt wider frustration, too. The response to foot-and-mouth seemed simply to kill, kill, kill. Vaccination seemed the most humane, most logical way, but its supporters were being drowned out.

That afternoon I cycled out along the causeway and in the evening stood in my normal lone sentry position in the Sign of Two Kirstys. In eight weeks I had failed to pierce the shell of this establishment. I knew the names of every person in the bar, had spoken at some time to each one individually, but I was peripheral, a hoverer on the edge, a non-member of the tribe. And then I asked myself. Did I want to be anything else? And did they not know that, come the end of next month, I'd be gone? Course they did.

I had no right to expect their acceptance.

Oh hell, but why not? I was a human being, I was living among them.

Why not? Because you weren't here just like anyone was here. You were here writing a book about Holy Island here and now, and that meant them.

Sure – and why not?

No reason. Except don't expect everyone to welcome you with open arms. OK?

And thus engaged in this lively debate with myself, I passed the time required to drink two pints of John Smith's.

On the third pint of John Smith's I mused long and hard about pub doors. Most entry doors into bars were glass-panelled, allowing the drinker-to-be some knowledge of the scene he/she was about to enter. A glass door also made it less likely those already inside would swivel their heads each time the door opened.

To walk into a bar via a totally wooden door could be disconcerting, an entry into the unknown. Both the Sign of Two Kirstys and the Lindisfarne had solid wooden doors.

But then didn't the Manor House? Yes, but this was normally propped open and entry was more stress-free. And the Ship had a glass panel, also making entry less of a trauma.

Such are the subjects on which the solitary drinker may muse after 57 days on a small island.

MONDAY, 12 MARCH 2001 – DAY FIFTY-EIGHT

Naming the Dead – A Stone Start

A Holy Island poem arrived from my Tyneside writer friend, Valerie Laws. It was rather fine and here it is.

Praise the Lord and Pass the Ammunition

The rainbow arch hangs in space
at Lindisfarne, a cannonball's leap
frozen in stone. Hail and rain rattle
the walls like shot, the sea keeps up
its cavalry charge. Cows graze
salt-bleached grass, descendents
of those spared by the monks
who spent more on gunpowder
than parchment.

Cold as steel, the salty air
that cramped their fingers
as they hefted the sacks
of black meal*, protection
against the devil's reivers.

Within, by the fire, Eadfrith
lit the pages of the gospels,
on calf-skin pricked with needles,
tattooed with inks. So slow a fuse

burning in red and gold, his truth
needing a little help from the gunsmith,
shielding the spark, so easily flaring up
and catching hold.

Valerie Laws

*Black meal was flour paid as protection money on the
Northumbrian/Scots border, giving the term 'blackmail'.*

I told myself the earth was slowly warming and each day the sun climbed a little higher in the sky and stayed there longer. And when would we see the first Holy Island bud?

In bed I read for an hour from the Buddhist book. I suddenly decided to spend three separate tides on that rocky outcrop, St Cuthbert's Island.

The decision brought me a strange kind of elation to counter the recent grumpiness. As to my reasons? I usually didn't examine these too closely but knew how all this was wrapped up with my exposure to religion on the island.

I was beginning to look beyond religion, a search for a strong and active spirituality which had nothing to do with a mute, unanswering God. I was beginning to know what I had suspected: that most religions were absurd and imprisoning. And if any one of them was 'right', what did that make the rest?

There was something else, too. A new frying pan. Mo had given it to me and I could now fry an egg without it supergluing itself to the pan surface.

I could enjoy an unbroken egg. And no need to thank God for providing it.

But I still went to see his pad. I was moved to visit the graveyard (and not only to check the disappearing dog vomit). I had a yen to look at the gravestone names. I played a little game. I made a list of what I thought would be the most common among islanders, then checked it against the facts.

My own list was Brigham, Patterson, Douglas, Lilburn, Kyle, Walker. I visited every gravestone, recorded the name. Only Cromarty had to be added.

And my house had a new occupant. Having cleaned and oiled Tim Hardin's yellow bike, I was loath to return it to its cold damp barn. From now on the bike would live in my hallway, where I would need to brush past it several times a day and each time mumble 'Scuse me'.

See how bitty this day seems? My son's visit had disconcerted me. So much so I felt humans could not counter it. Only sheep. I donned boiler suit and wellies and walked up the lane to the farm.

Since my last visit 180 ewes had lambed. Jimmy Patterson had had only three hours' sleep the previous night and I arrived to see him fresh from chasing off a trespasser.

'I couldn't believe it!' he said. 'Keep Out notices all over the place and there he was in the middle of a field of sheep, taking photographs of the castle!'

Any description?

'I think he was Japanese.'

Was he certain?

'Well, he looked Japanese. And just before he ran away, he turned and bowed to me.'

Midge the sheepdog was now on the scene. Jimmy and son Martin used him to round up another 160 pregnant sheep from a far field for the overnight pen.

In the barn Margaret was feeding a reluctant lamb. The implement was called a lamb reviver, a plastic bottle with a thin hose attachment that slipped down the lamb's throat to feed it milk. They'd lost only one lamb so far.

The sheep waddled their collective way round the barn. I gazed at their daft impassive faces, faces that posed no threat to any living thing. I thought of them in their thousands on the funeral pyres and wondered if there was a single species or creature on earth that could claim to have benefited from an association with humans?

Later I introduced the chisels to stone. I propped stone up on Mike Burden's shed. I took a pencil and wrote in the requisite letters. Stone ate pencil voraciously and I felt a sensation totally different from that of placing a poem on to paper. This poem would outlast me, my friends, my family, their families.

But this chisel now – it felt strange in my hand. There was no fusion between person and tool. I was like a driver using the clutch pedal for the first time, the skater slipping and sliding after the initial donning of the skates. The chisel was with me but not of me. I dared no more commit it to stone than chisel into my own head. The pencilled letters would wait a little longer.

I walked home, rang my mother in the Rotherham hospital. Her troublesome hearing aid was once more kaput. I found myself needing to shout at a volume that robbed all words of any warmth or intimacy. And even with the shouting the response was my mother's frail voice saying, 'Peter, I can't hear you. Peter. Peter.'

Three of the village pubs that night were shuttered and dark, all streets empty. Gloom seemed to be descending like a slow black curtain.

Only the Ship offered a welcoming light. And inside new landlord Frank Gregory was smiling. No matter he had taken over the pub in the worst weather for a decade, in the middle of foot-and-mouth and with power cuts rampant.

The two customers were Roger and Lesley Andrew. I'd been missing greatly Lesley's dad, Banjo Bill. He was due out of hospital the next day.

'A friend of mine,' said Roger, 'has designed a raised causeway for the island. It's built over open pipes through which the tide could flow. The causeway would give permanent access to the island.'

The silence that followed did not imply consent or agreement. The pattern of life on this island was dictated by the tides. This was an imposition gladly accepted – in fact, willed. An imposition which the island would have fought to keep. Holy Island looked to natural laws to protect it. In this it had a lesson for the modern industrialised world which believed, in its ignorance, that it could ignore nature as and when it saw fit.

Roger Andrew pursued the point.

'A raised causeway would be good for business,' he insisted.

'I'm business,' said Frank Gregory, with rather a good spontaneous line, 'and I don't want it.'

After the pub I walked out the mile to the dark mass of the castle. At this time of night, in the silence, the emptiness, you could believe that Holy Island belonged to you and you alone. And in a way it did.

Except no one could really own Holy Island, no matter what any legal document said. It was beyond such piddling legalities of humankind, which soon enough would turn to dust.

TUESDAY, 13 MARCH 2001 – DAY FIFTY-NINE

God, et al – Danger, Sculptor at Work

We all have that sense, at some time, of hurtling through space, spinning on a piece of rock on which we are condemned to pass our days. The sensation is a humbling one and, for me at least, can produce the feeling that, just for a short time, I'd like to get off.

Holy Island was a tiny microcosm of that. Another piece of rock stuck three miles out in the North Sea on which a tiny community scrabbled for its existence. One difference was people could get off (or at least most of them). In fact, I'd say it was vital. Otherwise you could go cuckoo. Sometimes I thought – hey, I'm going cuckoo.

Several people who did 'proper' jobs on the island chose to go elsewhere to live. Lyndsey Hackett from Lindisfarne Mead, for one. Rene Richardson, the island community officer, for another.

I had noticed how circumspect a lot of island people were, especially when talking to the likes of me, a nosy writer. Who could blame them? A man could also sometimes get the impression, common in very small communities, that no one on the island actually liked anyone else on the island. I didn't believe this was true but you did see how lethal human beings could be at close quarters, and the quarters didn't come much closer.

No place had left me so ambivalent. Holy Island fascinated me yet often the instinct was to run screaming across the causeway back to the mainland. In a society where change could be destructive as well as beneficial, the island had changed little. In the summer it sucked in tourists by the tens of thousands, yet when it had spat them out again their imprint was meagre.

A few miles down the coast, the old fishing village of Seahouses was, in direct contrast, a proliferation of chippies, amusement arcades and other tourist trappings.

Like most places that depended on them, Holy Island had a love–hate relationship with its tourists. As visitors, they were vital. But not really loved.

And here was I. Another visitor. But not even vital.

Back to Rene Richardson. Her job was as much diplomat as anything else, walking a delicate line, keeping a careful balance between the island's factions. Her base was the Heritage Centre, converted from a pub to create one of the island's few truly modern-looking buildings.

Rene had lived ten years on the island, running the then North View Guest House (now the Open Gate retreat and bed & breakfast). It was bought by Ray Simpson's Society of St Aidan and St Hilda, which also had its eye on an adjacent property, something a lot of islanders resented, not wanting further spread of what they called the God Squad. They feared becoming another Iona, the Scottish offshore island which many believed had now been taken over by the religious fraternity.

Many Holy Islanders clung tenaciously to their ungodliness. As I did, actually, but in a different way.

Personally, I didn't like the name of the Heritage Centre, which seemed to cling to the past whereas the building often looked to the future and hosted many of the island's social and cultural activities. It was now over-shadowing the village hall, which was falling to bits.

It was bright, airy, with a permanent eye-catching exhibition on the island's history, a touch-operated video screen to bring up either island 'characters' or bird noises, and the gospel room with the 'turn the page' computerised version of the Lindisfarne Gospels. (A small diversion: when the monks had created the intricate gospel pages, they'd made a small deliberate mistake on each one on the premise that only God was allowed to be perfect.)

In a way, Holy Island was trapped in the past, the only place it could take refuge, the only place it found security. Rene Richardson's job was partly to counter this but it wasn't easy.

I asked her whether the original Lindisfarne Gospels (housed in the British Library) shouldn't be returned here to their rightful home?

'Yes and no,' said Rene (see what I mean?). 'In one way it would be right but we'd never be able to deal with the numbers. And how many people would see them this far north?'

As to the island's future, Rene had helped raise funds to renovate rented houses for young islanders, to combat the holiday-home syndrome, and she'd done the same for the planned new island flats. She'd encouraged such groups as health, arts & crafts and (in the planning stages) a writers' circle to use the facilities. There was also massage and reflexology, which seemed remarkably modern. The centre was an art gallery, a meeting place, staged touring exhibitions (the current one was from the Channel 4 *Time Team* programme) and had its running costs met by the £2 entry charged to the thousands of annual visitors, half of whom, I was encouraged to learn, came from the island itself.

I stood in the middle of this accessible, bright, well-designed building and I felt a confidence in the island's future, an optimism about its ability to develop.

This wasn't the case everywhere.

And at the end of her working day Rene would drive back to the mainland and her home in the tiny Northumbrian village of Whitfield.

Stone was waiting. And chisel. I'd been procrastinating.

Because I knew this was not like writing on a typewriter or a computer. No Tipp-Ex. No 'delete' button. A chiselled letter was a chiselled letter. Best get it right.

In the Burden shed I experimented with small pieces of stone. I took the chisel in one hand, the small hammer in the other. The one did not seem to know the other. Intention and execution were far apart. A supposed straight line turned out a wiggly one. I either had the chisel angle too low (it skated across the stone) or too high (it dug a trench). The chisel, like an unbroken horse, had a mind of its own.

I'd found the phone number of a mainland stone-mason, Dave Rumble. I went home and rang him up.

'I'm finding this hard,' I said.

'Being a stone-mason is a seven-year apprenticeship,' he remarked, to which I added I had only a few weeks.

He gave me some advice, boosted my confidence. I returned to the shed, took up hammer and chisel and decided to be bold. On a small piece of stone, I carved out a word.

It was crap. That wasn't the word, you understand. That was a description of how it looked. The letters were faltering, loopy; they looked like the writing of a child asked to use their unnatural hand.

I tried again. No difference. I was growing impatient with myself, which made it worse. Luckily I was able to take myself to one side and whisper in my own ear: 'Just leave it for today, all right?'

Back home was a letter from the Parish Council, signed by Ian McGregor. It was hand-delivered. One beauty of Holy Island was that the entire population could be leafleted in the time it took to watch *Neighbours*.

The letter spoke of the two farms on the island living 'day to day in fear' and 'the 80 per cent of the community who rely on tourism finding business evaporating every day'. It also made official many of the walking restrictions thus far haphazardly imposed. You could walk in the village, the long way round to the Heugh, on the shoreline, on the Shell Road out to the causeway. To get to all the points of my favourite North Shore meant an 11-mile walk round the entire island. Right. That was what I would do, then.

One islander for whom walking was vital was 54-year-old George Kyle. I'd watched his slow recovery from his hip replacement operation. Two walking sticks gave way to one and soon, none. I realised my interest was two-fold. First, my poor mum recovering from her own hip-op (hey, that made it sound trendy!); and second, because of the nagging omnipresence in my own hip of Arthur. You'd forgotten about Arthur? Wish I could.

In the Ship that night the only customers were me, fisherman Richard Ward and his wife Karen (chef at the Ship), plus a roaring fire. At 8.30 p.m. Frank Gregory looked at his watch.

'May as well shut up shop,' he said.

I feared the island itself might soon be shutting up shop. There were now more than 200 mainland cases of foot-and-mouth reported, a sense of it running out of control. I feared we might face a fortress Holy Island.

WEDNESDAY, 14 MARCH 2001 – DAY SIXTY

Stone Breakthrough – Cash-Point Christianity

Taking such pains to carve a poem on to a stone in the middle of this national crisis might seem odd. I didn't think it was. I was always cheered by tales of people who managed to put on plays in war-torn and bombed-out cities, people who created music and poetry in concentration camps. It was when these things were abandoned that we were truly lost.

Good news! Banjo Bill was out of hospital. And grinning.

'Apparently,' he said, 'I had a heart attack.' They'd given him 16 stomach injections, pumping stuff in, and the dark bruises on his arms showed where they'd pumped blood out. He'd been told to take it easy. He was 84.

'On Friday,' he said. 'I'm making five gallons of wine.'

Bill was simultaneously robust and fragile. He inspired another oxymoron, too, because I felt protective towards him and protected by him.

At his age many people suffered loneliness and isolation. Bill's kitchen was busier than St Pancras station. Harm the Dutchman called every morning at 9 a.m. and stayed two hours, smoking a few packets of fags. At midday Jimmy Brigham (Clinker) knocked and sat in till 2 p.m., when he went off to the Manor House.

I was there most days. As was Jean Peart. Everyone got tea and wine, if they wanted it. Cheese often appeared. Plus Bill's home-made pickled onions. Was it because he had so little to do that he found time to write his music? (That's a joke, by the way.)

It was to his credit – but also occasionally to his cost – that nobody really thought of him as an old man. Back sitting in his kitchen, I realised how much I'd missed him.

Bill was as fed-up as me over the cancellation of the Howlers concert. His banjolele-playing was always a star turn.

One version of the 'real' reason for the cancellation was some people's dislike of me, a non-resident, being involved; but, as usual on Holy Island, seeking the truth to such a rumour just found you wandering deeper and deeper into a dark swamp.

And so to stone – day three! Here was my strategy. I would not expect instant results. I would patiently practise before committing myself to the task proper. I took a small piece of sandstone from the Burden garden and on it chiselled 'Mike & Anne'.

Anne looked at it closely and said 'Hmmm', which wasn't a bad thing to say when you sought diplomacy.

It was the writing of an infant baboon.

'Perhaps you could do a stone for our dead Labrador, Tessa, who's buried in the garden?' she said. I dismissed the thought that she'd made this choice because the dead were likely to get less upset.

This time the script was that of a habitual drunk.

'I'll try Tessa again.'

And something happened, a very, very minor miracle. Something linked between myself, the hammer, the chisel and the stone. It was only a beginning but it was progress. The tools and the raw material had come onto my side. As I chiselled TESSA the second time, my excitement grew. Something was transferring from me through to the stone. It was as if I'd discovered some secret, as if all around us were secrets but we passed through life mainly without discovering them.

The tools were responding. Hammer connected with chisel, transferred its energy through its length which then bit into stone, not now totally as some wobbly wayward thing but for the first time with some slight sense of control.

I tap-tapped and at each tap a small cloud of powdered rock rose up, which I blew away.

The work was slow, meticulous, rewarding. I liked the sounds of the chisel and hammer. I liked the small clouds of dust which were like history rising before my eyes. I liked focusing on the small, the particular.

There was something else, too. I felt strangely linked with Eadfrith, the Bishop of Lindisfarne, who at the end of the seventh century had scripted the Lindisfarne Gospels. Delusions of grandeur maybe – one of the great works of art from the Dark Ages and me in a garden shed – but it was there. I was unlikely to empathise from the religious aspect, so here maybe was connection. The careful creation of letters and words.

Creating, like Eadfrith, something that would survive, helped conjure his manuscript mates, too; Ethelwald, who'd made the binding, plus Billfrith the Anchorite, who sounded like the final man in a tug-of-war team but who had, in fact, added the ornamental gold and silver gilt. All three had been inspired by St Cuthbert, who himself had been inspired by God.

So what was my inspiration? The act itself. And there was a certain purity to that.

I was only a tyro chiseller in a small shed on a March day on a wee island. Newspapers were not anxiously awaiting latest development on my chiselling. Global stock markets would be unaffected. Were the chiselling not to be completed, not a single gasp of dismay would be heard throughout the entire planet.

None of which rendered it any less important.

Mike and Anne brought me soup. We all stared at TESSA. The letters were still wobbly, basic. And in my time I would never solve the problem of making letters deep enough or wide enough. But the imperfections, in a way, were part of it.

For the monks, imperfection had been a matter of policy. For me, it was an inevitability. And I understood Bill Donald's reference to all those rich but impoverished London businessmen de-stressing themselves with a chisel and hammer and realising how much more important it was than making money.

Not that chiselling was totally without stress. The commitment to the stone, that moment of no return, that first cut of the chisel; at such times I found myself sweaty-palmed at the possibility of error. But this was a healthy stress and led to the great pleasure of chiselling, the human's growing familiarity with the tools and the raw material itself.

Stone did not resist the act. It did not feel itself defiled, polluted, exploited, destroyed. It was not being used, unlike so many of the earth's raw materials, for profit or quick gain. It was a partnership and stone was being enhanced.

This sense, in however small a way, that you are relating to our world's basic 'stuff' in a positive, creative way produces a sense of great calm rarely experienced.

I worked all afternoon. I was oblivious to the outside. We could have been on collision course with an asteroid, bug-eyed monsters might have been rampaging through Marygate. Whatever extreme occurrence might have been going on – even a policeman walking up Fenkle Street – would have made no difference.

By tea-time, I had chiselled out the following: OUT OF T.

I would work on stone every day till completion. Not that I was obsessed with it. Just that it kept drifting back into my mind during the two religious events I attended that evening.

Noticed just how many religious events I was at? Good.

Every day at 5.30 p.m. evensong took place in St Mary's Church. This was usually led by David Adam and announced by that single tolling bell I found so comforting. There were a smattering of folk and three things were of interest.

1) Though it was called evensong, there was no singing.

2) The service was punctuated by several 'one-minute silences', a ritual I'd only previously associated with respect for the dead but which apparently had monastic origins, and which I'd experience again on the island.

3) David Adam's appearance: his black hooded cassock made him part Spanish Inquisition, part Hammer Horror film, part charismatic Holy Man.

Later – after a brief interlude to watch Arsenal v Bayern Munich on the TV – I was in the Heritage Centre for the second of the faith lectures, given by Ross Peart of the Open Gate.

The purpose of this series, as far as I could see, was for each speaker to explain what fired/motivated/drove him and her. And for each, in different ways, it was religion. Did we feel faith was irrevocably linked with religion? And if so, why?

Ross had been a Tyneside town planner but a blinding flash had told him to enter the church. This hadn't been entirely spiritual, as the next day he had a lump on his head.

Two prisons where he'd worked had been set on fire. Also one of the churches. Initially, he'd been a Methodist and then an Anglican minister, and his unconventional methods included preaching at bus stops and cash machines.

Several years of severe depression had eventually been explained by the mercury poisoning from his teeth fillings. He confessed to being a 'Jesus baby', loved Holy Island to bits and cycled and walked as much as possible on the island.

He ran the Open Gate with his wife Jean (who wasn't in the audience of nine), whose constant stream of visitors left little room for privacy.

One thing was becoming manifest in these lectures. I was tending to be more interested in the people than the religion.

After a long, long, dark and cold spell, spring was in the air. More than I realised. I'd stacked up the fire and on opening the door to the living-room later found the warmth embraced me like a furry animal.

I decided to sleep downstairs. Ironically, only days after being chilled to the bone the pulsing heat woke me hot and sweating at 2.30 a.m. and I was forced to retreat to the cool of the bedroom.

It remained my only Holy Island experience of needing to back off from the heat.

THURSDAY, 15 MARCH 2001 – DAY SIXTY-ONE

Celtic Excess – Late Night Sheep

Retreating before the heat? Pah! By midday the snow had come back.

I was 61 days in and with the help and generosity of various island occupants I was managing to keep the larder well enough stocked.

Back home in Cullercoats I was used to various local shops being open till 10 p.m. Here I needed to adapt to a 20-mile round trip across a causeway dictated by tides – and not even me making the trip. Teacher Caitlin White, Mike and Anne Burden, Derek Pollard and Chris Holbrook all uncomplainingly took away my scribbled lists and returned with the goods.

Unexposed to supermarket psychology, I spent a great deal less than normal and noticed no difference.

Plus which I used the travelling vans whenever they visited. I was now used to the Cuddy House being empty (me apart) 99 per cent of the time, used to the ringing phone being a rarity.

And often it was just at the times I convinced myself how well I had adapted when I felt someone approach and tap me on the shoulder. It was loneliness, the long removal from family and loved ones.

Other matters simmered gently. Each day my visit to the Post Office for my copy of *The Guardian* was just slightly less fraught as the incident with Malcolm Patterson receded. Jen Ward of the Manor House seemed to have distanced herself, though George still made (half) joking references to 'reading the proofs of the book'.

Up at Beblow Farm, tempers were short. A loose sheep was flying about in the yard (not good for pregnancy). Jimmy and Margaret Patterson, existing on minimal sleep, were trying to catch her. I could sense the friction.

'Why not come back later?' said Jimmy, quite softly, though it was difficult to disguise the sense of clenched teeth. I beat a diplomatic retreat.

A shaft of light in all the economic gloom. A new shop was being fitted out in Marygate.

'Only a fool would do it right now,' said Karen Munday, who had once lived on the island, been involved in it 21 years but had now moved off. She already had Celtic Crafts. The second shop would be called Sally's of Lindisfarne.

'Absolutely nothing Celtic in it,' said Sally. 'The whole Celtic thing's done to death. Especially as much of it's made in India and China.'

An uncomfortable truth hit me after talking to Karen, as I thought about her as another who left the island when business was done.

To live on Holy Island could drive you insane.

I returned to stone, two hours in which my hands froze, and the lettering progressed to OUT OF THE SEA/A HEART.

I was the only customer that night in the Manor House. George's permanent smile could barely disguise his low spirits. A few weeks ago he and Jen had clinched the purchase of the place, invested thousands in its improvement, had looked forward to the fruits of their labours and been rewarded with foot-and-mouth.

'Maybe they *should* just close the island down,' said George wearily, 'at least then we could claim compensation. This way, we have vanishing trade but can't claim a penny.'

Could he have imagined himself, one month previously, talking in this fashion?

At 10 p.m. I walked back in the dark to Beblow Farm. I slid open the door to the large barn and walked into the maternity ward of 170 sheep.

Before me was a large huddle of placid oval creatures. I could have lain amongst them without the slightest danger. They wished humans no ill will. The reverse was not true. We were slaughtering them by the million, in an increasingly dubious policy. The surviving babies would have a few weeks to enjoy themselves before being dished up on dinner plates.

For 15 minutes in that sweet-smelling sanctuary of a barn I allowed the sheep's placid nature to become part of me.

Jimmy Patterson walked in. Seventeen lambs the previous night.

'And look – she's just about to have her second.'

A sheep giving birth acted little differently to a sheep not giving birth. No shrieks of pain, no midwife yelling 'Push! Push!', no doctor yelling for hot towels (just what *were* the hot towels for?).

The sheep waddled about, munched straw, licked the first-born clean while from her rear, like a pair of slack braces, dangled the legs of the second-born.

Plop – out came the lamb. Twelve minutes later it was on its feet and walking. Slightly faster than a human. Against that, sheep weren't very clever and couldn't invent nuclear weapons.

Jimmy pushed a laxative down the lamb's throat.

'Sometimes they can't go to the toilet properly at first,' he said. 'They can swell up and explode.' Exploding lambs – sounded like a punk band.

The barn was soporifically calm. Steam rose gently from the backs of the 170 waddling sheep. Lambing was well into the second of three weeks here, while on neighbour Robert Brigham's farm it was just starting. Three weeks – 800 lambs.

I watched another birth. Jimmy threw the ewe gently on her back, exposing the great swollen bladder of her teats. He inserted a hand and as easily as taking a drink from a dispenser pulled out the lamb.

'Sometimes they come out backwards or sideways,' he said, and then grinned. 'But usually it's much easier than carving a stone.'

There's this strange thing called a lamb adaptor. When mothers rejected the lambs and didn't allow them to feed, the ewe's head was placed in a set of 'stocks', allowing the lamb to suckle the teats undisturbed. These stocks were in sets of four, like a square. A quartet of sheep's heads faced inwards, giving the impression they were locked in some serious debate.

I stayed in the barn almost till midnight. What did Jimmy think about foot-and-mouth and feelings on the island?

'I know it's hitting a lot of people as well as farmers,' he said. 'Feelings are running high. But talking of a tourist crisis right now seems a bit much. How many people holiday in the far north of England in March?'

I clumped home through the deserted village. Had I mentioned spring? Under a clear sky, which spread its bright twinkling diamonds across its black display cloth, temperatures had again plummeted. Car windscreens had crystallised into thick frozen fur.

FRIDAY, 16 MARCH 2001 – DAY SIXTY-TWO

A Dearth of Red Noses – An Island Rumbles

R ed Nose Day. And Dylan's seventeenth birthday. And the country reeling from foot-and-mouth.

And Holy Island receding from me, taking itself away. I had spent several weeks familiarising myself with its physicality. Most days I had spent two hours walking its coves, its footpaths, its dunes. Each day I felt myself getting closer to its small details, its natural heartbeat.

This was now in reverse. At the village edge, I spotted the distant white tip of Emmanuel Head. I could no longer simply walk to it. I wanted the great loneliness of the North Shore, the giddy cliffs of Coves Haven. I wanted to lie in the dunes and pull faces. I wanted to be alone on the footpaths. I wanted to inspect my totem.

And though I planned a journey round the island, this felt like a major exercise, not some impromptu foray.

The prospects of seeing any red noses seemed remote. Playfulness was not the first quality I associated with islanders.

I'd arranged another visit to the school, and was once again grateful for the unfettered imagination of children.

Molly was dressed as a fairy, a beautiful white satin dress and gossamer wings. Joel was a pirate, skull-and-crossbones hat, spotted scarf and a cutlass fit to fillet Blackbeard in seconds.

'Let's have a story,' I said, 'and we can have a collection.'

On Holy Island, with its concentrated population, such impulsive acts could bear fruit. Within minutes the audience was six: Caitlin, Molly, Joel, Joel's little sister Martha, mum Anna and little Martina Vierling, daughter of Dutchman Harm and Magda.

I told my story of Fatso the Skeleton and his unrequited love for potted beef sandwiches; everyone harangued parents for money and we raised £10.50.

My tungsten chisel was blunt. I sought out Richard Ward and Sean Brigham, secreted in a back building behind the Manor House where they made and mended their lobster pots – 200 in all. To buy them in cost £35 per pot, or a cool seven grand. The pots were a hymn to recycling: off-cuts of netting, plastic tubing bent to form three arches and secured on to wooden off-cut bases. The netting was interwoven round the arches with the speed and dexterity of a magician.

Richard resharpened the chisel on his oil stone. With a fresh appetite it bit into the stone anew and by that evening the carving read OUT OF THE SEA/A HEARTBEAT/OF, with only the word STONE to be added.

My son's birthday and, down at Chare Ends late afternoon, the Friday ritual – the gathering together of the kids. Nothing unusual in a group of kids and mums (no dads, alas) playing together. Except on Holy Island, with its ageing population, its intermittent sense of the slow, the deliberate. Against such a backdrop, the sight of these noisy, energetic, fizzed-up children was a welcome antidote. They yelled with excitement. The future held no fears for them, mainly because they had no time even to consider its existence. Theirs was the unfettered joy of the eternal present.

As they ran across the sands, as they tore round the four bases of the rounders game, their laughter and cries echoed out across the sand flats and the island's terrain and I wanted it to go on long and loud.

Anger and frustration were rife on the island. In the Manor House that night George spoke of 'ruination'. There was hostility to English Nature's decision to close both the Priory and the Museum, despite the lack of livestock near either of them.

I'd even heard suggestions that the island's sheep (all perfectly healthy) should be slaughtered, the farmers paid off and the island opened up as normal. The very sheep that had so calmed me the previous night.

And Banjo Bill Nelson was exhausted from the number of visitors following his return from hospital. I contrasted this with my 85-year-old mum lying alone in that hospital ward. All those miles away.

SATURDAY, 17 MARCH 2001 – DAY SIXTY-THREE

Anticlimactic Stone – The Poet is Summoned

I'd gone back to Sean Brigham's house till 3 a.m. Drink had featured in the programme.

So that this morning came the joylessness of a hangover, a listlessness that saw my attempts to sit down and write prove futile. In the middle of the futility came a knock at the door.

It was the musician Beryl Pain. Would I give a poetry reading on the island?

My instinctive reaction – which I checked – was to blurt out 'But I'm not a real writer! I'm a fraud! Look at that blank sheet of paper! Is that the sign of a proper writer?'

'Thank you very much,' I said. I had all the energy of an anaesthetised sloth. Beryl left and I tried writing again. After 30 minutes the page's whiteness was still unchallenged.

I walked out along the Pilgrim's Way, which felt glutinous underfoot, sticky, unpleasant. I felt about the same myself.

I looked for relief in stone.

For the first time the carving seemed a drudge. I actually finished the poem. OUT OF THE SEA/A HEARTBEAT/OF STONE. This was a watershed moment in my 100 days, a moment that vibrated with resonance.

I stood back and said, 'Huh.'

My invitations out to meals were few and tended to coincide with my hangovers. Thus it was again. Actor Phil Hall and his wife Mylee, who worked at the Queens Arts Centre, Hexham, where several of my plays had been performed, took me to the Lindisfarne Hotel.

I'd dragged my hangover around all day like a convict's ball and chain. How kind Phil and Mylee were. And what a drag I probably was.

And probably over-sensitive. So that when, at the bar, mention was made of my gardening pursuits and owner Clive Massey said, with a half-smile, 'Taking work away from the islanders', I laughed back but just kept thinking – is that what he thinks? Is that how the island views me?

And later, in the bar of the Manor House, George announced to the gathered folk, 'Hey, I caught him on the stairs at the Duck Supper – he was making notes in his book!' And he laughed out loud and I laughed out loud, too, but felt various pairs of eyes staring at me, as if I'd been exposed.

As if my clandestine *modus operandi* had been blown. As if writers *didn't* take notes!

Or was I just an ungrateful wretch? I'd been invited to give a reading. I'd been given a free meal. And all I could do was get paranoid.

Hey – it was bloody-well snowing again by closing time.

SUNDAY, 18 MARCH 2001 – DAY SIXTY-FOUR

Buddha and the Hoover

Despite the previous day's creative inaction, I'd banged on with the writing overall. At the expense of the house. This led to the haiku.
Second notebook
full. Dust on
the Hoover
After finishing it I cleaned the house from top to bottom and made a beef casserole. Its slow cooking through the day created such a delicious aroma I opened every door to allow each room to sniff it. I also went out several times for a few minutes, the better to smell it when I walked back in.

I'd also finished the seventh of the books given me by northern writers. This was the tweely titled *A Path with Heart* by the long-standing American Buddhist Jack Kornfield and was a gift from poet Linda France.

If I had to pick one religion where I found an affinity, it would be Buddhism. No 'supreme being', for one thing, no slavish worship of some remote 'almighty', no adherence to the doctrine (as stated in the catechisms) that 'the chief end of man is to glorify God'.

Contrast that with what Kornfield wrote: 'It is what you know deep inside you that is right. Do not be satisfied with hearsay, or tradition, or legend, or what is written in great scriptures.'

Discovering what was deep inside you wasn't easy and these words could easily give carte blanche to misguided zealots ('It was the voices speaking to me!' and so forth). But basically I liked the Buddhist approach, more a way of life than a religion. Unless you were properly in touch with yourself, how could you be in touch with others and the rest of the world?

One of the book's great strengths was in relating Buddhism to the here and now, the nitty-gritty of our own Western culture, as against merely being relevant to shaven-headed monks in Nepal.

Nor was the book some trendy West Coast 'How to . . .' manual. It promised no easy fixes. 'Enlightenment' was a long, hard path and different for each of us. But whereas reading of most religions depressed me with their limitations on human potential, Buddhism excited me and also put into context everything I was doing on this island, from carving stones to sitting in refuge boxes, to hoovering the carpet.

It was a weighty tome – 355 pages. And I knew it was just a start which I may or may not choose to pursue. But never once did it preach or make me feel servile. I am probably too volatile ever to become a good Buddhist. But it was the best I'd get.

That day's newspaper ran the story of the North Shields trawler the *Christinne Nielsen* sinking 125 miles out in the North Sea. I'd worked that boat, written a poem about its crew, which was framed in the wheelhouse. I now had one poem on a stone. Another at the cold bottom of the ocean.

My Sunday routine now normally involved a languorous reading of the papers in the Island Oasis Café, outside which Eddie Douglas sucked money into his charity tin and directed island trippers to various destinations.

Occasionally Neil and Cathy would emerge with a fresh cup of cappuccino to fortify him. Outside the café looked dull. Inside it reflected their own cosmopolitan nature. They were well travelled, multi-lingual and though Cathy's family had island roots she was probably its first member to practise tai chi.

Dutch visitors could get Dutch coffee, Spanish visitors Spanish coffee and so on. I liked sitting in the café. My horizons expanded.

One curio was the sticking door. The door was self-willed. When it stuck, customers tugged and pulled in vain and Cathy's mum Gladys was summoned. For her the door opened without fuss. Another curio was Neil's 'coffee bang'. This had to do with the percolator filter and was loud enough to turn every head in the place. The few who didn't turn were (you realised) locals and used to this regular loud noise.

I skimmed through 34 supplements, munched two home-made scones and got my head together for that night's poetry reading.

This was a night of Culture with a capital C. Me, the large piano, Beryl Pain, an audience of 20, baritone Keith Currie and violinist John Thomas. A soirée, no less.

Mozart, Schubert, Brahms, *et al* were also present via their music. The featured composers ranged from the modern Geordie, Eric Boswell, through to such obscuranti as Hulay. Beryl was on the piano.

I'd never given a reading like this. A private house. The power of Keith Currie's voice, coupled with the sound of the violin and piano, seemed altogether too great for the four walls to contain, as if this performance demanded a concert hall, a tiered audience of thousands.

How would my own single voice sound in comparison? Close on the heels of an aria from Mozart's *Magic Flute* I read my nonsense poem, 'Bum'.

Singer Keith Currie, with a voice as rich as molasses, cut a nautical look in his blazer, while violinist John Thomas had a craggy, slightly academic air and a dry wit.

It felt good to be reading. As if, after nine weeks of describing, defining and encapsulating other people on this island, here, for a few moments at least, I was defining myself, and with a captive audience, too. I was in touch with myself. Just like the Buddhists said I should be.

And I'd written a traditional 5-7-5 syllable haiku for the occasion.

Twice daily the tide
thinks deep over swallowing
the island laid bare

I read it out. One problem in reading a haiku out loud was that just a single dry tickly cough in the audience and they all risked missing it.

After the music and the poetry there was wine, chocolate biscuits and chat. After they've given a reading, male poets always want beautiful women to approach them, buy their books and hang off their every word. A beautiful woman called Anne from Berwick approached me and bought a book. A few moments later I turned to give her the chance to hang off my every word but she'd gone with the tide.

The evening contained an entertaining island anecdote from council chairman Ian McGregor that would have been worthy of a Compton Mackenzie book. When Ian had first moved to Lindisfarne in the 1960s, he'd wondered why so many front doors were painted the same shade of green. Later he discovered that some time since a boatful of green paint had been washed up on the rocks.

There was one strident voice among islanders (which I won't name) and it rose above the gathering. Kill all the sheep on the island, said the voice. Let's get back to normal. The loud demand left us all looking at our shoes, unaware of just how to respond. I didn't know why but there was something in that final incident, a cold-blooded justification of mass slaughter after listening to beautiful music that reminded me of an evil dynasty that stained the world 60 years ago. They liked their high culture, too.

MONDAY, 19 MARCH 2001 – DAY SIXTY-FIVE

One Z and Two Noughts – Listing

I always got excited at my own poetry readings. I had never quite grown used to the extraordinary fact that people were actually coming out to listen to something that I had written. Lots of poets were pretty blasé about this and hunched around morosely. That was too cool for me. I've never been cool. So the excitement usually saw me downing a few drinks. This wasn't with any befuddled, romantic idea of aping a kind of Dylan Thomas-like self-destruction, it was just the adrenalin. Which invariably was followed the next morning by listlessness.

I cooked a listless breakfast, wrote 1,000 words listlessly, sat in the back yard reading the paper in a manner I can only describe as listless.

In such a state I should have stayed well away from stone. I didn't. I wanted to finish the carving off with 'PM 2001'. I carved my initials then worked backwards on the numbers. The '1' was fine, the two '0's I made diamond shape and they looked fine. The '2' was a disaster. It didn't come out like a '2' but a 'Z'.

What I had chiselled was the enigmatic 'PM Z001'. People were likely to take the final '1' as an 'L' and hence read 'PM ZOOL'. This read like someone's name. The author of the poem, for instance.

I imagined, in centuries to come, historians puzzling over the existence of the poet PM ZOOL. Looking him up would prove fruitless. PM ZOOL'S entire poetic output, it would be decided, was one small chiselled poem on Holy Island.

I sought a second opinion – Anne Burden's.

'Oh, no one would notice that!' she said. 'They'll take it as 2001.'

And with that one statement, the potential future reputation of PM ZOOL lay in ruins.

Walking on the causeway, I waved to Ross Peart returning in his car. His father was ill in Durham. He'd been to visit. I thought of my mother. The image of her, shrunken alone in that hospital bed haunted me. I considered another visit to Rotherham.

On this island I carried my other world around with me like a sack of spuds.

How did those global explorers manage? Did their 'other' world not matter to them? Or was it getting away from that other world that motivated them? Were they only really happy trekking up mountains, through jungles or navigating oceans? I knew I wasn't like that. Something drove me to get away. And then kept tugging me to get back.

I sat up contemplating such things till 3 a.m. By which time I was almost too knackered to make cocoa.

TUESDAY, 20 MARCH 2001 – DAY SIXTY-SIX

Owning the House – Village Green Fingers

The vernal equinox – the start of spring. In celebration I broke open a new toothbrush and clicked on a new razor blade. I also examined the Boots Original Shaving Bowl I had bought for my duration. I had shaved from this bowl for 66 days. In these 66 days my brush had made only the very slightest impression on the shaving soap surface. In such time, a shaving stick would be halved in length, a tube of shaving cream would be all but rolled up. A pressure can of shaving gel would have spluttered its last. My Boots Shaving Bowl had hardly broken sweat. It was clearly magic; capable not only of outlasting the island but possibly the writer.

This product endorsement, ladies and gentlemen, comes totally free of any financial or other remuneration from the manufacturers.

I was two-thirds of the way through my 100 days. I felt less need to rush at things. I thought of a field of cows. Chase after them and you'd always be distant. Simply lie in the middle of the field and the cows would eventually come to you.

I always tried to force-feed events. Sometimes they had to just happen. Sometimes an event could happen, small, insignificant, and in the whole room possibly only you were aware of it and for you it was important. It was at such times you realised life wasn't at all like they taught you it was – but by the time a lot of people realised that, they were already dead, if the dead *can* realise anything.

Take this morning. I sat up in bed and stared at myself in the wall-mounted mirror on the opposite wall. The head on the pillow staring back wasn't mine but that of my father in the morgue.

I shot out of bed. After such an event you didn't want to hang about. The image stayed with me. Like it would.

You probably want to know about the Cuddy House water system. This was given to untoward behaviour. Long after I'd run the taps or flushed the toilet huge deep gushing sounds could be heard, like some vast subterranean river or thousands of gallons deciding to move themselves from one tank to another. There was no logic to the sounds, nor timing. The water welled up at its own bidding, like some great restless beast, like some kraken that was calling out.

The water apart, after 66 days, the house was mine. I did not own it, nor seek to profit from its sale. The house and I belonged to one another for the duration. After 100 days the arrangement would cease.

It was not my identity but someone else's stamped on it. It was totally unlike my Cullercoats house of muddled clutter, shop window dummies, huge murals and mountains of books.

I had made no effort to change the furniture, shift things to my own perspective. In some ways I had lived in the house like a ghost, moving from room to room without a ripple.

Yet now I knew it and owned it, just as it owned me. I knew where things were in the house, which floorboards creaked, how long the bath took to fill, the vagaries of the solid fuel fire, the house's silences and its noises. I cleaned it like you might bath a baby. At different times I walked into different rooms and simply stood still. This was part of it. I knew all houses ultimately belonged to themselves. But the house and I were under a short-term mutual ownership scheme, one which an estate agent would fail to understand.

My gardening services were again in demand. I was employed to cultivate the small strip on the outer wall of Eleanor Jarven's cottage opposite the Manor House in the Market Square. Eleanor was a woman of nervous energy due a hip replacement (a lot of it about). She pointed at the strip, handed me some secateurs and with a vague kind of wave said, 'Oh, you know, sort it out' – not the kind of indeterminate instruction to give a gardener of my monumental ignorance and potential destructive power.

I downed a ham sandwich at the Manor House, scrounged the use of trowel and brush and set to, hoping not to destroy any flowers of long Latin nomenclature.

The Holy Island Market Place was the village focal point and its only wide-open space, the grassy stretch along Fiddler's Green apart. It was like four small village greens in one, each criss-crossed by paths. There were two sycamore trees, a war memorial, several benches on which to while away the day (which today was warm and sunny). Most of the buildings which faced on to it were painted white and most had taken a few steps back the better to give the green a sense of spacious tranquillity.

If asked to name one item most people would remember it would be the impressive stone Cuthbert Cross in honour of the saint.

My garden strip was south-facing and in the gentle warmth of the sun my two hours tending the plot were among the most enjoyable of my 100 days. Various reasons: the clement weather, plus the steady drift of island visitors, several of whom stopped for a chat. They all took me as a gardener. I wanted to be taken as a gardener.

I always wanted to be taken as one of the resident group on such occasions. If I walked through the foyer of a hotel hosting a dental conference, I would want everyone to see me as a dentist. At college I once sat through an incomprehensible physics lecture basking in the thought I would be taken as a future physicist. It was the only motive to be there.

I don't want to be a dentist. Or a physicist. Only at times such as these. A gardener, too.

As a gardener, I received the favours (drinks-wise) of a brace of women. Next door in the distinctive terrace was the house of Eleanor's sister, Sarah. After an hour's work I knocked at the door and said, 'I am your sister Eleanor's gardener. Feel free to offer me a cup of tea.' I got one. Plus a chocolate digestive.

A short while later, Chris Holbrook emerged from the door of her house, the Stables, and offered more tea and chocolate.

I'd arranged to paint the following haiku on a small piece of sandstone for Chris and Derek's garden.

Apologising
to every dug-up worm
the new gardener

My plans for a poetic take-over of Holy Island were gathering pace.

That afternoon I broke the law, cycled out to Snook House and, contrary to foot-and-mouth regulations, headed on foot across the dunes to the North Shore.

Here's my defence.

1) This spot was at least two miles from any livestock.

2) I wore the identical clothes I wore on the farm, clothes that had not left the island for ten weeks.

I wanted/needed the North Shore's vast silent emptiness, wanted to empty myself into it. I could scarcely see the breaking waves on the horizon and it took me a full 12 minutes of fast walking across the beach to reach the sea. Solitariness, which could terrify the human race, was also at times its friend, that sense there was nothing else, not in the whole world.

The Book Club met that night at the Heritage Centre. The fact I hadn't read the book, Philippa Gregory's weighty historical tome, *A Respectable Trade*, did nothing to discourage me. I went to everything, remember?

WEDNESDAY, 21 MARCH 2001 –
DAY SIXTY-SEVEN

A Plethora of Poems – God and Lambs

H oly Island handyman Jimmy Middlemiss had offered to secure stone in the small plot outside my front door. Naturally, the stone/poem would become so famous worldwide that desperate attempts to chuck it into a car boot to be flogged secretly to a millionaire art collector had to be resisted.

Its resting place had to be permanent.

This was the day of the poems. I was normally a lazy poet, excusing my small output on the flimsy reasoning that it was only bad poets who produced hundreds of the things.

I'd been invited to provide a poem for the Heritage Centre's Holy Island millennium quilt, a series of muslin squares in words and visuals created by islanders and visitors.

I decided on my 'Twice daily . . .' haiku and worked all morning doing it freehand on to the muslin, along with my freehand map of the island. The day was cold, overcast, a wind honed to painful sharpness. I banked the fire high, snug in my cottage.

I felt secure, warm – and poetic. Having finished the quilt square, I set to completing the poem I'd written about the Manor House garden (the one I'd worked on), probably the only piece of Mortimer verse to contain a cabbage.

In the Manor House Garden
a new cabbage,
arisen.
Contemplated by St Aidan,
salted by the sea,
shadowed by the Priory.
It shares the wind
that wastes the castle,
shares the island's clenched survival,
clinging tight to fragile roots.

I also decided this day that I would spend Three Tides for Cuthbert, a triple visit to that rocky outcrop involving spells of up to eight hours at a time on that exposed bareness.

I had marginalised myself from a large island (Britain), to a small island (Lindisfarne). I would now take the process further and marginalise myself to a tiny island (St Cuthbert's).

Cuthbert had retreated to the island to commune with God and fight demons. Neither had proved their credentials sufficiently in my book. Cuthbert had grown even more extreme. On Hob's Thrush (the alternative name for the island) various people had waded across to seek his advice, forcing him out to the more remote Farne Islands (south-east of Holy Island), where he lived in a shelter open only to the sky.

So why exactly was I planning three – probably uncomfortable – tides on this small outcrop?

No doubt I'd find out. In time.

The weather remained foul all day, a day to cook bangers and mash and stick the bangers into the mash to protrude the way they did in the comics of my youth.

That evening Ray Simpson gave the third faith lecture at the Heritage Centre. He was the only Holy Man with a Peter Mortimer bathroom haiku. I found myself drawn to the large Celtic cross round his neck. This cross seemed to announce him before his actual physical presence made an impact, so that a caricaturist asked to draw him would simply draw the cross.

Ray was an intelligent, humorous man, though the ambitions of his Society of St Aidan and St Hilda were viewed with suspicion by many island residents.

He spoke of the new Celtic Christianity, the new interest in monasticism, how religion gave his life a meaning, in a similar way that writing did mine. Maybe it was all as simple and as complicated as that.

But, again, I found the man more interesting than the religion. And guiltily, while he spoke, my gaze was increasingly taken by the millennium quilt hanging behind him, on which now my haiku square was secured.

The lecture prompted another haiku that day. It was this Holy Island and religion thing – it wouldn't let me go. That, and the natural world.

The granite church
crumbling. The breaking wave
still breaking

Late at night came the call of the sheep. I was getting used to it and past 11 p.m. walked the lane to Beblow Farm.

My sheep would be waiting. My harmless, docile, non-threatening sheep. I needed them.

The barn's sides rattled and shook in the fierce wind as I walked the darkness of the lane. It was a wild night and to slide back the barn door to the sweet smelling calm, the soft rustle of sheep among dry straw, was pure delight.

I wanted my world to be as simple as that of the sheep. Except their world no longer was simple. We humans had seen to that.

Margaret Patterson was on duty while her menfolk caught up on much-needed sleep.

'I just wish they'd get on with this foot-and-mouth slaughter,' she said. The words sounded strange in the peace of that barn. I was increasingly disturbed by the hundreds and thousands of animals slaughtered, many in perfect health, all suffering from a recoverable disease.

One pursued fox could bring out the protestors in their thousands. Where were these same protestors when a million animals were killed just to make sure a few rich individuals stayed rich?

Three hundred ewes had now lambed. I spent half an hour in that barn. It seemed a haven in a troubled world yet in many ways was at the very centre of that same world.

A special foot-and-mouth meeting had been called on the island by council chairman Ian McGregor. This was high-powered stuff, with MP Alan Beith due to appear, plus big cheeses from English Nature, English Heritage and the National Trust, guardians of virtually all the island's public sites and properties.

Emotions were running high, proposed solutions often light years apart. The time of the meeting wasn't quite high noon. But it may as well have been.

THURSDAY, 22 MARCH 2001 – DAY SIXTY-EIGHT

Poverty Cages – A Beckett Encounter

The skies were still leaden and sunless; the only resistance to the depressingly inevitable return of winter was the occasional defiant trill of a bird.

In the dining-room of the Lindisfarne Hotel at the Duck Supper, as well as the variety of males on view, I'd noticed the striking giant paintings on the wall.

Owner Sue Massey referred to them as 'my pension', original works by north-east artist Sheila Mackie to illustrate an edition of *Beowulf*, the oldest surviving poem in the English language. Though not set in this country, *Beowulf* probably originated in Northumbria in the eighth century.

People who complain that modern poetry 'doesn't rhyme' should take note that 1,200 years ago neither did *Beowulf.*

Sheila Mackie's paintings were used for the shorter translation by Edwin Morgan, which actor John Glover used for his stage version of the poem.

If you don't know *Beowulf*, it's a rattling good yarn about the eponymous hero and his life-and-death struggle with the monster Grendel. When Grendel cops it, his mum comes looking for revenge. I'd recently read Seamus Heaney's brilliant version.

Mackie's paintings were technically excellent collages which celebrated Anglo-Saxon art. But they failed to capture the great narrative drive and the often horrific sense of adventure of the book, with all its carnage and turmoil. The painter's art was too much like art.

The village was deserted. Huddled in their workshed, Sean Brigham and Richard Ward carried on with the seemingly Sisyphean task of making/mending the lobster pots, or 'poverty cages', as Sean called them.

The pots were piled outside, where they had been known to trap blackbirds. They even trapped birds when underwater. Cormorants had been found in the submerged pots, lured to dive after the bait and unable to escape.

The ex-vicar of Berwick and driftwood icon-creator, Mike Burden, was 65 in a few days' time. Banjo Bill, not quite obeying doctor's orders to take it easy, said to me, 'You write some lyrics, I'll write a tune, we'll tape the result and give it him on his birthday!'

Thus was born one of the great songs of the twenty-first century, from one of the great partnerships. Rogers & Hart, Leiber & Stoller, Rice & Lloyd Webber – make way, please, for Nelson & Mortimer, laying down cool music from Paradise Studios. The song was called 'Pension Book Blues'. For the music, Banjo Bill bastardised the 'Happy Birthday' tune and for the lyrics I just bastardised most things else. This was how it went:

> They gave me this book
> and it's got the name Mike on
> though I'm still working hard
> making beach driftwood icons
> it doesn't matter a jot
> from today the bad news
> is there ain't no escaping
> the pension book blues
>
> Chorus
> Don't try to refuse
> those years you can't lose
> from today you'll be facing
> those pension book blues
>
> Time was, I could run
> just a little bit quicker
> in Berwick they called me
> the speediest vicar

where once I was lightning
now I must cruise
'cos there ain't no escaping
those pension book blues

Chorus
Don't try to refuse . . .

And so on . . . Both Bill and I agreed rehearsals were needed. The Howlers concert may have been cancelled but you couldn't keep true performers down.

One of my island jobs was to help paint Neil and Cathy's Island Oasis Café window frames prior to them being erected. The couple, who were off the island a good deal, handed me a set of keys and said just go ahead. The frames were inside the café.

This all led to a strange meeting. Of little consequence, but strange.

I let myself in via the café's front door (the sticking one). A few moments later, a second individual let himself in via the rear door. We stood and looked at one another across the empty café. I had briefly been introduced to this man by Ross Peart. His name was John Basham and I seemed to remember he was an expert on birds. He was a small figure in a long black coat half-tied with string. He wore a grey woollen hat pulled over his head, which I noticed was half-shaved in a peculiar manner (the head and not the hat). Under his coat he wore a blue boiler suit and this was fastened with the kind of thick belt a weight-lifter might wear.

His voice was slow, deeply sonorous, and had the kind of deliberation that suggested he had picked out each word individually from a bag. He reminded me of a character from a Samuel Beckett play, a connection reinforced by the intensity of his features.

Our conversation across the empty café floor went something like this:

'You're John Basham, aren't you? Ross Peart introduced us, remember?'

'No. I don't remember that. I'm very anti-social.'

'Aren't you an expert an birds?'

'I'm not an expert on birds. I know nothing about anything.'

'I was wondering if you knew where any paint-brush cleaner might be?'

'I might know that, yes.'

He bent down behind the café counter and produced some paint-brush cleaner. He then asked me: 'Would you like a cup of tea?'

And I did.

He probably had as little idea as to why I was in that locked-up café as I did him. I drank my cup of tea and began to paint the frames. He said nothing and pottered about, moving this and that.

For half an hour we both continued thus, speaking few words. I'd then done all the painting I could and it looked like he'd done all the shifting about that he could.

'Goodbye, then,' I said.

'Goodbye.'

I left via the front door, which I locked. He left via the rear door, which he locked. And that was that.

The inclement weather (is 'inclement' ever used for anything other than weather? Like 'desiccated' with coconut?) again demanded a hot fire.

I'd arranged to rise early the next morning and go for a spot of mussel-gathering with fisherman Richard Ward and Frank Gregory of the Ship. I had little idea of what this entailed but then this was fairly normal in my preparation for events.

That evening I read a book, wrote letters to friends, stared into the fire and let the shivering world outside go hang.

FRIDAY, 23 MARCH 2001 – DAY SIXTY-NINE

Mussel Power – United Island

Despite my two parties, house visitors were still rare. Most days I was the only presence. I now took for granted eating and cooking alone, waking and going to bed in an otherwise empty house.

I was almost ten weeks away from home. I drifted in my solitary orbit. I knew many of the island people, some warm and friendly, some hostile, some indifferent.

Often, because I was a transient, they moved in and out of my existence like ghosts. My position as a writer made some people curious, others wary, as if 'no comment' was the only response, even if I was just asking them to pass the salt.

The situation felt strange to me. Anonymity is the best option for a writer (which was why many did their best work before they were famous) and in normal day-to-day living I made no big deal of what I did on this planet. Here, though, it seemed flagged up all the time, an inevitability. My position of 'writing about the island' defined me much more than my own personality. It was like that giant St Cuthbert cross which Ray Simpson wore – you saw it coming before you were aware of the man. All of which left me in a sort of limbo.

Limbo or not, I was up at 6 a.m. for the mussel-gathering. The day (surprise) was again grey, cold, damp, this beast of a winter refusing to loosen its grip.

I'd delayed my planned Three Tides for Cuthbert, having little inclination to suffer death by hypothermia, though a similar fate, I concluded, might await me on this morning.

By 7 a.m. myself, Richard Ward and Frank Gregory were heading out of the harbour in Richard's tiny boat. Richard's mood, considering he'd dropped his mobile phone in the sea and just injured his hip in a jetty fall, was upbeat. Frank Gregory was wearing a pair of giant waders which stopped just short of his chin.

The sky, the sea, the castle, the harbour and probably our faces were painted various shades of grey as we phut-phutted out from shore. Seals bobbed up and down alongside the boat like targets in a video game.

Our destination was the Beacons, on a piece of jutting mainland reached by no road and probably one of the least-walked-on stretches of sand in the UK.

We were a few feet from shore when I made to get out.

'Don't,' said Richard, restraining me. 'This is steeply shelved. We're in twenty feet of water.'

The mussel beds were visible only one hour each side of high tide. They rose up from the sea like unmoving whale backs, small black islands where the crunch of mussel underfoot was like walking through rice crispies.

The mussels were gunged up with all sorts of goo. Collecting and cleaning them with bare hands on a cold damp morning rated fairly low on the Pleasure-o-meter.

There were millions of mussels round Holy Island. Each tide they appeared, begged people to come and collect them, and, getting no response, disappeared again.

I could never decide if it was to the island's great shame or credit that it seemed uninterested in developing the great mussel potential. Thus mussel-gathering was the occasional preserve of daft blokes on the occasional morning. Though all these mussel beds were owned by the island, generally they remained as unvisited as the moon.

We crunched on, filling our plastic buckets. Eider ducks skimmed and scudded about in search of, according to Richard, their favourite food, hairy Mary worms.

And soon enough the sea was lapping back in, preparing to cover over once more this source of foodstuff to which, for once, humans seemed indifferent.

By 8 a.m. I was back home, cooking breakfast and thawing out. For several hours my hands would tingle from the slow return of blood. I cooked the food as if wearing boxing gloves.

The foot-and-mouth emergency meeting was called for 11.45 a.m. at the Heritage Centre. All council members would be present, as well as the MP Alan Beith. The National Trust were there for the castle, English Heritage for the Priory and Museum, and English Nature for the 8,000-acre reserve, all affected by the disease's restrictions.

Feelings were running high and the mood was prickly as traders, hoteliers and others gathered in the foyer. I anticipated some resentment at my presence and it came.

'How come you are here? Exactly which island business do *you* represent?' asked Jen Ward and another islander. I stood my ground and held up for them my official invitation from council chairman Ian McGregor.

The odd person was stirring things up, loudly berating the officials and predicting they would sell the island up the river. The signs were not good. But the meeting was. And just as a previous public meeting had shown me how quickly the island could flare up into conflict with itself, so this one showed its ability to unite.

The room was crammed to bursting, with the officials sat in a line at the front table as serious-faced as any politburo. It soon became apparent that a good deal of work had already gone on behind the scenes.

The National Trust and English Heritage declared the castle and the Priory would be open by 1 April. English Nature offered to open the sand dunes to the west of the Big Bank (a location, not Barclays). They would provide free disinfectant, matting and fencing.

In the room were hoteliers, farmers, shopkeepers, mini-bus drivers, café-owners; the entire commercial momentum of the island gathered in this small space. And in that room, in a response to the obviously constructive offers made by the statutory bodies, the atmosphere changed. It seemed that at that very moment a group consciousness rose up, a realisation that in the face of this dire threat, cooperation and not conflict was the answer.

How long this group consciousness would last, no one could say. Maybe it would dissipate once they walked out the room. But it was there and it was a small shaft of light, an instant of optimism that was felt by all.

Plus which MP Alan Beith seemed much less of a weasel than many of his MP colleagues. No political point-scoring, no treating the islanders as election fodder. My suspicion that this might be an MP who was also a human being was reinforced a little later when I learned he was to play a trumpet at the head of the Holy Island Jazz Festival procession.

The optimism, of course, was in context. George and Jen Ward walked straight from the meeting to learn of the cancellation at the Manor House of 25 Canadians booked in for three days. This brought their losses thus far to £10,000.

Two small incidents that day. Stuart McMurdo spotted in the Sign of Two Kirstys with a pint in his paw – signifying the end of his current radio- and chemotherapy treatment. And Jimmy Brigham telling me he'd been off the island.

'But, Jimmy,' I said, 'you never leave the island!'

Because normally he didn't, and remarkably seemed none the worse for it.

'Aye, well,' he replied. 'And why should I want to?'

Which gave me a lot to think about.

That evening Banjo Bill and I honed 'The Pension Book Blues' to greater heights of perfection in readiness for its public performance.

He'd been suffering from a poor tum and blamed salmonella eggs. Bill's theory was that if he drank a whole bottle of red wine there'd be enough acid to kill it off. So he did. And there was.

SATURDAY, 24 MARCH 2001 – DAY SEVENTY

Fire, Work with Me – The Two Banjo Bills

Marking off the days of my stay often saw me playing little number games; the statistics of how long gone, how long to go. This day, 24 March, was a new watershed. I was due to leave the island on 23 April. This was now the last '24' I would face, as with every other number coming up.

Now, dear reader, I know you will find the following hard to believe but it is true.

This day, this 24 March, presented itself with a cold grey face, a huge unbroken slab of dirty sky, an oppressive immutability, a sense of always-has-been, always-will-be. There had never been any weather apart from this. Nor ever would be, forever and ever amen.

This drabness drained the life from you. For the previous week I'd walked very little, even in the small area people were allowed to walk. I had hardly been conscious of or looked at the mainland. I had been aware of little beyond my own small isolated world.

I rose and changed the bedsheets, an act which always brought more happiness than you would expect. I'd made the fire each day of late in defiance of the terrible weather. It was an irritatingly difficult fire to light. I had an old open range in my Cullercoats kitchen, where it was easy to build a deep structure of paper, wood and coal, and where the bottom draught was a healthy one. The grate here was wide and shallow, with too few gaps for a draught. I needed to build a precarious pyramid. I also needed to employ those items which a true fire-maker scoffed at – firelighters. These were like having stabilisers on a bike or a machine for making hand-rolled cigarettes; something a purist wouldn't entertain, like putting blackcurrant in Guinness.

Here they were essential, though, as various abortive puff-cheeked attempts could testify. Even then, with a mix of paper, firelighters, driftwood and coal, I was required to lie flat on my stomach for 45 minutes nurturing the tentative flame, rearranging, adjusting, adding, fortifying, blowing, fanning. More wood here, move the coal there. Without this nurturing the fire simply gave up the ghost.

This was not a fire for a busy executive or any person on whom the world made big demands. Off Holy Island me and this fire could not have co-existed.

More rehearsals with Banjo Bill. Boy – we were good!

On Saturdays I afforded myself little extra treats. On this day I cooked roast chicken with three veg and also had a rice pudding which I pretended to be surprised by when I plonked it down on the table.

And I'd been keeping up my yoga schedule. I looked for a balance in yoga; it gave some control over my excitability but I knew if I got too cool, too together and in harmony, I'd probably do nothing but look out with a self-satisfied expression and have no need to write.

A strange evening followed at Banjo Bill's, one that haunted me. He'd spoken of a film called *The Miner*, shot half a century ago as part of a National Coal Board recruitment drive at Hilton Mains pit in Staffordshire, where Bill had been colliery manager. Part of the film was narrated by the much-missed Derek Guyler.

I was sitting with Bill and his son John as he loaded the film when in walked Ross Peart. He was, in the spirit of the film to come, carrying a lit Davy lamp kept from his own childhood. The lamp's light shone in the gathering gloom as Ross announced quietly, 'My father died today.' He'd been crying that afternoon, he said, but was now OK. This patently would be untrue but he was thinking of us. His wife Jean arrived and in a somewhat unusual atmosphere the film began.

Ross's circumstances only added to the strong sense of mortality in that room. The film, shot in black and white, belonged to another age and not only because it showed a time when there was a strong mining community. There was also the post-war feel of Brylcreem, short-sleeved Paisley jumpers, short hair, brightly polished shoes. Mineworkers pedalled their lumbering, heavy bikes to work. We saw them packed like sardines descending in the cage, film of them working at the face or relaxing in the Miners' Institute, the hub of any mining village. They drank at the bar, played billiards, their wives and children were seen in the Institute's various leisure and cultural activities, a choir, art classes and so on.

More shots of the miners' wives in floral pinafores cutting thick slices of white bread in front of blazing coal ranges (which may or may not have been easy to light) while short-trousered children resembling urchins from a West End Victorian musical looked on.

A handsome, young, dark-haired man with an obvious air of authority was smoking a pipe and addressing the trade union officials.

'That's me,' said Bill.

Three things combined in that room. My father's recent death, the death that day of Ross Peart's father and the sense of the two Bill Nelsons, one on that screen, one sitting in this chair. The film had been made before Stanley Matthews' Cup final, before the Queen had been on the throne. Churchill had still been prime minister.

And there he was, in his early thirties, addressing the meeting and waving his pipe. Bill Nelson.

'And I've still got that pipe. Look,' he said and produced it off a shelf. The film finished and we all sat silently. After a few moments Ross relit his Davy lamp and disappeared into the night with it and his sadness. Bill talked about the making of the film.

Bill Nelson then and Bill Nelson now were two different people from two different galaxies. Yet here he was, sitting in his chair, glass of wine at his side, banjolele at the ready. And time rolled its inexorable way on.

I was still haunted by the film later that night in the Sign of Two Kirstys.

Around 11 p.m. the door burst open and in came a noisy gang of island fishermen fresh from their day out at the Glasgow Fishing Exhibition. Probably – and quite rightly – they'd spent the whole enjoyable day without the need to dwell on mortality.

SUNDAY, 25 MARCH 2001 – DAY SEVENTY-ONE

The Two North Seas – A Burden Ballad

I had this growing suspicion that the sun had fled to another solar system entirely. There was, of course, a residue of light (it took some time to get here) but soon that would be exhausted. After which our world would simply be switched off like a television set (assuming you are one of these people who ever does switch off the telly). There would be a little time when we would be that white spot at the centre of the screen. After which, nothing.

How else could I explain the sun's total absence for the fifth successive day? Zilch. Nothing. Not one single ray. Not for one single nano-second.

I am not the kind who dreams of endless Mediterranean sun. It would be boring. But just a glimpse, please. And remember, my dad was now a part of that sun.

My desires were in part fulfilled later that day. The sun peek-a-booed round a cloud then reluctantly, like some nervous child pushed forward to do their party piece, made its way centre stage. It was too shy to remain there for long, just long enough for me to stand in the middle of Marygate, close my eyes and feel its almost forgotten warmth on the skin.

After which I had my customary Sunday papers read and snack in the Island Oasis Café. Neil and Cathy listened to my John Basham 'strange encounter' story.

'John gives an important sense of the surreal to the island,' said Neil, which was right. The full name apparently was John Bulwark Basham and he was a true eccentric in that he seemed delightfully unaware of the fact. He had also sculpted two large hedges round the café. At the front was his 'hedge car' and at the rear his 'hedge train'. The car especially had proved a huge attraction, photographed by so many people that Cathy had come up with an ingenious idea. All photographers were asked to make a donation to charity. A £400 cheque had already gone to Amnesty International, with more coming in all the time.

With a jigsaw, Neil had cut out the wooden letters for the new café sign. Him creating letters in wood. Me in stone.

Later, on my Sunday perambulations, I noticed a small pot of mussels in vinegar on the Manor House bar.

And was there a single drinker in that establishment who paused for one moment to consider the huge sacrifices endured by the island writer to bring these mussels to their palate?

No, there wasn't.

There was, though, a new Holy Island pleasure to be discovered that afternoon – high-tide cycling.

When the causeway part that ran alongside the island was underwater, there was still a narrow sand strip between the water and dunes navigable on a push-bike. Eventually, of course, the causeway took leave of the island altogether and there was no place left to go except back. But this gave almost three miles of deliciously deserted cycling, the exhilaration coming in the sure knowledge you would encounter absolutely no one.

I cycled to Snook Tower, parked the bike and again leapt across the dunes to see my much-missed North Shore. The view this time was totally different from the great flat desert of sand seen at low tide.

The sea had become schizophrenic and divided itself. It lapped at my feet and I saw it stretch away to the north for several hundred yards until it ended again, divided in both directions by a raised-up sandy strip. Beyond the strip was the sea again – the second wave, as it were – and it looked as if you could just plonk a deck chair on that sandy strip any old time and just snooze the day away right there, in the middle of the North Sea.

My bike journey to Snook had been a painless wind-assisted whisk from the village. On the return journey the wind shouldered against me like a resistant rugby scrum and I got back home truly cream-crackered.

Mark this day well. For on it was the first public performance of 'Pension Book Blues', live and to an invited audience at the house of Mike and Anne Burden.

For his birthday party, Mike Burden sported a snazzy shirt and lively pair of trousers that transformed him from the shapeless cords and baggy old woollen jumper (often with holes) image. Not that this spared him the song. There were demands for an encore. What could Bill and I do except bow to the will of the people?

MONDAY, 26 MARCH 2001 –
DAY SEVENTY-TWO

The Brigham Touch – New Age Island

Hey – what was this? Some mistake, surely? No. I rechecked the evidence and, sure enough, through my bedroom window was some *blue* sky.

To half-mix a metaphor, though, it was a false dawn. By the time I'd had breakfast, the weather had drawn its familiar grey curtain across and the temperature was a shimmering one degree.

I'd decided to dump the small stone I'd reserved for Chris and Derek's garden. I'd fetch the one earmarked for me by Jimmy Brigham on St Cuthbert's shore. No good for carving but this poem would be painted.

I trundled the Burden barrow down Jenny Bell Lane and along the shoreline to the base of the tip. The Brigham stone was taller and heavier than my carved one but at least it was on the right side of the island.

I dragged and lugged it on to the trolley then negotiated the 20 metres of large, strewn rocks which resembled a collapsed city. I say negotiated but in attempting to straddle the first rock, the stone fell off. As it did on the second. It would need securing. I walked back to the village and scrounged some fishermen's twine from Richard Ward, still at his poverty cages. En route I passed Debbie Luke, mother of school kid Molly.

'Mind,' she said, 'you're walking a bit funny.'

This, of course, was Arthur. Arthur went most places with me. He liked the cold and damp, as it made him stronger. It's fair to say I loathed Arthur. He'd almost stopped me running and, quite honestly, I didn't trust him further than I could throw him.

'On the island,' said Molly, 'we call that the Brigham hip.'

And I was about to lug up the Brigham stone.

I secured the stone to the trolley, which I slowly bumped over the large boulders. The trolley sank deep into the sandy mud, causing tracks as deep as trenches on the Somme. There were two alternative ways of movement: drag the trolley behind me, bent over like a worker ant, or pull it walking backwards. Either way, going was slow and I was relieved to find bird man Ian Kerr to help me up the sloping sand to Jenny Bell Lane. From there I trundled up the footpath, past the church and down Church Lane towards the Market Square and the Stables.

Various curious people asked me what I was doing. When I replied, 'I'm making a poem' they tended to enquire no further.

No answer at the Stables so I left the stone trussed up on the trolley by the front door. It felt like returning some ransom hostage.

Something of note happened that day at the Post Office. Little by little, almost imperceptibly, the atmosphere between Malcolm Patterson and me had changed. At first our post-spat exchanges were almost non-existent, possibly a monosyllabic grunt, a stiff-backed formalism. Slowly, titbits of conversation filtered in: it was a cold day, yes; the tide was high today, yes. Not much, but an improvement.

On Holy Island such things move at their own speed. Any attempt by me at an over-hasty reconciliation would have been met by either embarrassment, hostility, incomprehension or any combination of the three. But slowly the occasional phrase became the occasional sentence and now, on this day, when he took my money for the newspaper Malcolm said, 'Thanks, Peter.'

The use of my name was a major breakthrough, a symbolic gesture. We both knew it. Neither would mention it. I restrained myself from committing what would have been a totally disastrous act – to give Malcolm a hug – and left the shop.

I'd booked a reflexology session with Christinne Holbrook at the Heritage Centre. Her weekly sessions also took in aromatherapy and massage – a rare nod from the island to alternative culture.

Holy Island did offer retreats but they were all Christian. The multi-faith, multi-cultural life of mainland Britain had made few inroads on Lindisfarne, partly through the island's history, partly its isolation. On the mainland Christianity was an enfeebled and ailing beast, often with a great deal less energy than other religions. On the island, it had a stranglehold.

But this, in terms of medicine, was an alternative and walking into Christinne's prepared room was a most non-Holy Island experience. There was a soothing water fountain, a scented oil light burner, subdued lighting; soft Eastern music was in the background. I stretched myself out on the couch. Chill-out time.

Reflexology works through finding meridians and chakras; these are located via the feet or, as Christinne put it, 'Your brain's in your big toe', the kind of comment I'd often had to suffer. For one hour she applied different pressures to my feet, the effects making themselves felt in various parts of the body.

Did any native islanders book in for sessions, I wondered?

'A few women – the men would be scared stiff.'

Me, I was all for alternative medicine. British doctors had suffered a drastic decline in status; once perfect pillars of society, they were now often seen as suicidal, alcoholic, overstressed, out of touch. And it took years of dedicated training to get to that state.

The thing was, I had a decreasing faith in pills being the answer to anything.

As Christinne Holbrook put it, 'It's hardly ever just medical. The state of mind is vital as well.'

Not something the giant drug companies want putting about.

The reflexology left me fresh, recharged. I walked round the village that night. Three of the four pubs were closed, only the Manor House open. More than ten weeks since I arrived, Easter looming, but the night-time village was often as silent and dark as that first Sunday in January.

And if I needed late-night company, it would have to be the sheep. I liked the sensation of walking the dark lane at this time. Entering that barn put me in touch with something I couldn't define, beyond words or reason but something essential, as if it compensated for many of the things that fell short elsewhere.

I struggled with my place on this island, my reasons for being here, my identity. I could walk in with the sheep and all this meant nothing, as if the mere fact of my having walked up to the barn meant that I was accepted.

Approaching the barn at this time was visually dramatic. Its slatted sides leaked strips of yellow light across the farmyard and the lane. The barn rattled in the wind, a dark bulk, a fortress for its mild inmates.

Sheep were an unregarded species. Their faces manifested no nobility, no braveness, no mystery, no savagery. Their sideways chewing was comically ludicrous. They showed in their behaviour not a vestige of independent thought. They gathered together diffidently, the occasional 'baa', the odd rustle of straw, the wind's night-time rattle against the barn sides. The smell was sweet, slightly dungy.

For humans, sheep were useful, utterly harmless, non-threatening. All of these sheep were healthy, fertile. And new mothers.

Kill the lot of them, said some on the island.

TUESDAY, 27 MARCH 2001 –
DAY SEVENTY-THREE

Cuthbert Grief – Postal Drama

The constant severely cold weather slowly forced a sartorial functionalism on me, so that my daily garb was increasingly dark blue jumper, dark thick trousers, my rainbow colours confined to the wardrobe.

In this aspect, I was coming to resemble the islanders. In other ways, not.

On this day I had company – Mike and Anne Burden's black Labrador Charlie, while they were off exhibiting their artwork in Musselburgh.

On the village grapevine I'd heard some rumblings of discontent over my planned Three Tides for Cuthbert. I never had any idea which of my actions would upset who or why. On this occasion, some thought I planned to take a tent (no tents allowed on Holy Island).

I was stopped in the village street by a local with whom I'd had hardly any dealings. I assured her there would be no tent.

'But you are going to spend time on the island?'

'Yes, three tides.'

'And then you're going to put it in a book?'

'Probably, yes.'

'And then every bugger'll be doing it.'

'Well,' I said. 'Not sure how many would want to. Anyway, odd people have spent tides there for the last 1,300 years.'

'And who told you that?'

'I thought most people on the island knew it.'

'Aye. Them as don't belong here. Them as aren't Holy Islanders. Them as interfere.'

She walked away, leaving Charlie to stare up at me. For several moments I was unable to move. I had the sense of an undercurrent on this island, an entire section of the community sullenly hostile to me, a mainly unspoken hostility occasionally manifesting itself in something as non-threatening as me sitting on a lump of rock. These were people I did not know, people I would occasionally see hunching themselves along the street. They were people who felt the island belonged to them and that the likes of me were interfering outsiders.

Suddenly, in the village street, I longed for the anonymity of the city, the ability to lose yourself in a large conurbation.

I longed there and then to flee across that causeway, a pox on Holy Island and all that it stood for. Because there was something deep down that was beyond me, that was beyond anyone who came here not content with merely accepting 'the package'. Well, that package had been bought by enough people, from writers to documentary-makers to trippers. Buying the package left the island blissfully undisturbed, left the place – or sections of it – 'unpolluted' as it were. A dangerous state. And then I remembered the flipside, the loneliness and isolation many suffered in modern city life: old people found dead in their homes after a month, the daily rat race, the drained faces of the commuters, the sink estates, the crumbling schools, the violence of the filthy streets, the sense of despair. And I realised why so many would come here and desperately *want* to buy the package, and why there was so much vested interest in perpetuating it.

And who were these island people, except human beings brought up in a particular way of life, one that was resistant to change, resistant to nosy strangers? What to me was a writer's curiosity, to them was interference.

But I also argued this: my Three Tides for Cuthbert was entirely my own affair, time spent on public land freely accessible. And though I was keen to accommodate and appease local feeling, there was a limit.

Those who didn't like me spending three tides on Cuthbert's island could, ultimately, lump it.

And with this thought came the realisation I was now much better equipped to deal with the island's knock-backs. The village street tirade had momentarily floored me. But like those Russian dolls, I was back upright fairly quick.

Which was just as well for Charlie, who wanted his regular walks up the Heugh. I noticed his slight limp.

'Moi aussi, Charlie,' I said. Not being bilingual, he failed to respond.

That evening, as I left Banjo Bill's, I caught a glimpse of something that crossed two separate cultures.

The manic wind was whistling its freezing way round the village streets. Mercury had plunged down the thermometer as fast as a broken lift, the rain was beginning its icy spit. Few people were abroad, the odd dark hunched figure scuttling out of one door and into another.

Except these two laddos. They were striding out towards the Manor House, seemingly oblivious to the elements. Above the waist they wore only skimpy, short-sleeved football tops. This was the kind of obligatory macho gear worn by thousands of young Geordie weekend drinkers as they staggered their way round the unique Bigg Market area of Newcastle, where one bar was never more than a quick vomit away from the next, and where you were never certain if those wobbly figures up the narrow alleyways were being sick or having it off.

What united the young bravados was the dress sense. Coats or other protective gear was taboo. Even when the weather turned skin to a bubble wrap of goose pimples, even though the snowstorms may be arctic the message was – shirts only. The females did their bit, often wearing little more than two hankies.

And these two laddos had brought that culture to Holy Island. Where it didn't really fit. No peer group for psychological support, for one thing. More severe weather, for another. They were, in many ways, out of their element. They sat in the Manor House bar contemplating their longish walk back to their bed & breakfast.

It was Jen Ward who came to their rescue, as the ferocious weather showed no signs of abating, persuading them to borrow two topcoats. If their names were ever revealed, their Tyneside street cred would be gone. The secret is safe with me.

I had named the stone for Chris and Derek Blush, from its distinctive pink appearance. They liked it but had now gone off the original haiku.

'We'd like something – well, a bit more philosophical,' Derek said.

Oh well, just like that then. A poet's lot, etc.

Holy Island society is – willingly – dictated by the tides. Many people got the crossing times wrong. I came to realise this wasn't just stupidity. There were several tide tables presenting the information in different, often confusing, ways. Framed tables were posted at various points round the island, updated every month. These had two columns, the first 'Open From', the second (in red) headed 'Danger – Incoming Tide'. The Post Office published its own annual tide booklet showing the time and height of each tide and a reminder at the bottom of each page: 'The causeway is closed for TWO hours before high tide until THREE hours after.'

This wasn't always strictly true.

A third set of tables was available on single printed sheets. These gave safe crossing times but no heights. I came across a fourth set, which only residents saw, provided by weekend islander QC Paul Batty. These gave the real low-down on every tide, such as the odd times (on really low tides) when the causeway wasn't even covered.

Suddenly I had a brilliant idea. Commission an artist to create a 'tide clock' in the village centre. According to Derek Pollard it had been suggested the previous year. People didn't want it.

That night the insect whirr of the air ambulance helicopter was heard, as a collapsed diabetic staying at the Open Gate had to be lifted off.

I also learned that three millionaires owned properties on the island and between them spent about as much time here in a year as it took to gather mussels. My sympathies swung suddenly to the islanders.

Rain and wind lashed the streets. I ran home pell-mell from the pub, coat pulled up over my head, thinking of the minimalist protection of short-sleeved footie tops.

WEDNESDAY, 28 MARCH 2001 – DAY SEVENTY-FOUR

Maternal Pull – A Brace of Haiku

I woke at 4 a.m. I blamed Derek Pollard. Him and his damned haiku. It demanded to be written. I sat up in bed with pen and paper. Half an hour later I dozed off again, a pattern I repeated several times till 6 a.m., when I felt the haiku was complete. I stared at it, the feeling it had been written by someone else.

Captured
in the lovers' kiss
the cartwheeling virus

I read it again, trying to get some purchase on it. People expected writers always to be able to define and explain what they'd written. Not always possible.

The poem had a sexual content. I'd had none of that on the island. Maybe this was my anguished cry. Foot-and-mouth was in there, too. Work it out for yourself.

I read it out to Derek on the phone.

'That'll do nicely,' he said.

I needed to see my mother, eight weeks in that Rotherham hospital room. She needed to see me. Some things were that simple.

Mike Burden ran me to Berwick station. The east coast main line train whizzed south. Holy Island appeared briefly to the east, an offshore glimpse, mist-shrouded, hunched into the sea like a dream, a memory, a ghostly evocation. Was I ever there? Did it even exist?

Passengers on the train looked utterly normal. And totally strange. This sense of Holy Island being another planet was reinforced when, south of Tyneside, the seemingly permanent grey, cold weather fell back, the sky spread itself blue, bright sunlight blessed us.

Rotherham, never the most fashionable of towns, seemed suddenly almost Mediterranean.

And from my own small Holy Island world, I was going to the even smaller world of my mother in her two-month, small room confinement.

I brushed her white hair, as delicate as smoke, I rubbed vaseline into the rock-hard pressure sore on the sole of her foot, I adjusted her hearing aid, which most times seemed purely decorative. Her hip operation had left one leg four inches shorter than the other.

I examined the special built-up shoe made for her. It sent a shiver of fear through me, evoking those Saturday matinée villains of my childhood ABC Minors.

My mother was less tearful than on my previous visit. The cast for her broken femur had been removed, the drips were gone and she was able to sit in the bedside chair. From the window she looked out across a concrete space to another window and the back of a woman's head in a small office. My mother talked about this woman, this head, how it moved during the day. She talked with the obsessive detail of a Samuel Beckett character.

When I left I stared from another window across this concrete space and waved to my mother. She waved back, a weak hand raised like a fluttering moth, her image imprisoned in that window frame.

I had still not told my mother the duration of my Holy Island stay. This with-holding of information, this deceit, burned inside me like swallowed bile.

Yet, overall, I was less vulnerable than on my previous Rotherham visit. Being off the island brought a perspective. I lay in bed at the house of my brother Alex and his wife Helen, knew that I was stronger, knew I feared much less the return.

And though the relative domestic 'luxuries' were welcome, I was not clinging to them. In fact, my mind was racing over the final quarter of my stay.

I woke again in the night, and again was writing in the small hours. The result was the small, simple haiku:

To Cuthbert's island
the longest
journey

THURSDAY, 29 MARCH 2001 – DAY SEVENTY-FIVE

The Curtain Recloses – The Cautious Christians

G ood news for my nephew Matthew – a reconstruction operation after one year should restore him almost to normality.

Good news for me, too. A big fat juicy cooked breakfast plonked in front of me by Helen.

Back at the hospital, my mother asked, 'Have you finished your book?'

'Nearly,' I lied.

Each time you say goodbye to an ageing parent, it could be the last time. Who ever knows such things? When I'd mentioned my father, my mother had sobbed. I'd told her off, saying he wouldn't have wanted that at all. She agreed and still sobbed.

I did say goodbye and waved to her through that same window, after which the endless hospital corridor seemed doubly endless.

The blue sky and sunshine travelled with me until north of Newcastle, where the grey clouds, the gloomy mist and the cloud were waiting in ambush.

According to Mike Burden, who met me at Berwick station, they had never been away. We drove over the causeway, towards the half-focused grey line of the village crouched beneath the lowering grey sky.

I realised I had only dreamed the sunshine. Lindisfarne was in the permanent clammy grip of some dreadful grey phantom from which escape was impossible.

The Cuddy House was cold and unwelcoming and sulking from me being away. I was chastised. I felt unable immediately to readjust to it and was grateful for Mike Burden's offer to eat with him and Anne. I still felt unable to return home later and made my way to the Manor House bar.

In which were gathered more young Christians than you could throw a crucifix at. Dozens of them – on the island for an international convention – squashed round every table. I sat at the bar, chatted to George Ward and realised

30 minutes later that not a single young Christian had come to buy a drink.

'Came in an hour ago, bought one drink each,' said George. 'They've never moved since.'

I also realised that many of the young Christians, since I'd been in, had been staring at empty glasses.

Here was a matter of some conflict. Drinking among the young was on the increase. They started younger and increasingly moved at an early age to the 'harder' drinks, encouraged by feckless landlords offering triples for around £1.50, which meant that for under a fiver a youngster would have drunk nine whiskies. Now here were some upstanding youngsters showing splendid restraint when faced with the evil drink. As against that, George had a bar filled to bursting (several locals looked in and went away again), a place teeming with people but with the till remaining resolutely shut.

Finally he moved out amongst them, gathering up glasses. Without these to stare into, the young Christians seemed to lose the will to continue with their display of iron-willed in-house non-indulgence. Very quietly, and without the hint of a bellowed song, they all stood up and left.

I'd noticed on the way onto the island that plastic fencing had been erected by the road to the castle. This was due to open 1 April. Also the Priory. The island was fighting back.

FRIDAY, 30 MARCH 2001 – DAY SEVENTY-SIX

The Invader – Indian Excess

Part of me hated planning ahead – I moved rapidly away from anyone talking about future retirement, pension plans and so on but part of me needed the excitement of something coming up; writing a new book, a new play, planning a new venture.

On the island I tried to let myself go with the rhythms, without feeling I had no rudder. Thus I planned on the Saturday my much-delayed 11-mile perimeter walk round the island. Soon after that I would tackle my Three Tides for Cuthbert. I still had the poem to paint for Chris and Derek. And I still planned to deepen and improve the carved letters on stone number one.

I had sought no publicity while on the island, being such a shy retiring chap. Seriously, I wanted none. Once I was off, no problem. I'd abseil naked from the Tyne Bridge if it might help the book. But only after I'd finished my task.

Word did get out, though, and I had a phone call from a student called Brian Smith, who wanted to do a 20-minute film project on my unusual poetic creations as part of his thesis at Sunderland University. He would call it 'An Artist, A Chisel and 100 Days'. And Brian was ever so grateful when I agreed on the phone. Secretly I thought it might be good fun. And a new face. And me on celluloid. And nothing spoilt.

Meantime, I'd finished the latest in the books chosen for me by northern writers. Elizabeth Bowen's novel *In the Heat of the Day* was the choice of poet Sean O'Brien.

My books achieved one of two things. Some helped define my place on this island, to have a religious or geographical relevance. Others removed me entirely and reminded me of the world outside. Each was necessary and Bowen's novel did the latter. It was set in wartime London – an era just out of my consciousness – and centred on Stella, who discovers her lover Robert is suspected of trading secrets to the Germans. The purveyor of this news, Harrison, is in a position to ruin Robert but is prepared to spare him if Stella gives herself to him (Harrison).

This is a very English novel; its characters at times echo the polite restraint of *Brief Encounter*. Bowen died in 1973 and has an almost alchemic skill in creating real gold from the base metal of the daily drudge. Her densely written descriptive style and evocation of wartime London are both remarkable and unlike the style of today's young bucks. Not a great deal of action, and hardly likely to pose a threat to John Grisham, but a beautifully written book, a sealed volcano of emotion. In both time and place it sucked me right away from my tiny island to the bomb sites, the air raid sirens, the black-outs and all that repressed emotion of the English.

I imagined few in this country read the novel today. Especially men.

At the door stood Brian Smith. Slung from his shoulders and at his feet was some serious-looking video equipment, tripods, cameras. Technology had come knocking. He was an affable, slightly shy young man without edge.

Over the next hours he filmed me with the carved poem, the quilt poem, the garden poem, the bathroom wall poem. He filmed me measuring up Blush ready to paint the new poem.

And I was always talking, talking. I stared into the dark eye of the camera hour after hour. I waxed lyrical and unlyrical about my life on the island. For though I wrote down a great deal of what I was doing on the island, I realised how little I talked about it. And by talking, in many ways, I defined it.

Partly, I was sad. The camera would record, would take away, would expose to others. This was the first step in the process, my removal from a state of innocence. I knew now there would be no going back, as if, in however small a way, my experience on Holy Island would begin to 'leak out'. Just as it had to. Otherwise why come to write a book?

But knowing it and experiencing it were different. Everything had been enclosed. Even the notebooks I wrote in remained on the island. No longer. Brian Smith was the harbinger of the new chapter. He would carry across that causeway a part of me. And it could never come back.

This was an important day on another count. I ate a meal which, unbeknown to me, would affect my whole future. Among the supermarket food in my last delivery was a fillet steak under cellophane.

Back in Cullercoats I never ate supermarket meat, relying on the wondrous creations of our local butcher Peter Darling.

The steak had been dyed a florid red, the paper-thin slices fanned out to make it seem more substantial. I grilled it with tomatoes, mushroom and onion. As I ate it, a terrible truth dawned.

The steak had no taste whatsoever.

Had it been given to a blindfolded person, he/she would have been unable to identify it. To say the steak was offensive was to imbue it with some active characteristic it clearly lacked. It was thin cardboard.

It was a grilled beermat. And it was in order to create this utterly tasteless abhorrence that we had turned our farms into vast factories, had crowded our stressed cattle into sunless sheds, had fed them the slurry of other beasts, had visited upon our land a plague of biblical proportions.

I tossed this 'meat' into the bin. It would, soon enough, albeit metaphorically, return to haunt me.

That night a lively crowd of Tynesiders was in the Manor House bar and easily outdrinking the previous young Christians in the celebration of a fortieth birthday. They were resident at Lindisfarne House, where naturally I wangled myself an invitation. Two abiding memories of that party. First, I was almost moved to ring the *Guinness Book of Records* for the largest amount of Indian food moved over a distance of 50 miles (they'd brought with them from Tyneside enough foil containers to carpet the entire back room). Second, there was live music.

How I'd missed live music!

How important to sing or dance every single day of your life. My monastic Cuddy House existence was against a backdrop of silence or the occasional telly or radio programme. I needed to shake down, needed music's unique power of release.

I bet St Cuthbert never tried it. I bet it would have done him good.

SATURDAY, 31 MARCH 2001 –
DAY SEVENTY-SEVEN

The Long March – Mortimer Island

I stayed late at the party and woke at 10 a.m. feeling particularly sluggish. The same piece of grey sky that had taken up residence outside my bedroom window some time in the fourteenth century was still there. The inclination was to roll over, sod the planned circumference of the island, go back to sleep.

And indolence almost won the day.

Except this walk was important to me. First, I was still denied access to much of the island and walking round it would reacquaint me with it. Second, it was a ritual, a way of confirming my relationship with the place. This was like dancing round the maypole (though my walk had little to do with sex). To walk totally round the island was to lay some claim to it.

Holy Island was both the place and the people. It did well to distinguish the two. And for this expedition, I had no interest in the people.

Partly because of foot-and-mouth, partly as a personal challenge, I vowed I would do the entire circle without once stepping on to the land mass itself; rocks, beaches – no footpaths, no fields.

I made cheese and onion sandwiches, a flask of tea, packed fruit and crisps. I felt suddenly melancholic, realised such preparations were done normally for long walks with Kitty. I pictured myself, all day walking alone, felt incredibly sorry for myself, picked up the phone to speak to Kitty. A tinny answerphone message.

I slung the bag over my shoulder.

'Right, I'm off then,' I said, because that was what I would do at such a time, even though in this instance there was no one to hear it.

It was to prove a walk of two halves. Pleasure. Followed by pain. But first, a small miracle. As I walked through the village and approached Chare End, the clouds thinned and began to be pulled apart like candy floss by kids. Streaks of blue appeared, sending islanders rushing to their reference books. But, yes, it was – *blue sky*. Last seen when, exactly? Few could recall. Village elders were quizzed.

More of it appeared. And more. Look, great chunks of it. Look, the entire sky – blimey.

I'd set off two hours after high tide, the best time to ensure passage over all beaches and rocks. There was a keen westerly wind in my face. With a bit of luck, later it would be at my back.

On the mainland Cheviot was still snow-flecked, hunched like some giant plum pudding. The keen wind made rippled silk of the marram grass and already a stream of weekend visitors was driving across the causeway. I spotted the horse Najana out on the flats. A horse galloping across a flat landscape. Had it not been for that bank advertisement, it might have seemed quite enticing.

It took me an hour to reach Snook Point, the island's western extremity, swollen like a glass-blower's bubble. About 80 metres off Snook, I discovered another island. This sizeable area of tufted grass and sand was not that much smaller than St Cuthbert's but where was any reference to it on a map? Who had ever mentioned it?

I strode to its highest point and announced to the air, the birds and the sun: 'I name this Mortimer Island. May it exist as a totally independent state.'

By this I meant it must be free of all power blocs, nuclear treaties, trade agreements, cultural exchanges, town-twinning. It was to have no flag, no national anthem, no passport control, no armed forces, no entry in the Eurovision Song Contest, no McDonalds, no enormous Sunday newspapers (I was getting carried away).

Later, the font of knowledge for most things on the island, Jimmy Brigham, explained that Mortimer Island (not its name) had slowly grown through the shifting of sand, after which the grass took hold. The channel between it and Holy Island was growing narrower. Eventually, he said, the two would be joined. Which could mean an end to its independence. Also near Mortimer Island, added Jimmy, secreted in the sand dunes, were the remains of a witch's cottage.

The long curve of Snook Point slowly shut out all sight or sound of the causeway traffic, in preparation for the great lonely magnificence of the North Shore. The sea had scuttled off so far to the north as to be evidenced only by sound, and again there was the strangeness of those huge tree trunks, seemingly tossed on to the sand by disaffected giants. Some were 30 ft long, three feet thick. The trees, not the giants.

No sign of human life. To the south, Snook Tower peeped its mysterious head over the dunes as I made my way to the distant jut of Snipe Point, a favourite seals hang-out (though not this day).

The sand was as flat and smooth as a snooker table and the wind (now behind me) snaked it past my feet ankle-high in curves and twists.

I'd been walking more than two hours and in bright sunshine. I was ready for a rest but this exposed terrain offered no protection from that wind prior to the headland. Sand gave way to rock and rock it would remain for another two and a half hours, at first flat, easy, but growing stranger, half-hollowed shapes like decayed teeth. The going was slower, more difficult. And then, darting from the rocks and making a quicksilver dash for the grassy shore, was the red streak of a fox.

A fox? At the seaside? But foxes didn't have days out at the seaside. Sometimes, yes, said Jimmy Brigham later in the Manor House. Foxes would often lurk round Snipe Point. They waited for the unsuspecting birds to fly up when the tide came in. Then the foxes got 'em.

'Shot a fair few foxes at Snipe Point myself,' said Jimmy.

I rounded the point – welcome relief from the wind. With tired legs I flung myself down in the dunes. And looking round, the strangest, least likely species to be seen, the creature that would really have surprised me with an appearance here, would have been a human. There was none.

It seemed a long time since I'd planted my totem. I found myself nervous that it might not still be there, as if I'd planted it in the middle of some vandal-torn sink estate, not here, on the wild side of Holy Island.

Unable to use the headland path, I was forced round the extremities of Castlehead rocks, which slowly lowered themselves into the sea over a half-mile reach. It was here my Cullercoats Rock Scrambling Veterans Certificate came in useful.

On the other side was Sandon Bay, a mildly curious name as it had no sand. It did, though, have my totem, still standing proud by its porcupine bush. I had created this totem. Initially, to mark stone's location. Now it stood in its own right. Now it laid claim to part-ownership of this island. Like I did. Ownership would last till the elements finally beat it to the ground. Till then it was a creation growing from the island as much as the castle or the Priory, and with as much claim.

History was what happened. Now, as much as then. I lay my head against it. Ate my sandwiches. And I photographed it, the bright sun-rays creating a spiky halo behind it. The photograph is on the book's rear cover.

After 20 minutes, I set off again in the belief my journey was two-thirds over and wondering just when, if ever, I would see totem once more.

Progress down the eastern shore, past Emmanuel Head, proved a nightmare. The surface on this one-and-a-half-mile journey was neither rock nor shale but an endlessly shifting mix of small boulders constantly moving underfoot, creating the impression of me as a staggering drunk. I was reminded of those kiddies' playpens in fun pubs, half-filled with coloured plastic balls. They made falling over fun. Try it for one and a half miles.

I tottered past Bride's Hole, staggered and lurched past Sheldrake Pool, slipped and wobbled past Scar Jockey. During this time, Arthur began to talk to me.

'I don't know why you bother. It only hurts, let's face it. Put your feet up. Admit it, Arthur's won.'

'Sod off, Arthur.'

The final irony was that a few feet from my right shoulder was a perfectly passable, flat footpath. I was sworn not to step on such a surface.

Alongside this footpath, a gaggle of sheep had wandered down to stare at me and for a short time they ambled along as I stumbled and wobbled my slow progress.

It was for the benefit of these sheep that I had eschewed walking on that footpath. And did they show even the slightest gratitude for my concern? None at all.

Occasionally Lindisfarne castle would appear through the dunes, disappear and reappear again some 30 minutes later. By all reasonable laws, each appearance should have seen it closer but this didn't seem to happen.

My leg muscles ached, my body grew sticky under the black greatcoat. Arthur was having the time of his life. Eventually I rounded Castle Point, under the lumpy arse of the castle itself. Two people on a rock were waving. It was Michaela and Terry Dale, who'd hosted the previous night's party.

'Having fun?' they shouted. How did they guess? From the castle I walked along the shoreline past the harbour, up through the village and into the soak of a long bath. The circumference had taken four and a half hours and I was pretty whacked.

My endeavours illicited little sympathy from Jimmy Brigham later in the Manor House.

'You didn't finish the circuit,' he said. 'What about St Cuthbert's beach?'

My tired limbs stretched out in Banjo Bill's as I supped a glass of his wine. He'd bought a bread-making machine. Eighty-four years old, he made his own wine, made his own beer, pickled his own onions, made his own music. Now he was making his own bread.

At that moment, his energy levels seemed twice mine. I closed my eyes; the flash of a red fox, the claiming of Mortimer Island, my totem piercing the sun. I began to drift away. Bill woke me up, refilled my glass.

SUNDAY, 1 APRIL 2001 – DAY SEVENTY-EIGHT

The Island Reborn – The Painting of Blush

It was some April Fool joke, this – in the middle of the night someone had turned my legs to stone. Very funny but I'd quite like the originals returned.

Not so easy. My walk to the bathroom mimicked that of the *Wizard of Oz* Tin Man prior to oiling. I walked like a *Thunderbirds* puppet. One small sight in the bathroom cheered me. I'd brought with me a jar of 100 cod liver oil pills. My life had been measured on this island not in coffee spoons but in these same pills as the jar slowly emptied. For the first time I could see the jar bottom.

And I was into my final month, April. For the first time in recent memory, I awoke to bright sunlight. Something had happened to the island, a rebirth.

With the tide open all day, visitors were out in plenty. Hector Douglas's island shuttle bus (round the village, up to the castle) was up and running. Outside the village store the proprietor Garry Watson had placed a sign 'SUMMER IS COMING!' and attached to it several bright balloons. Tables and chairs had been put out in the Manor House garden and the Ship had opened, for the first time, its beer garden.

Only the public toilets in Crossgate failed to enter the spirit, stubbornly still displaying the CLOSED FOR WINTER sign.

It was, I later realised, a halcyon time; the arrival of more clement weather but not yet the arrival of the thousands (i.e. people).

I walked up Marygate. Eddie Douglas was hovering with his collecting tin.

'I've got those photographs from the islanders' exhibition,' he said and I thought, blimey, I've escaped. Then he added: 'You can have them if you make a donation to the air ambulance.' And the tin was stuck under my nose. I was a beaten man and shoved a fiver in.

Why didn't they just let Eddie Douglas run the National Lottery? Much better than crooked Americans or the grinning Richard Branson.

It was my day for painting the stone, Blush. This penchant for giving nicknames – to stones, to pubs, to injured hips, to gardens – was, I realised, merely a mimicry of island behaviour. I'd never known a place where so many people had nicknames and on my mental list went a note to pursue this further.

Blush was propped up in Chris and Derek's summer-house. I again had with me for the day the Labrador Charlie, and while I painted Blush, Charlie reclined on the lawn. The glass summer-house took the full heat of the afternoon sun, a rare luxury which I indulged shamelessly. All afternoon I painted a bit, slept a bit, painted a bit, slept a bit. Charlie took only one nap. It lasted two and three-quarter hours.

Chris had provided hammerite for the painting. Blush's surface was ridged, uneven. At first the hammerite flowed evenly from the brush, the first maroon letters taking shape without problem. Soon both brush and paint grew glutinous, each stroke depositing either nothing at all or a large lump like a blood clot. After every third letter I cleaned the brush thoroughly in white spirit and shook the paint tin as if it were a cocktail. Letter by letter the poem took shape. Charlie was so excited he almost considered opening one eye.

I should have been excited but wasn't. The previous day had drained me. When the poem was complete I stood back and studied it. I yawned. Instead of the exhilaration at the birth of a new stone poem, there was a sense of ennui.

'Right then,' I said drearily, 'that's that.'

Part of my mind was on the next day, for which I'd planned one of two alternatives. I would either set sail in the early hours on Tommy Douglas's trawler out of Seahouses or I would embark on my Three Tides for Cuthbert.

I phoned Tommy Douglas and learned that he and his sons Mark and Paul were likely to be at sea for three days. This would have broken my rule of spending at least part of each of my 100 days on the island itself.

I realised how little I had wanted to go and experienced a great sense of relief at being given a get-out. Except why did I need one? The idea had been my own. No one was wielding a big stick, ordering me to go.

The same applied to St Cuthbert's Island. This would entail rising at 5.30 a.m. to beat the tide. My body was screaming out not to be given some demanding physical task the next day. Why not listen to it? Why start the Three Tides the next day?

This was a startlingly obvious solution I had not even contemplated. No boat, no island. I felt slightly giddy at the decision, a condemned man reprieved.

I knew what it was. It was this daftness, this sense that if I didn't keep doing things all the time, somehow the world would end. Actually, it wouldn't.

So I went to bed at 10 p.m.

MONDAY, 2 APRIL 2001 – DAY SEVENTY-NINE

Other Refugees – Other Sculptors

Had I gone to St Cuthbert's Island early that morning I would have been soaked and frozen. The brief interlude of fine weather had gone and I woke at 8 a.m. to an angry spat of rain at the window and the sky as grey as elephant skin.

I had needed the long sleep and could still feel vestiges of it in my body. I read a bit of my next book, rolled over, grabbed some more sleep. How indolent I was becoming.

My plan for this day was to have no plan whatsoever. The day would lead me by the hand and I would follow. I finally made it downstairs where my living-room was shivering with the cold. I spent 45 minutes creating and nurturing a healthy blaze.

A knock at the door. By now I realised I rarely expected callers. Solitude, such an unwelcome guest in the early days, had by this time made himself so much at home sometimes I'd go all day and hardly notice him sat there.

It was Ross Peart with a little-known leaflet he'd unearthed. It bore no date but was written by Paul and Sally Nash and was titled 'Encountering God – Spending High Tide in a Shelter on the Pilgrim's Way'.

Someone else, it seemed, had had a similar idea to my own. But with two major differences. The Nashes had spent the tide in the pedestrians' box, not the motorists' refuge – there were two of the former, redolent of machine-gun towers, and one, if you remember, had been declared open by John Selwyn Gummer. Second, the main object of the exercise for the Nashes had obviously been to draw close to the Creator, something that had hardly crossed my mind.

The pamphlet first offered some practical advice on becoming a temporary refugee. Thereafter it was heavily laden with religious references. There were some poems from David Adam, a few quotations about silence and solitude.

My own objective had been to get close to the experience itself. I'd been fascinated by the small details, the bubbling brickwork, the trapped flies, the silky spread of the tide, the growing sense of isolation and remoteness. God didn't seem to have any place in this – though, of course, for believers, God had a place in everything.

Good luck to such folk. In all honesty I hadn't wanted God there, He would have got in the way.

I'd never been inside the Priory Museum. Education had put me right off museums; as boys we'd been forcibly dragged round stuffy, dusty, boring places, made to stare at and take notes about bits of leather said to be a Roman soldier's sandal strap or a sliver of rusty metal reputed to be from an Anglo-Saxon brooch.

Things had improved. The Priory Museum was a smart place, information and objects presented in a lively modern way.

In spite of that, my own attention was drawn to some objects which in my adolescence would have produced only long yawns. These were carved stones from the seventh and eighth century. And if Banjo Bill's mining film had linked me to another age, so too did these. I drew on my own sculpting experience, imagined these stone-masons, 1,300 years ago, tap-tapping out the letters, the small rising clouds of dust.

I ran my fingers along the grooves and wondered if, 1,300 years on from now, anyone would do the same to my poem. I was linked to these stones in a way which, without my Holy Island experience, would simply not have been possible. And how many things created so simply by humans lasted 1,300 years? Who could ever touch the most sophisticated IBM PC from 2001 in the year 3401? Or drive the most advanced luxury car of our own time? What evidence would be left of a 2002 jumbo jet?

Yet here were these stones.

And the only slight personal annoyance was the fact that, despite having been carved 1,300 years ago, the sculptors had been far superior to me.

That night I called at the Wild Duck to pick up my latest shopping. I must have recovered from my indolence. Lesley offered me a glass of wine and we ended up drinking the stuff till 4 a.m.

TUESDAY, 3 APRIL 2001 – DAY EIGHTY

Farewell Then, Dead Beasts – A Stone Disaster

The decision I made on waking this morning could well affect the rest of my life. I had had no idea I was going to make it. It arrived like a bolt from the blue and it arrived with the power of a thunderbolt.

Through my head were running the following: foot-and-mouth, e-coli, variant CJD, swine fever, bovine TB, mechanically recovered meat (slurry), Campylobacter, factory farming, Big Macs.

I was sick of the whole thing, the entire filthy agri-industry. I was sick of the whole meat process that infected both animals and humans, that condemned beasts to miserable lives, awful deaths, that produced for us tasteless fodder that made us prone to all manner of diseases, that left us open to heart attacks.

The decision was made. I would eat no more meat on Holy Island. Possibly I would eat no more meat ever again (I wasn't quite up to such a cataclysmic decision at the drop of a hat). And me, a guzzling carnivore, a robust meat-eater whose chicken dinners sent adults and children alike misty-eyed, whose lamb hotpot brought the neighbours flocking from their doors, whose sugar-and-mustard pork chops produced mass salivation in half of Tyneside.

What did it matter if one lone individual decided to give up meat? Would it even affect the great scheme of things? Probably not. But it mattered to me, there and then. It made me feel slightly less helpless in the face of the great slaughter.

As if there was some little thing I could do. And I was doing it.

I made a plan. I would record (for you, dear readers) every remaining meal eaten on the island. To eat meat would mean I would need to lie brazenly in print.

Maybe I was being rash. But rash, I concluded, was better than rasher. Here was the menu for this day, Mortimer's Meatless Life, Day One.

BREAKFAST – fried egg and potatoes

LUNCH – cheese and tomato sandwiches

EVE MEAL – grilled cod on rice with cheese sauce. Plus some fruit. And three gallons of tea.

That atrocious supermarket steak had not been totally in vain.

I had been paying small calls on stone, attempting to deepen the letters with my broader chisel. My letters were skinny little things. I tapped here, tapped there. I realised I had made an early, if basic, error. I had tapped inwards and not outwards, and for this I was condemned. My script would always be spidery. Never would I achieve the chunkiness of the seventh-century masters. But I could tinker.

On this day I did more than tinker. For some reason all sense deserted me. I stared hard at my letters and found myself wondering why I had failed to chisel out the bottom stroke of an E? What had I been thinking of?

I set to with the chisel, slowly carved out the bottom stroke, nice and straight. I stood back to admire it.

Had a malignant spirit been at work? Was last night's late wine to blame? Or was it the prospect of nut cutlets stretching into the future?

It had not been a letter 'E'. It had been a letter 'F'. The line now read not OUT OF THE SEA but OUT OE THE SEA.

This did not make much sense.

I stared in disbelief. I had been working on stone for a full month. In 30 minutes of self-inflicted vandalism, all this work was undone. Various emotions gripped me. One was panic. Another was the strong desire to beat myself senseless.

I looked away from the stone. Then looked back, some desperate half-thought that this was all in the imagination. The 'F' was still an 'E'. I looked round the garden. No one. I was finished. I was all washed up. I was a walking disaster. I should never have come to Holy Island. I walked out of the shed. I mouthed 'Wha—?' and walked back in again. I could not calm down.

It was the Burden neighbour Jimmy Middlemiss who came to my aid. Jimmy was a handyman. I found myself wanting him to be unbelievably, exceptionally, supremely handy. He looked at the errant letter, thought a moment. He suggested surgery. I would need to use some sand and cement, some of the stone itself, powdered, and some adhesive.

I would try the next day. I was in no state at that moment. My incredible blunder had unnerved me. I found myself wondering if certain island forces had been at work, that even now were cackling in delight at the outcome.

I told myself to stop thinking tosh. The fault was all my own. I was able to write nothing and instead filled a hot bath, intending a long soak.

But it was one of those days. Within two minutes I had to abandon the bath. I'd decided to wash in it a purple Nepalese top I'd been wearing. Within seconds the colour had run so much I was sitting not in a bath of water but bilberry juice in which, had I stayed long, I fear I would have turned the colour of a nice dark plum. I was inept. Hopeless.

And that night in the Manor House, Jen Ward asked me: 'Are you still intending to go on St Cuthbert's Island?'

I nodded glumly.

'There are some in the village think you shouldn't,' she replied.

At that moment, such folk weren't my main concern.

WEDNESDAY, 4 APRIL 2001 –
DAY EIGHTY-ONE

Stone Surgery – Preparing for Cuthbert

I was awake feverishly early. Stone had not let me sleep. Stone was obsessing me (is that grammatically correct?).

What had caused me to take up that chisel? It was, I concluded, some malevolent power but one which I had created myself and which I now needed to counter, as if I had been carrying with me some negative energy about the island.

Everything about my relationship with this island found some echo in stone, in the object I had desecrated. And by damaging it, I had damaged not just the carved poem but something more essential.

Whatever had driven me to that destructive act had to be countered. There was no rest till then, and without this remedy something was irretrievably damaged.

I was nervous, unsure of my ability. I walked down Jenny Bell Lane for a distraction, to check out tide levels for my planned St Cuthbert's Island stays. The sweet smell of new-mown grass in the churchyard soothed me, as did the single tolling bell of St Mary's. I returned home, donned my boiler suit, prepared to face stone.

A knock at the door revealed Derek Pollard, recipient of another Mortimer stone.

'I thought I'd invite you round for tea,' he said. 'I've got juicy big steaks.'

For 80 days I'd eaten meat on the island. The day after I ceased came the steak invitation. How about some fish?

But first – stone. Jimmy Middlemiss provided the adhesive, some sand and cement. Rarely had I felt so nervous. Carefully, I took a shallow chisel to the rear base of the stone (which would eventually be underground) and shaved off a pile of fine powder. I took a small paint brush and lined the bottom of the errant groove with adhesive. I decided to forego the sand and cement but dipped a finger into the powdered stone – like a schoolboy with sherbet – which I then pressed on top of the glue. A second layer of glue, followed by a second layer of pressed powdered stone. Slowly the chiselled groove filled in. I pressed a third line of glue, third line of powder and finally a fourth. The line was now flush with the stone surface. It also, miraculously, seemed the same colour and texture. Like a skin graft, stone had been healed with its own properties.

I left it to settle a moment, then blew it, half-afraid it would all vanish in a puff of powder. I could scarcely believe it. The wound was healed, the errant chiselling scarcely visible even to a knowing eye.

My Holy Island exile was back in balance.

'Anyway,' said Anne Burden, as we celebrated with tea and biscuits, 'even Henry Moore makes mistakes sometimes.'

What a journey stone had taken me on. From that first minute I had spied it in Sandon Bay, physically, artistically and mentally it had challenged me. And were its challenges now complete?

I'd finished the latest of my northern writers' books. This was *The Red Badge of Courage* by the late nineteenth-century American writer Stephen Crane, donated by poet Michael Wilkin.

A background of war apart, it was difficult to think of a book more removed from Liz Bowen's *In the Heat of the Day*.

Crane – whose fame rested mainly on this book – was a traveller, poet, essayist and journalist, and his short novel centred on Henry Fleming, a unionist private in the American civil war. Even this broke with convention; most war books of the time centred on the officer ranks.

Reading the harrowing, vivid and totally convincing descriptions of war on the front line, it was difficult to believe Crane himself never saw action; this was the dirty, dishevelled, bewildering and mainly futile world of a humble foot soldier.

Nor is Fleming a hero – the red badge of the title is a head wound inflicted on him by one of his own ranks as Fleming attempts to desert. Later his fellow soldiers believe it to be a wound of great bravery and the man feeds on this. He is an early anti-hero against a backdrop of army officers shown as bungling and cold-hearted.

The book, described by the author as 'an episode', has little plot or character development, virtually no women. Its fame came from newspaper serialisation; two separate endings, the better of which is fiercely anti-war.

Ironically, it pre-dated an American film industry which mainly glorified war and violence and helped produce the world's most gun-soaked nation. Even more ironically, the book itself was filmed – or should we say butchered – by John Huston in the 1950s, with Audie Murphy in the lead role.

Plenty of guns on Holy Island, come to that. But in the main people had more sense than to aim them at one another.

On this day, the island school would close for Easter and not reopen till the day of my departure. I made a final visit. Caitlin had organised a treasure hunt. We scoured the grounds for chocolate eggs which we promptly ate.

I retold Blubberloop for the final time, Molly and Joel spread out at my feet like starfish. We painted some Easter eggs and I took one home. I felt sad at the end of my unofficial work in this, the country's smallest school.

Joel and Molly didn't look sad at all. Why should they?

That evening at the Stables I ate tuna bake and looked out into the garden where Derek had already planted Blush.

One totem, one poem now planted. A second poem to come.

Later was the third in the series of faith lectures at the Heritage Centre, given by Andy Raine of the island's Catholic church and a Christian dancer, a man whose hippy appearance made him fairly distinctive in the village streets.

Andy had come to the island from his Barnard Castle home on a circuitous route and after a spell with the Salvation Army. He said that God had spoken to him.

I had trouble with people who claimed God spoke to them. Why some people and not others? And how did God differ from the 'voices' some unfortunates tend to have been tragically guided by?

But then I realised I was having trouble with these lectures overall; not the people so much as the basis. I wasn't enthused. They didn't tap into my own life passions, the things that excited and moved me, which, I was becoming increasingly aware, had very little to do with religion.

BREAKFAST – Weetabix, marmite on toast

LUNCH – cheese and tomato omelette

EVE MEAL – tuna bake

THURSDAY, 5 APRIL 2001 – DAY EIGHTY-TWO

Small Travels with Charlie – A Change of Plan

For what reason was I planning my Three Tides for Cuthbert? I had no real answer to this. Except it was all to do with me, my time on this island, the whole religion thing. Would that do?

Packing my bag for the first tide, I felt strangely nervous. I had two books, a flask of cocoa, crisps, binoculars, chocolate, a plastic sheet from George Ward, two black bin liners. Oh, and Charlie the black Labrador.

St Cuthbert had gone to the island for solitude, to find God, to fight demons. He finally retreated to the even more remote Farne Islands to the south-west. Poet Andrew Waterhouse had remarked (quite wisely) that anyone who spent that much time in isolation would find it hard to differentiate between the voice of God and hallucination.

My first tide was in daylight and the day itself had dawned bright and sunny. I wasn't fooled and pulled on two pairs of socks.

A knock at the door revealed Ross Peart bearing a book.

'Do what Cuthbert did,' he said. 'Read the Psalms.'

He handed me the New Testament, which I put in my bag. I liked Ross's religious banter. Secretly I think he hoped to convert me but was never evangelical about it. The bible lay tucked between salt and vinegar crisps and a Penguin.

On the shoreline Charlie and I waved goodbye to his owner, Mike Burden, and walked across the 400-metre-wide channel which was rapidly filling with water. It was 9.30 a.m. High tide was 1.30 p.m. I would be on the island till around 5 p.m.

Once across that channel there was no return. Soon the water would be knee-deep, then waist-deep and finally neck-deep. Cuthbert was reputed to have stood hours long in this deep channel, casting out demons, which would need to be pretty hardy to survive anyway.

The island was bleak terrain, tortured volcanic rock on the top of which was tufted spongy grass whose uneven surface and hidden potholes made walking difficult. The stone remains of Cuthbert's cell were slightly sunken, offering some slight protection from the wind which was, it appeared, on a 24-hour-a-day, 7-day-a-week contract. At one end of the cell was an impressive oak cross erected 60 years previously. Several people had carved their initials on this. I assumed they were Christians, as the carving was very tasteful. On the south-west side a well-trodden path led on to a small peninsula from where Charlie and I were able to view the rapidly flooding basin, as one by one the sand-banks were silently swallowed.

How big was the island? You could probably throw a cricket ball from one end to the other. Were you so inclined.

The sky seemed massive. The view back to Holy Island took in the Priory ruins, St Mary's church and the row of desirable properties named Fiddler's Green. Through the binoculars I could trace the progress of the Dinky-sized cars on the distant causeway. This would continue till 11.30 a.m. To the west, across the water, lay the mass of the Northumberland mainland.

Despite being several hundred yards from Holy Island proper, St Cuthbert's offered little privacy. Strollers up high on the Heugh could look over and down, and on various occasions during my stay I found myself eyeballing them, binoculars to binoculars. The Fiddler's Green properties could also see almost everything you did.

The island was almost litter-free; one light bulb, one plastic water bottle. A solitary fisherman's box had been washed up on the rocks and I watched as the tide slowly edged up to reclaim it.

The wind was south-west, which meant the most sheltered spot was crouched down right opposite the imposing cross, whose presence seemed to be demanding some reverence.

To appease it, I opened the Book of Psalms.

It had probably been 40 years since I'd read any Psalms. I suspect I was not alone. I read 80 of them. At times the blank verse was akin to declamatory poetry, or even rap, and I could imagine them declaimed before a frenzied audience.

The Psalms were capable of creating extreme reactions – as in Waco, Texas – but to be fair so too were Leeds United. God was pretty vengeful and warlike – in Psalm 4 he will 'break the teeth of the wicked' and in Psalm 11 'on the wicked he will rain fiery coals and burning sulphur'. In this edition, the word LORD was always in uppercase. There was a great amount of uncritical adulation of said LORD, such as in Psalm 42: 'as the desert pants for you, so my soul pants for you, O LORD'.

Too much of this kind of thing, I thought, and the LORD might just get a wee bit bored. Good and evil in the Psalms was as cut and dried as in a standard western. At times, the imagery was beautiful, as in Psalm 65: 'The grasslands of the desert overflows/The hills are clothed with gladness/The meadows are covered with flocks/And the valleys are mantled with corn/They shout for joy and sing'. Without a single mention of the LORD.

The power of language in the Psalms was capable of sweeping people away; one reason they have been all things to all people. People look to justify themselves and do. I could imagine the Jewish soldier going into battle fortified with this line from Psalm 73: 'Truly God *is* good to Israel.'

I was crouched down into the shelter. I read a bit, snoozed a bit, drank some cocoa. I nibbled. Whenever Charlie spotted someone on Holy Island, he barked. On one occasion, through the binoculars, I tracked a nun making her way to the prayer holes where I'd cast my bread upon the water. She sat for a few minutes, then went back. Whether this was due to Charlie's barking or the deteriorating weather was unclear.

Clouds were gathering. The temperature was dropping. I stood up to stretch my limbs, walked round the island, ate an apple, read more Psalms, fed Charlie.

By 1.30 p.m. (high tide) all evidence of sand-banks, protrusions of rocks and the like was gone and the island size reduced by one third. The occasional shaft of sunlight was still in evidence but only just. The estuary was now fully swollen with water.

Across this water, in a lonely field, cropping the grass, was Najana. As the weather grew worse, the more isolated and lonely the horse became.

Come to that, so did I.

By 2.30 p.m. the clouds had shut out all sun. By 3 p.m. the rain had begun. I sat on the plastic sheet, pulled on the big black coat, tucked the bin-liners round my trousers.

The wind was keener. The gloom intensified. I thought no more about reading. I drank the last of the cocoa, savouring its precious heat. My limbs began to stiffen. Occasionally I would stand and walk about but I was then at the mercy of the ever-growing wind which, on this exposed island, met no resistance. The walks were brief.

At 4.30 p.m. through the binoculars I observed a small procession making its way down Jenny Bell Lane. It was Mike Burden, his wife Anne, plus a family from Mike's previous Berwick diocese who'd asked him to scatter the ashes of a deceased member.

There was something bizarre about me, stood shivering on this hunk of rock, staring through the binoculars, hearing across the water the occasional carried word of the incanted ceremony, witnessing Mike hold up a small casket which he then emptied into the wind.

The wind first carried the ashes out across the water then allowed them to drift down to their resting place.

The group stood a little longer – impossible to know if anything was being said – then made its way back up the lane. I felt strangely protective towards this small family group who I never had, nor ever would, meet. I felt strangely positive about Mike Burden – now retired – having agreed to do this for them.

And I also felt, I realised, as I turned to huddle back down, absolutely frozen.

The extreme weather forced me at 5 p.m. to make two attempts to wade across the shrinking channel. Twice I was forced back as the water lapped over the wellie tops. By this time my body was shaking with the cold, my clothes were wet and St Cuthbert's Island had lost a small amount of its appeal. My breath was frosted and my limbs moved stiffly.

At 5.30 p.m. Mike Burden appeared on the shore and whistled for Charlie. The dog was fast off the blocks and weaved his way through the water like a dolphin.

And if Charlie could go, I could go, wet socks or not. I'd had enough. And I'd lost my mate. I set off.

Before I reached the channel's middle, water was flooding into the wellies. I didn't give a damn. I needed warmth, shelter. I made my way home, ran a hot bath and lit the fire.

My original plan had been to spend three consecutive tides on the island. This would have been total folly and would have entailed returning to St Cuthbert's in five hours' time for another eight-hour exposure – this time through the night. My body would not have taken it. Superman apart, no one's would.

Part of me was miserable, dejected, another part sensed this testing time on the island had been worthwhile, even necessary to my Holy Island stay.

But I had to accept the three tides would need to be staggered. Not for the first time in my life, I realised I was no saint.

BREAKFAST – tomato, fried egg, beans, fried bread, Weetabix

LUNCH – Mars Bar, apple, crisps, cocoa, fruit

EVE MEAL – sardines, mashed spuds, peas

FRIDAY, 6 APRIL 2001 – DAY EIGHTY-THREE

The Aftermath of Cuthbert – Watchers on the Shore

Despite the hot bath and a long sleep, I woke the next morning as stiff as a rusted hinge, and my limbs probably made a similar sound. The weather forecast for the next two days was truly appalling.

I realised I was 57, not 25, and though I wanted, like everyone else, for the flame of eternal youth to burn ever in me, the day on St Cuthbert's had left me like a snuffed-out candle.

Part of me had an affinity with Cuthbert and those early monks, in that willingness, desire even, to suffer such deprivations. Yet I had little idea what I was trying to prove.

Was there, deep down, some sense of guilt at the privileged lifestyle of the West, conveniently ignoring the plight of two-thirds of the planet, some need to atone? Or was it a case of ignorance being bliss, simply not knowing what lay in store? In which case, why was I planning two more St Cuthbert ventures?

Ross Peart called. Had I read the Psalms? Lots of them, yes.

'Next time,' he said, with the kind of good advice he'd often given me, 'don't take Charlie. The dog's good company but it means no birds or seals will come close.'

The decision was made for me soon after when Anne and Mike Burden announced no more island ventures for the pooch.

'We don't feel it's good for Charlie.'

'So what about me?'

All day my body offered thanks for me not taking it to the island again immediately. Only Arthur demurred. Perfect conditions for him.

And there was a present for my next tide from Stuart McMurdo – a waterproof COASTGUARD coat, said the word printed on the back and various broad luminous stripes the colour of scrambled egg. When I put it on I became a different person.

I asked Stuart about his bowel cancer. He was having further surgery.

Holy Island had been given various names and there were always people keen to give it more. Magnus Magnusson in the 1980s had tried hard with a book and television programmes to make stick 'Cradle Island'. Few had taken to it. Now I picked up a new tourist leaflet designed on the island which labelled it 'The Thousand Acre Isle' and my suspicions were this would go the same way.

Part of Mortimer's paranoia while on Lindisfarne was of being constantly observed and judged, that my every act was noted and recorded by some amorphous body established purely to note down all behaviour of nosy incomers such as I. The truth, of course, was that people had their own lives to live but anyone in a similar position to mine will know what I mean.

The paranoia was fed with the discovery of just how many people had been observing my St Cuthbert tide. Anne Phillipson, of home-baked loaf fame, who lived on Fiddler's Green, told me she'd watched me various times through binoculars, and Ross Peart had come to the shore twice to take a look. Unbeknown to me, the Dutchman Harm had whistled for Charlie and, had the dog responded, he could have been drowned. Jimmy Brigham had twice walked the shoreline and watched me. Visitors had asked who was the strange person on St Cuthbert's in the long black coat, to which he'd given one of two replies: 'St Cuthbert' or 'Robinson Crusoe'.

I'd been in total isolation. In full public glare.

The great grey slab of sky, which on this day spat down various cold showers, failed to move at all, pushing down on the island like some hydraulic press.

I needed to walk off the stiffness, an expedition that led to a totally unexpected example of being 'observed'.

I headed along the causeway, crossed the dunes and came to my beloved North Shore. I then walked out across the huge beach as far as a stranded tree trunk with long thin branches. It sat on the sand like some scabrous giant insect about to leap on its prey, its bent legs primed for a sudden leap. Rain began to spatter down again. I turned for the long walk back to the dunes.

Someone had been watching me.

At the base of the dunes, some 100 yards west of my path, sat a female figure in the kind of red coat that haunted most of us after watching *Don't Look Now*.

I walked in a straight line to my path. Something told me not to approach her – for her sake more than mine. This was a lonely, isolated spot and if I felt surprised to see this person I imagined (assuming she were not a spectre) her reaction to seeing me.

As I walked back into the dunes, I realised I was now behind her. My partner Kitty had educated me a good deal on the risks single women faced all the time. Would this red-coated figure remain sitting? Would she move to make herself less vulnerable? Who on earth (me apart) was crazy enough to come out here on a day such as this? Especially a lone female. Was she, indeed, a ghost?

On the walk back to the village, I wondered if my eyes had played tricks. A solitary woman? Out there in the dunes? On this freezing cold day? It made no sense at all.

The image was still strong in my mind that night. Jean Peart was away and me and Ross dined out at the Manor House. For some reason two middle-aged, heterosexual men rarely dined out together, unless to clinch a business deal.

At the base of the dining-room window was one of those gunshot splatter-marks that reminded me of the stick-on facsimiles on car windscreens when we all pretended to be Chicago gangsters. This was a single spatter and was real, an errant shot from an island wedding ceremony during which, for some reason, islanders fired live ammunition in the air to celebrate the nuptials. Odd shots went adrift.

It was later in the Sign of Two Kirstys that I was approached at the bar.

'I was the woman in the red coat,' said this female. This was her story.

She and her partner, on the island for the weekend, had walked to the North Shore. He'd gone off to look at Snook Tower, leaving her alone to smoke a joint. She'd looked up across the wide empty beach and suddenly seen this figure with a flapping long black coat and straggly white hair striding out. The man stood examining the trunk of a tree for several moments then strode back. He hadn't looked like an islander, and when he'd disappeared into the dunes she'd got on to her partner via the mobile.

This strange meeting was made stranger. The couple were staying at the Retreat, where Kitty and I had stayed the previous year and where the idea for this book had taken root. They invited me back, where I sat till 3 a.m., drinking wine. They produced a big bag of home-grown weed, the first I'd indulged in on the island. Getting stoned seemed just right. I lay back and let a pattern form in front of me. The pattern had begun in this cottage as a vague idea and was now on Day Eighty-Three of its execution.

Past and present combined and seemed to make perfect sense, just as at other times they made none at all.

My eventual walk back to the Cuddy House took all of six seconds, just long enough to realise that in this truly appalling weather it would have been a very dead left-handed book-writer that ended the night on St Cuthbert's.

That small, red-coated figure in the lonely dunes – would I ever see her again? Or should we accept the necessary transience of such fleeting, important moments?

BREAKFAST – porridge

LUNCH – mushroom omelette

EVE MEAL – Manor House salmon steak

SATURDAY, 7 APRIL 2001 – DAY EIGHTY-FOUR

The Holy Island Bubble – Weddings & Deaths

All night the rain had continued. Nor would it cease this day. I awoke with as much energy as an arthritic skeleton. So torrential had been the downpour nationwide that half the football fixtures had been washed away and the Grand National was turned into a four-horse mudlark. I was too listless to place a bet. Banjo Bill and George Ward picked the winning horses.

On this same day the island hosted a wedding and a death, and I had no connection to either. The death was of 82-year-old Gert Main, a good friend of Banjo Bill's. A muffled bell rang its sad tone across the island.

Meantime the weddingites (from Hull) made merry, the ceremony in the castle at 10 a.m., the reception in the Manor House. An island of contrasting moods. I was unable to write a word. I had planned the long walk out from Snook Point to Goswick, where the great sand flats were said to contain many wrecks of both ships and cars, and were also given to pockets of quicksand.

The expedition, like most other things on this day, could wait. That evening I stood at the bar in the Manor House. A group of islanders were gathered in conversation. It felt as if their language was an exclusive one, that almost subconsciously it included certain people and excluded others, and I was in the latter category. And I suddenly thought, in my day-long torpor, that maybe the island and I were losing interest in one another. Maybe I'd been here long enough for both sides.

I slouched my self-pitying way home, opened the door and was thinking of an early bed. Something stopped me, though, turned me round and sent me up to the Ship, where the wedding party and others were whooping it up in a ceilidh.

Immediately on walking through the door the music lifted me, as live music had a few days ago. The ceilidh band was Bellow and Bows. A caller invited people to take the floor for formation dancing. I realised the only fun in this kind of dancing was in not being able to do it.

As the caller barked his impenetrable instructions and the dancers were expected to duck under an arch, twirl twice, change partners, skip the length of the room or whatever, an amiable and necessary anarchy took over. Dancers bumped into one another, were left stranded, failed to link, missed the arch. Every cock-up caused great hilarity and laughter. Had the dances been done properly (something I have yet to see), a dull efficiency would have taken over.

People only liked doing these dances for the precise reason that they couldn't do them.

Fisherman Tommy Douglas was at the bar. I'd made several unsuccessful attempts to get on his trawler. Maybe he didn't want me. I asked him.

'Drive down with my son Paul to Blyth on Wednesday,' he said. 'The boat's moored there. We'll come back Thursday, OK?'

Blyth was a small port 40-miles south. Suddenly I felt less rejected and, to reflect the mood, the band struck up with such life-enhancing numbers as 'Whisky in the Jar' and 'The Wild Rover'. The whole pub was on its feet whooping and yelling and there, on the dance floor, a full 14 hours after their nuptials, were the bride and groom, neither in the first flush of youth.

'In fact,' said Roger Andrew, 'I think the groom's older than you.'

After the final number the band leader offered kind thanks to 'all the people of Holy Isle'.

An immediate cry went up: 'This is Holy Island!'

Like I said, the island already had two names. And that was quite enough.

BREAKFAST – porridge, marmite soldiers

LUNCH – too hung-over

EVE MEAL – cheese and potato pie (for its alcohol-soaking qualities)

SUNDAY, 8 APRIL 2001 – DAY EIGHTY-FIVE

Tricks of the Tide – The Taunting of the Lambs

A conclusive argument for laying off the drink: the previous day I'd woken with a hang-over the size of Shropshire to face a day of weather most foul.

This morning, after very moderate amounts of alcohol, I felt fresh and invigorated. And the sun was shining brightly. Simple.

I read in bed till 8 a.m., did 40 minutes yoga, ate, sat down at the typewriter and to compensate for the previous day's inaction rattled off 2,500 words as if from a machine-gun. The painful memory of my first Tide for St Cuthbert I'd stashed away and now, in more clement weather, I was ready for my second. I had learnt some lessons:

1. Wear leggings under the trousers
2. Take soup instead of cocoa (more heat)

3. Wear three pairs of socks

4. Stay dogless (thanks, Ross)

I packed my grub and belongings and donned Stuart McMurdo's COASTGUARD coat. It made me look official. From my house to the shoreline was only half a mile, then 400 yards to the island across the channel. Yet there was still the nervousness of embarking on an expedition as I slung the bag over my shoulder and clomped off in the wellies (spare boots in the bag).

I had an important psychological boost this day. If I survived the tide I was invited for a Sunday meal at Wild Duck Cottage with Roger and Lesley Andrew.

And I was better prepared; the mild weather for one, plus my arrival at the shoreline well in time. The tide had hardly begun to finger its way round both sides of the island.

I sat on the tufted grass, bided my time. Jimmy Brigham walked past with his Labrador Susie. We chatted on. I watched the two fingers of water grow closer, touch, expand. Jimmy left. I took in the white fluffy clouds, the sense of spring. I watched the Sunday visitors climb the Heugh, I studied the contours of the distant mainland. For 40 minutes I sat peacefully then rose and began to walk across.

I had left it too late. A truth that dawned well before halfway, as the water rose higher and higher and finally lapped over my wellie tops. I stopped. I knew people on the shore were watching.

And me in the dayglo yellow stripes of my COASTGUARD coat. All official-looking. At such moments a man is given to strange thoughts. My own fixed on the mercurial speed with which water could penetrate through three thick pairs of socks.

Within a nano-second all three were soaked. And me with eight hours on the island.

Stopping was no use. I pushed on, my feet sucking and squelching in the wellie bottoms as more water poured in. It seemed I crossed three oceans before the level began to drop and I was rising up towards the island.

I scrambled my wet-footed way up the rocks, across the tufted grass (which was as difficult as walking on a mattress), then dropped down into the sunken recess of the cell.

I was cursing my own incompetence for having sat day-dreaming so long. Cursing, though, would fix nothing. I peeled off the three pairs of saturated socks, which resembled dead fish, wrung them out and laid them in the sun on the rocks. I poured the water from my wellies, looked at my pale naked feet.

From the bag I took two black bin-liners. I wrapped one round each foot the way fairground folk wrapped up their toffee apples. I then placed my feet inside the (mercifully) bone-dry boots I'd carried in my bag. The feet felt remarkably warm and cosy. But would they last eight hours?

Two pairs of the socks on the rocks (which sounds like a strange cocktail) were brightly coloured. They may have been taken as semaphore flags.

After this initial shock I settled down, took stock. Ross Peart had been right. Suddenly I had many birds as neighbours, some of which I could name. Off the western shore floated a semi-circular flotilla of cuddy ducks. Their gentle coo-cooing soothed me and I was, I confessed, pleased to be Charlieless. The sun was warm on my skin. I took up the binoculars and scanned the distant causeway.

Where, at 2.40 p.m., some 40 minutes after safe-crossing time, I spotted what at first looked like a small swarm of blackflies but was in fact a group of motorcyclists heading towards the open causeway like bats out of hell. Even at this distance, I could hear their impatiently revving engines. As they neared the flooded part of the causeway they slowed down, stopped. They seemed to be in consultation. ('Hadaway, man – yee gan forst!' 'Nah, man, yee gan!'). Two moments later they set off again, slow at first, into the water.

I plotted them as they passed my refuge box and as they came close to the mainland, and grew in confidence, they opened the throttle, doing the final 200 metres trailing long white arcs of spray.

I was sucked so much into this motorcycle drama that when I lowered the glasses I was surprised to be back on my island among the peace of the gently cooing ducks.

I also had a flock of Brent geese on the furthest outcrop of island rock. If I moved further away from them, they moved further up the rock and on to the island. I did the opposite, they waddled back, leaving a seemingly exact space between bird and human. The only way I changed the formula was to rush them, which scattered them like chaff. This was exceedingly childish, which I knew as I did it. I tried an alternative, lying so low in the cell as to be hidden from them. I did and spied them slowly creep upwards. This smacked of cheating. I wondered if anyone was watching me from the shore.

The estuary was by now in full flood. I saw Ross Peart, plus Roger and Lesley Andrew, walk down to the shoreline. Ross shouted across. I began to shout back but the raised voice seemed wrong for the island's serenity, so I waved the socks instead.

It was clear these were too thick to dry (oh, for intelligent socks). Time for Plan B. I pulled two pairs of the damp socks on top of the bin liners, then replaced the boots. The third pair of socks were still unpleasantly saturated.

This meant the inside of my boots got wet but the feet stayed dry.

I had with me a huge heavy tome which Roger Andrew had said I would find useful. This was *The RSPB Complete Book of British Birds*, with a foreword by (who else?) Magnus Magnusson. It was an exhaustive list of our indigenous species and, for me, totally useless.

My day was passing, despite the accident, in more pleasant fashion than Tide One. For eight hours this small island belonged to me and me alone. Like all possessions, this was temporary and the agreement would be happily rescinded when the tide receded. But for that spell, no one on the planet had a more legitimate claim.

I read, I sat. I walked, I ate a banana, an apple, I slurped some delicious tomato soup with buttered bread. I picked up a piece of driftwood and chucked it into the water to measure the tide's speed.

The loud 'ker-plash' again emphasised how peaceful was my day. I identified curlews, black-headed gulls. There were others but my main mates were the eider ducks and the Brent geese. I liked the way the eiders waddled to the water's edge, like some fat character from a Donald McGill picture postcard.

The island was like a lung. As the tide came in and ate its lower reaches, it shrank, as if expelling breath. Later the tide went out, the island size grew and the lung was breathing in.

By 5 p.m. the day had settled into one of the most pleasant of my 100. My feet (which would later emerge from their wrappings as wrinkled as two walnuts) were warm and secure. And the lack of wind meant the tide receded faster.

There was a dreamlike sense to my solitariness, a state reinforced in the final hour as an extraordinary sound carried from somewhere across the water in the direction of the mainland.

This was a lonely and haunted wailing, a soft ululation, ghostly. It seemed to plead to the listener and appeared as if from thin air. I scanned the sea but could find no trace of the source.

It was the sound of Holy Island seals and at that moment I fully understood how the story of the sirens had come into Greek mythology, those deadly mermaids whose songs lured sailors to their doom and whom Ulysses cheated.

Composers had used whale sounds in their music. Why not seals? This was the seals' farewell symphony, timed almost perfectly for my moment of departure from the island. I redonned the wellies, waded the shrinking channel without mishap and was met on the shore by Lesley Andrew, and a few moments later in the bar of the Manor House by Roger, Banjo Bill, Ross Peart and Banjo's mainland friend Jean.

The meal was roast lamb. I watched Roger carve the juicy joint back at Wild Duck Cottage; the curves of meat fell away as thin as stamp hinges. Combined with the tart smell of the mint sauce, this was guaranteed to send any recent veggie half bonkers.

I kept my salivation in check, filled the plate with vegetables and, in compensation and to reward my willpower, pigged out on double portions of jam roly-poly *and* sticky toffee pudding.

After the enjoyment of the solitary exile, the bonhomie of a full dinner table. The day could have been a microcosm of my whole stay on Holy Island.

BREAKFAST – kippers, toast and marmalade

LUNCH – soup, fruit, crisps, chocolate

EVE MEAL – you've just read it

MONDAY, 9 APRIL 2001 – DAY EIGHTY-SIX

The Passing of Eddie – Owning up to Arthur

For the final time, I changed the bedsheets. After today, only one more Monday on the island. I had only to pause now, whatever the activity, just for a few seconds, to feel that gentle tugging at my sleeve. It came from my home. My son. Kitty. My sick mum.

How lucky I'd been on my second tide. The skies this day had once again pulled across their grey curtain and the island descended once more into gloom. Again, I postponed my planned trek across the expanse of Goswick Sands.

I planned my Third Tide for Cuthbert for Easter Monday. I would get on the island soon after 5 a.m. (8 a.m. high tide) and I'd have done my eight hours and be back home before most people had decided which Bank Holiday traffic jam to get stuck in.

On the radio, Karen Armstrong was talking about her new book on the life of Buddha. The last thing Buddha wanted, she said, was for anyone to 'worship' him. I pricked up my ears. Buddhism was like a raft that might get you across a river. Once across, you didn't expect to lug the raft about for the rest of your journey.

This seemed a radically different look at religion and slightly different to 'panting for the LORD'.

I looked peaky, said Ross Peart. I should go for a run. I hadn't done this in almost ten weeks, mainly because of Arthur, and I missed the post-running buzz, the toxin-purging adrenalin, the tired stress-free aftermath.

Arthur had pulled the plug on that. I decided for once he could go hang and set off towards the estuary mud-flats.

I spotted Eddie Douglas and his collecting tin as I approached the Island Oasis Café. Some laws on Holy Island were immutable. One was that within more or less 24 hours the tide would twice advance and recede. Another was the impossibility of passing Eddie Douglas without (a) a charitable contribution, (b) a chat or (c) preferably both.

When in less than hospitable mood, people had been known, upon spying Eddie, to scuttle off on long detours round the village, or jump into the back of passing pick-up trucks. What nobody would attempt was simply to *walk past him*.

I now had the perfect excuse. I was out running. No money. No time.

Such incidentals did not deter Eddie. He attempted to flag me down.

'One minute, lad!' he shouted.

'Can't stop now, Eddie – I'm out running!'

I could scarcely believe I had spoken the words but I had, and I was past him, and I felt the exhilaration and guilt of having transgressed some great Law of Holy Island.

It was possibly this that caused me not to dwell on Arthur during the run. I was obsessed with Eddie and what tactic he might employ on my return. A lasso? A trip wire? An invisible force field?

There was no sign of him on my return, however, and for a few daft minutes I felt guilt that my rejection had led to such loss of face by Eddie that he had thrown in the towel.

Not so.

Arthur was none too pleased I'd been running. He wanted me to stop and told me so. I knew he'd do all in his power to bring it about but I didn't know how strong Arthur was. This was the very last time Arthur would allow me the luxury of running.

It was a day for frenetic domesticity: washing clothes, vacuuming all rooms, cleaning the kitchen, lighting the fire. I was hanging out the sheets when a woman appeared in the next yard and asked me about rubbish collections. She was a holidaymaker, in a wheelchair, and while we chatted her husband/partner appeared in the kitchen doorway. He was black.

Among all the islanders, the incomers, the God Squad, the daytrippers, the birdwatchers, the delivery men, the pilgrims, the holidaymakers – among all that large range of people for whom this island was a long-term or a temporary home, or a special place to visit, hardly a single one, in our multi-race Britain, was black.

Holy Island – the Isle of White.

Despite Arthur, most of my body felt good post-run. I had my Sunday brunch in the Island Oasis, walked up Marygate. By this time school-teacher Caitlin had moved in with fisherman Sean, an interesting mix.

'I spotted you out on the sands,' said Caitlin. 'Aren't you a bit old to run, Pete?'

As if Arthur wasn't enough.

I wallowed in the luxury of a spanking clean house that night, read in front of the fire, drank cocoa, went early to bed. If you'd knocked at my door, offered to buy me free drinks all evening, I'd have declined.

BREAKFAST – cornflakes, boiled eggs

BRUNCH – toasted cheese sandwich, scones and tea

LATE NIGHT – cereal and milk

TUESDAY, 10 APRIL 2001 – DAY EIGHTY-SEVEN

Foot-and-Mouth Low-down – Seals at Last

Foot-and-mouth had become an ever-present backdrop to island life. Thus far the county of Northumberland (of which the island was part) had fared better than neighbours Cumbria and Durham. General consensus on the island was that the outbreak would not get through the natural barrier of the causeway and the tide. It never had. But local businesses complained it bit deep into tourism (the staple industry), notwithstanding that early April was hardly peak time. It also created tensions; the closure of Sanctuary Close, for instance, by farmers Jimmy and Margaret Patterson. Some villagers had pulled down the sign.

Not that there weren't always tensions on this small island. I learned of various long-running feuds which meant one particular islander simply never spoke to another nor went on their premises.

But despite the disinfectant mats, the posters, the restrictions, the fencing, 95 per cent of visitors could do what they always did: walk round the village, visit the castle, the Priory and the Museum, stare at lumps of ancient stone, digest great wedges of historical fact.

The average Holy Island holidaymaker was a different animal to the frequenter of Blackpool or Whitley Bay. There was an almost total absence of loud 'yoof' determined to bellow and vomit their way to a good time. Lots of well-behaved family groups, birdwatchers with serene expressions and anoraks, coaches disgorging a collection of white heads, walkers in thick red socks and sturdy boots, also some seekers after salvation and spiritual uplift.

The ex-journalist in me decided to find out some facts. Armed with a notebook, I stuck a foot in the door of each hotel and invited them to spill the beans.

At the Manor House Jen Ward, suffering from a bad shoulder, said takings had plummeted by two-thirds – just as she and George had bought the property with big expansion plans.

'We've already lost £10,000,' she said. 'The farmers will get compensation. What will we get?'

Like elsewhere the Manor House was fully booked for Easter but on the night of my survey only 3 of the 13 rooms were let.

'And normally we'd be full!' said Jen.

At the Ship, where Frank and Pauline Gregory took over in the middle of power cuts, the severest weather for a decade and foot-and-mouth, the situation was better.

'But we only have three rooms,' said Frank. 'They're all fully booked. We'll survive.'

I drank a cup of tea with Sue and Clive Massey at the Lindisfarne. They'd just celebrated 29 years in the place – though, given the circumstances, the verb 'celebrate' might have been optimistic.

'In one recent week we took £465,' said Sue. 'Same week last year, that was £4,500. That's a 90 per cent drop.'

They'd put on hold their expansion plans for two more bedrooms and a new lounge bar and estimated they'd lost 500 bed/nights.

At the Sign of Two Kirstys (OK, OK, if this is an official survey, we'll call it the Crown and Anchor), Jill and Paul Turner had recently renovated the dining-room to find March bookings down by 50 per cent and April thus far down by 20 per cent.

The Crown had four bedrooms. Despite foot-and-mouth, from here on they expected they would all be full.

At the Open Gate bed & breakfast, a big factor in the dropped income was the closure of St Cuthbert's Walk – that 65-mile spectacular trek I had originally planned before the death of my father.

'Many of our customers book in here after doing that,' said Ross Peart. He peeled off some statistics. 'We've lost £2,626 so far – 13 per cent of our annual turnover.'

It was more than just financial, though. For the first time ever there were restrictions on some of Holy Islanders' native soil, as if something of their birthright was being denied them. And for which they themselves were blameless.

Shoot the sheep, said some. Shoot the government, said others. Shoot the Ministry of Agriculture, said a third lot. One thing was certain. Whatever the complaints, the dreaded disease itself was not on the island. Which was more than could be said for great swathes of the northern mainland.

Seals, to my knowledge, have no fear of foot-and-mouth. The previous day they had chorused for me. Now they decided to put in an appearance. Lesley Andrew phoned excitedly from Wild Duck Cottage and I found her staring through a telescope across the wide estuary to the mainland.

A small colony of maybe 20 seals was basking on a sand-bar halfway across the water. Occasionally they would slip down out of sight on the blind side, then reappear.

Seals were born for water. On land their movements were highly comic. They looked like sack race contestants asked to race on their stomachs. Their bodies gleamed like wet roofs.

Approaching the huddle was a small motor boat. As a group the seals disappeared into the water and I saw them bob up to the surface like little black dots. In 100 days it was my only actual sight of these strange and lovely creatures.

BREAKFAST – Weetabix, marmite on toast

LUNCH – cheese and green peppers on toast, yoghurt and honey

EVE MEAL – cod curry and rice

WEDNESDAY, 11 APRIL 2001 – DAY EIGHTY-EIGHT

Swallowed by the Sands – Becoming Visible

Now I know you'll find this almost impossible to believe, dear readers, but the day dawned cold and grey. It seemed I'd been planning my long walk across Goswick Sands for weeks. Waiting for good weather seemed as pointless as waiting for Margaret Thatcher to turn socialist. I decided this would be the day.

Goswick Sands lie to the north-west of Holy Island and stretch away forever from Snook Point. I suspected they would be a place of great solitude and so decided (with the Burden permission) to take Charlie, despite him being present meant no birds would be.

My planned fishing trip with Tommy Douglas had never come to fruition. I later came to realise this was the right way of things. Tommy and his sons were trawlermen and sailing on a trawler would replicate my experiences for my book *The Last of the Hunters*.

In that way, it would have been a safe option, even if the terribly harsh and dangerous life on a trawler can hardly be called 'safe'. But safe in that it was familiar territory, whereas the remainder of my 100 days, for better or worse, should see me stepping into the unknown, which is exactly where a writer should always step, however painful.

And now I was on the last leg, within the final fortnight, my mood altering. Holy Island and I were becoming more equal partners. For a long time it had been no contest.

Ross Peart ran Charlie and me out to Snook Point. No one had done as much for me on this island as Ross, even though he sometimes told me off. We bid him farewell and struck out.

To our left (the south) a production line of cars was heading across the causeway on to the island. We were now into the Easter holidays, the island's character was changing rapidly. My empty outpost, my place of exile was metamorphosing into a holiday destination.

For the islanders, the money-making time of the year was approaching. For this reason, they welcomed it. For other reasons, they didn't.

And the contrast on this day between an increasingly crowded island and my own experience couldn't have been greater.

I was armed with one packet of crisps, one Mars Bar, one apple and a pack of doggy chews.

In the channel between Holy Island and Mortimer Island ('Live free forever!'), half-embedded in sand, was the skeleton of a sheep, and, if you could blot out the temperature and overhanging cloud, it smacked of a scene from the Arizona desert.

As we strode out from the shoreline, Charlie seemed reluctant to leave it behind, as if fearing what lay 'out there'. He skulked round the edge of the dunes, stood stock still and stared at me, skulked some more, and only after some vigorous shouting and the threat to withhold the doggy chews did he venture on to the huge empty wastes.

The corrugated sand was drenched. I splashed through in my (luckily) waterproof boots. A series of tall thin fishermen's poles, from which they would suspend salmon nets, stood gaunt against the sky. From here to the Northumberland mainland (to the north-west) was about three miles, a good hour's walk. The sea was about one mile to the north and to the east lay the expanse of the North Shore.

The huge sky and the reflected water seemed to give out more light than the air could hold. As we walked on, the causeway and the line of cars grew ever smaller, more distant, behind us.

On the North Shore I had found the solitude exhilarating. Here it seemed tinged with menace. I knew there were odd pockets of quicksand and I knew that dotted around these sands were unexploded bombs. Locals had assured me that unless I went off straying I should be OK but I wasn't certain what was straying and what wasn't. Except Jimmy Brigham had told me to look out for a white hotel on the distant shoreline and use that as a marker. I squinted and took the small white dot to be the same.

The sand soon became furrowed and soft and I found myself plodding through running channels of water. The furrows became deeper, dramatically folded like some of those vivid scenes from a desert. We came across the first shipwreck, a rotting wooden hulk half-buried in both sand and memory.

Slowly, undramatically, and unrecorded by the world, this anonymous vessel was being taken by the elements. It had come to grief at this lonely desolate spot from where it was doomed never to move, except into a slow disintegration.

Further out was a rusty, barnacled chassis of some vehicle, again half-buried. Despite the advanced state of corrosion, the four large tyres were remarkably unworn. The RAF had dropped some vehicles here for target practice, so while some wrecks were by default others were by design.

I knew what was disturbing me. Each time I paused out here on these vast flats, where I sensed a person could just die and rot away as undramatically as a boat or a vehicle, there was just a slight sense of sinking. It was just sufficient to unnerve me, to make me not want to stay too long in one spot, as if the terrain were simply waiting to claim whatever object or person stayed too long on it.

To cheer up, I ate my apple and fed part of it to Charlie, who was bounding out across the sands, his pawmarks leaving deep impressions.

We came to a sudden wide channel of water which blocked our way. I wondered about shedding shoes and socks to ford it. Except that with the incoming tide – due in a few hours – the channel could easily deepen and widen and leave us stranded on the far side. According to the map in Richard Perry's Holy Island book, we were staring into the Swinhoe Goat.

This troublesome goat forced us to abandon the plan of heading towards the white hotel and instead we followed it down its length towards the distant breaking waves. My hope was that the goat would eventually open out into some shallow, passable delta. But its route took us farther and further away from the mainland and sucked us more into isolation.

Charlie ran in wide circles. I lured him back, took the doggy chews from my bag and fed him. I was pleased to have him with me. Finally, we reached the seashore. This was a strange sensation; to be by the breaking waves but not on some deck chair-crowded beach, not even in some unspoilt South Sea paradise with the palm trees waving nearby, but on the edge of some secret sea, some forgotten sea, some sea totally unwitnessed. And out there in the waves, which bashed against it constantly, was a vast black hulk of a wreck, a ghost ship looked on by few human eyes.

We could go no further. The Swinhoe Goat was still a deep channel and I was anxious to head back. Despite the presence of Charlie, I felt too alone. Too vulnerable, as if to be here too long was to become a part of the place, to become forgotten. Far, far back from us Snook Point was a hazy, distant outline. And I wanted to be off that edgeless expanse. I made a plan. Charlie and I would strike out for Mortimer Island, stretch out in the dunes. I would be treated to a Mars Bar, Charlie to a clutch of doggy chews.

This cheered me a little. As did whistling, though the sound leaked away to nothingness. We walked for more than 40 minutes. As we neared the dunes of Holy Island, as if in relief Charlie took off and disappeared into the hillocks. For five minutes I called him to no avail, a small panic growing in me at the memory of those dogs swallowed by the collapsing rabbit holes. I was beginning to rehearse my announcement to the Burdens when he reappeared.

And after the anxiety, the disappointment. As we lay in the Mortimer Island dunes I discovered I'd lost the Mars Bar and realised I must somehow have dropped it when I took out Charlie's chews. It was out there somewhere. It would be lifted gently by the tide, carried, dropped. It would sink slowly into the sand, it would suffer the fate of all objects out there, lying in its grave with only the vast sky as witness.

All the time I had felt the sands wanting to claim something from our foray, needing to take for their own some small part of what had ventured on to them. They had taken the Mars Bar, which, I told myself, could have been worse, even if I was bloody peckish.

We walked back along the causeway to the village, Charlie looking as knackered as I felt. As I lay in a hot bath, Goswick Sands were already turning into a slightly disturbing dream.

Later I called on Banjo Bill. He'd had a bad night, was breathing with difficulty. I showed him some yoga breathing exercises which he promised to do.

And suddenly I realised Bill was the substitute for my dead father. I'd sought solace in Bill. His was the territory I could visit to make my mourning less painful. He was my refuge, a man of almost the same age as my father, if a very different man. His energy and humour were an affirmation; also a denial of the dark shadows of my father's death.

It was this day that had produced the realisation. The day when ghost ships had loomed before me. And the ghost of a parent.

That night was the final Lent lecture on faith given by the Holy Island vicar, David Adam. David was slim, short, dressed in black, a quietly dramatic look, his open face always twinkling with mischief. He was deeply religious but also, I suspected, something of an iconoclast. Significantly, he was a fan of Welsh poet R.S. Thomas, whose religious side also had those contrasts.

David Adam gave an amusing talk. He poo-pooed any idea of God talking to him. Such things didn't happen. He came from a family of gypsies, was an ex-coal miner and confessed life's myriad small mysteries fascinated him.

When I tried to pin him down, he often side-stepped me with humour. He'd written a play which I said I'd like to read but he never showed it to me, which didn't surprise me.

He was a serious man with a sense of the absurd. I wondered how orthodox religion managed to contain him, and perhaps sometimes it didn't, or perhaps for him it wasn't a problem. He was, throughout my stay, the elusive imp – never unfriendly, but each time I got where he was, he was somewhere else.

Ross's wife Jean had returned to the island after ten days away on her native Merseyside where a close, lifelong friend had died. I knew how difficult she found the island sometimes, how readapting to its culture and demands was not easy. She'd often been a barometer for my own unease, the first person to whom I'd confessed Holy Island life wasn't quite the spiritual peace and calm of all those books and documentaries.

But then how could it have been?

I'd not visited the Sign of Two Kirstys for several Wednesdays. I did this night and suddenly I was not the outsider. Artist Nick Skinner presented me with a selection of his framed prints, postmaster Malcolm Patterson chatted to me freely, Stuart McMurdo made a present of the COASTGUARD coat he'd loaned me.

What had happened?

Time had.

BREAKFAST – toast and marmalade, orange juice

LUNCH – Goswick Sands snacks (minus Mars Bar)

EVE MEAL – self-assembled tuna and tomato pizza

THURSDAY, 12 APRIL 2001 – DAY EIGHTY-NINE

Nicking the Names – The Christians are Coming

The very first mention of my 100-day exile had found its way into the media, a small news item in the *Berwick Advertiser* about the writers' workshop I'd been asked to run on the island. I'd also been contacted by Tyne-Tees Television, who'd heard of my venture and wanted to come and film. The agreement was that nothing would be shown until I'd upped and gone.

My remaining days were filling up. I'd decided to throw a final bash on the eve of my departure. I was determined to invite all sorts to this, many of whom normally would never mix. Part of this was mischief, to see what happened. I'd mentioned the number of nicknames on the island. As far as I knew no one had recorded these for posterity, so who better than me?

I went looking for Ian McGregor or Jimmy Brigham, either of whom I suspected would provide a comprehensive list. Ian McGregor got the short straw (I found him first) and we arranged a high-powered meeting over a pot of tea in his house. As we chatted, postman Dick Patterson turned up and got roped into the consultative committee.

Most of the people featured in the following list were still alive; some were in family groups. The derivation of some nicknames was unclear, that of some others too disgusting to reveal here. Father and son often had different nicknames. Some people were never known by their married name. One woman, Nellie Brigham, was always referred to as Nellie Hall. She had arrived on the island at the age of 15 and, according to Ian, never once crossed that causeway in her remaining 65 years. This fact haunted me and continues to do so; an entire nation's history unfolding just across the water and not once did she venture to see it. Nor, as far as I could tell, did she go insane.

I've grouped the names according to family. If the same name is repeated, it means a different generation. The nickname is in italics. Some individuals were greedy enough to have two nicknames, in which case I've put aka (also known as).

Jimmy *Clinker* Brigham
Jimmy *Clinch* Brigham
Lily *The Duchess* Brigham
Robert *Bobo* Brigham
Jack *The Dog* Brigham (aka *Tee Rig*)
Nellie *Nellie Hall* Brigham
Meggie *Meggie Hall* Brigham
Ralph *Dancer* Wilson
Ralph *Rufus* Wilson
Ralph *Wee Raf* Wilson
Thomas *Ta* Douglas
Thomas *Tinko* Douglas
Nancy *Moose* Douglas
George *Dougsie* Douglas
George *Goff* Douglas (aka *Dukes*)
George *Stoat* Douglas
Eleanor *Lady Belmont* Glover
George *Dodo* Kyle
George *Step* Kyle
Robert *Gow* Kyle
Lucinda *Lulu* Kyle
Eleanor *Hal* Luke
Norman *Slim* Luke
Matthew *Dougie* Drysdale
James *Commander Crow* Drysdale
William *Wonker* Drysdale
Phyllis *Poppy* Drysdale
James *Maggie* Drysdale
James *Snyder* Henderson
George *Bash* Moody
Thomas *Booner* Cromarty
Douglas *Dowser* Cromarty
Joseph *Lang Joe* Cromarty
Robin *Tim* Henderson
George *Wheeler* Lilburn
George *Lil* Lilburn
Charlie *Cha Pate* Patterson
Brian *Farmer* Patterson
Selby *Sparrow* Allison

Jimmy *Skipper* Walker
Henry *China* Walker
Matthew *Douglas* Johnson
. . . and finally . . .
Ian *Whacky* McGregor

There was statistical support here for the claim that Holy island was weighted towards the male of the species. Of the 44 people, only 7 were female.

Nicknames were virtually a lost art form in the UK proper. Here 44 were conjured (admittedly some belonging to the dead) on an island of 150 people.

Compiling the list with Ian McGregor was great fun. And surely the least controversial pursuit of my 100 days . . . Except that on Holy Island a non-islander could never quite be sure what was liable to upset the locals. The next day Eddie Douglas stopped me in the street. Word had got out about my list. Was I planning to put it in the book? Yes.

He shook his head.

'There will be them as won't take kindly to that.'

This was Maunday Thursday and the island was gearing itself up to its Easter bonanza. No fewer than 25 Christian events were due on Lindisfarne over the next few days, from the austere Stripping the Altar to the celebratory dancing round St Aidan's statue, led by Andy Raine. And although foot-and-mouth had seen the cancellation of the official cross-country pilgrimage to the island, many northern cross walkers were still expected to carry their burden over the sands this very day.

All this on the day a national broadsheet poll revealed that 43 per cent of the UK population did not know why Easter was in the calendar – except, presumably, for the settling of vital football promotion and relegation issues.

This statistic emphasised Christianity's long-term crisis in our country. Had the religion not been so firmly entrenched within the UK's rigid establishment, the poor beast would surely have perished long since. And Holy Island, where it all began, was where now it retreated to.

The church had little meaning in the rough and tumble of most people's lives. Christian clerics were mainly a removed species, pontificating with abstracted irrelevance. Church pews were sparsely sprinkled with the elderly, the eccentric, the sullenly devout. For whatever reason, the Christian church did not fill our spiritual vacuum. The trouble was, neither did much else, despite the efforts of *Big Brother* and the National Lottery.

The term 'non-believer' tended to be used in a negative way, as if the Almighty was the only thing worth believing in. I saw it as a positive, the first step towards taking responsibility for our own actions. And the other things you might choose to believe in were countless.

I believed in Banjo Bill, for a start. His breathing had improved and in his kitchen I ate some of his home-made bread, chewed on his newly pickled onions, slurped down his freshly fermented wine. I had to complain about the cheese – it came from a shop.

Bill drank and ate very fast. I liked that in an 84 year old and hoped I could maintain my own input velocity for another 30 years or so.

Being old was no joke (something the young, luckily, have no concept of) but Bill's home had few of the usual octogenarian signs: no support rails, no raised toilet seat. His groceries were found on high shelves as well as low. He walked upstairs to sleep. He cooked his own meals and seemed to entertain as often as (though in a different way to) Cynthia Paine.

Larkin wrote with stunning simplicity of the old: 'something has gone out of them'. Bill had kept hold of much of it. Another point of contact was boxing. Bill often stayed up all night to watch it on Sky and was impressed when I told him I'd been Nottingham schoolboy champion.

And the grub he'd laid out for me this day was perfect for a tyro veggie. The suddenness of my decision to turn vegetarian had left no room for preparation, plus which my shopping access was limited. But not a vestige of singed flesh had passed my lips in the past two weeks. I'd like to say it left me bursting with health but thus far the effects were all psychological. The decision had left me in a better frame of mind. Like most intelligent people, I raged against the farrago of foot-and-mouth but at least now I put my vegetables (and fish) where my mouth was.

Meantime, hundreds of gallons of disinfectant were polluting our rivers and streams, toxin-filled smoke was belching into the air, rotting carcasses shovelled into mass graves risked infecting the soil and, blimey, it looked like Coventry might go down. What could a man do?

Go to St Cuthbert's Island, of course. Which would be my plan for early Easter Monday, by which time Holy Island might be crawling with Christians, making mine a rather upside-down retreat.

BREAKFAST – porridge and honey
LUNCH – cod curry and red wine
EVE MEAL – Banjo Bill's platter

FRIDAY, 13 APRIL 2001 – DAY NINETY

Activities Holy & Unholy

For 90 days I'd tried to keep some island routine. Routine had both negative and positive aspects.

It imprisoned many wage slaves to a dullness and predictability as they trod the same path day after mind-numbing day. Creative artists who totally abandoned it found they often ended up creating nothing.

My own daily routine attempted to include the following: around 25 pages of the current book, 30 minutes reading the newspaper, write 1,000 words in rough (often very rough), about 30 minutes on yoga, a healthy walk, a visit to at least one pub (if open). After which, it was often time for bed anyway.

I'd become accustomed to a semi-monasticism, more used to silence, the importance of solitude. I am by nature gregarious, needed people far too much to consider long-term a Cuthbert-style withdrawal, but I noticed in the house the radio and telly were on less frequently.

The house knew I would be leaving soon. It was totally relaxed about the whole thing. I was getting that way.

Good Friday. Friday the thirteenth – strange combination. And as the visitors flocked to the island, so the Lindisfarne hostelries lived up to the British reputation for catering.

In most of the hotels food was served 12–1.30 p.m. and 6–7.30 p.m. – three hours out of twenty-four at a peak tourist time. Little wonder many foreign visitors looked bemused.

Various services at St Mary's church. In fact, you could gorge on religion much easier than food. I walked into Ray Simpson's devotional service where the congregation were sat in total silence.

It is rare for us in Britain to practise group silence, unless as a one-minute mark of respect for the dead, where often it is interrupted by yahoos anyway.

I enjoyed the experience. The sun filtered its rainbow colours through the stained-glass window. There was a barely heard ticking noise from the heating system. Those keen of ear (and eye) might hear (and see) a single butterfly banging its fragile wings against the window inscribed with the motto *Pro Rege et Patria* – For King and Country.

A door squeaked.

And an idea came to me. A weekly two-minute silence, nationwide. Not religious, not in remembrance of anything or anyone specific. Just to put us in touch. With ourselves.

The silence was ended by Ray Simpson popping up in the pulpit like a jack-in-the-box. As always he wore the big Celtic cross but also a dog collar and clerical black, which imbued him with a certain dignity.

He declaimed several prayers somewhat sombrely, then walked round the church in a circle bearing a makeshift wooden cross. I happened to know he'd been desperately hunting for one earlier and was thinking of yanking the one off the garden wall of the Open Gate, until Ross Peart offered to knock one up.

This day was defined by the two extremes of UK behaviour on a religious holiday. At the one end were the very pious and at the other were those determined to get bladdered.

Banjo Bill's son, John, was up with daughter Jo and her friend Nelly, and the three of them were slowly getting sozzled in the Manor House, the Ship and the Sign of Two Kirstys, but not particularly in that order.

All-day drinking wasn't usually my style. Nor did I want to spend all day in church. And I fancied young female company. So I flitted (and flirted) between the two, church–pub, church–pub.

I missed Kate Tristran's Liturgy Hour at St Mary's – preoccupied with a pint of John Smith's – but caught some of David Adam's Way of the Cross.

He and Derek processed from Marygate round the church and through the 13 stations of the cross with a somewhat glum congregation in their wake. At each station they paused and prayed. This was a solemn affair but at times David Adam's humour undermined it. At one stage he took the cross from Derek, handed it to Barry Hutchinson of the URC church, winked at Derek and whispered 'You can have it back later', followed by a quick smile.

I trudged round with them and en route studied *Hymns Ancient and Modern*. Even the latter were often the former, if you get my drift. I expected Charles Wesley's words to be sprinkled with the likes of 'thee' and 'thou' but I also found such archaisms in the likes of George B. Caird (1918–84) with 'did'st' and 'thy', G.W. Briggs (1875–1958) threw in a 'thee' and the still-living J.K. Gregory (1929–) contributed 'giveth' and 'liveth'. And here we are in the twenty-first century.

As I was musing, the procession had moved on to station seven. And, I estimated, in one of the pubs, the trio would have moved on to drink seven.

I tracked them down to the Sign of Two Kirstys, where Nelly was in top voice doing her impression of Kate Bush's 'Wuthering Heights'. Later, the trio's exuberance would earn them a chastisement from the management in the Ship.

I dropped in and out of their sessions and later joined them at Wild Duck Cottage for a tasty fish pie, where about ten generations of the family seemed gathered round the table. Nelly was looking as pale as a peeled potato and groaning from the excesses but, showing remarkable powers of recovery, was back out there again within the hour.

Meantime, things were still going on the God front. At St Mary's the latest service was about to get under way and a good time had been had by all dancing round St Aidan's statue in the churchyard. Thus the world spun on its axis and, in different ways, Holy Island passed its Good Friday.

BREAKFAST – honey nut cornflakes, scrambled egg

LUNCH – cheese and tomato sandwiches

EVE MEAL – fish pie, strawberries and ice cream

SATURDAY, 14 APRIL 2001 – DAY NINETY-ONE

The Chisel Chap – North Shore Trio

In what now seemed like a different century, my very first week on the island, I'd walked up through the ice to the remote Snook Tower, found my letter of introduction impossible to post and brought it back to leave at the Post Office. And now, nearly three months on, there was a reply. I had a phone call from the Tower owner Sue Ryland, who offered to meet me the next day.

Meantime, another mainland visitor, Bill Donald of the Kelso Tool Company, whose chisels and advice had helped me in the creation of stone poem. Stone at present was leaning nonchalantly against the living-room wall, patiently awaiting to be properly positioned outside. Bill, who came with his wife Sue, was a craggy Scot – an adjective invented for that race – and he cast a critical eye over my craftwork.

'Hmm,' he said. 'It's very – individual.'

This sounded like diplomacy. If he thought it was crap, why not say so?

'No, no,' he added. 'It's not bad at all. But the letters might need a bit of deepening.'

As if I had a JCB or something. I'd tried deepening them with the larger chisel. To little avail. What did he suggest?

'Possibly a future visit from a stone-mason – just to reinforce what you've already done.'

Bill was one of only three specialist tool-makers in the country. It wasn't a profession my careers master had ever mentioned at school. His tungsten chisels found their way round the world and I was proud owner of two of them. I showed him where I'd made the cock-up on the 'F'.

'I can't believe I was that stupid,' I said.

Sue asked to buy one of my books and I signed it.

'You've made it out to Mike and Sue,' she said, handing it back.

The island was obviously getting to me. Unlike the errant 'F', the errant dedication was remedied with Tipp-Ex.

That afternoon I took another walk to the North Shore. I'd never gone there with anyone else but Jo and Nelly said they'd like to come. They confessed to never walking anywhere and turned up in footwear more suitable to Legends Disco.

How far was it, they asked. About five miles there and back, I said, and saw the blood drain from their faces quicker than water through a colander. For a few seconds I felt like the native islander amused at the antics of the townies. Except I was a townie myself.

They stuck at it and I took a photo of them on the insectoid tree trunk which adorns the cover of this book.

That evening saw a strange ceremony at St Mary's church. I walked through the churchyard, which was brilliantly ablaze with flowers, in sharp contrast to the church interior. Where yesterday a service had been conducted in silence, today one was conducted in darkness. This was Easter Vigil and Holy Fire. The darkness brought some practical problems. Those reading the lesson up front were armed with those tiny torches doctors use to examine the interior of your ear. When not scanning the text, at times they would shine up directly below the face, turning the owners into Hammer Horror film extras.

The congregation was asked to sing various hymns but apart from those with torches, and possibly a few blessed with night vision, plus the odd clever dicks who knew the words anyway, we had no idea what to sing, couldn't read the book and thus babbled even more incoherently than normal.

The darkness was symbolic – a precursor to the resurrection and the coming of light. David Adam led the congregation out of the church (this doesn't happen much in Christianity), down Jenny Bell Lane and on to St Cuthbert's beach, where a vigorous bonfire was being whipped by a lively wind, sending its cartwheeling sparks out towards the Heugh. Meanwhile the sunset was burning itself into the Kyloe Hills across the dark waters on the mainland.

We all stood upwind of the sparks and there was more incantation on light and fire. I realised this concentrated mainly on light – not hard to work out why. Unlike some religions, Christianity and fire were uncomfortable bedfellows.

Fire was to do with eternal damnation. Fire was what awaited those of us who'd fallen out of line. As such, making too much of a celebration of it wasn't on.

Still, various people carried candles in jam jars and after a short time at the fire, side-stepping smoke and sparks, the procession made its way back up the hill.

Christianity improved out of doors. Once it was freed from those forbidding, enclosing four walls, all that internal echoey chanting and singing, once it was in touch with the wind and the sun it seemed less restrictive.

As we walked, I looked back at St Cuthbert's Island, now withdrawing into the dark; I thought of my two tides gone, my one still to come, and wondered if any of the assembled had spent the duration there.

The church enclosed me again. In more ways than one.

Before I'd come to Holy Island various people had wondered (as indeed had I) whether there would be much to write about in winter – the island, dark, shuttered, few amenities open. The reverse had proved true. As the influx of cars across the causeway grew, as the village filled up and became much more 'active' in the accepted sense, my interest waned, my pencil grew blunt. Often I had little incentive to go out of the house, as if the place had been taken away, commandeered.

That evening in Paradise Row, Banjo Bill's house was busier than St Pancras station on Bank Holiday, as the various generations of family took their leave, babies, children, teenagers, adults, senior citizens.

I wanted them all to uproot, make their way to Rotherham, crowd round my mother's bed, make lots of noise, leave her exhausted.

I wanted my mother to be unable to cope with so many visitors, to put her hands up and shout, 'If I could just have a few minutes peace!'

I drank that night with Jo and Nelly in the Manor House, where's Jo's trilling mobile phone cost her a £1 donation to the air ambulance box. This was a house rule of Jen Ward's. In theory, someone could have refused. I couldn't see it happening.

And later, they asked to see the first draft MS of the book. It felt strange, someone else leafing through the 95,000 handwritten words, like exposing some fragile infant to the world for the first time. In almost 13 weeks I had shown the MS to no one and couldn't help but feel apprehensive until it was once again safely stashed away.

When Jo and Nelly left in the early hours I realised that all night I'd felt as randy as a butcher's dog. My testosterone levels – maybe to do with the cold climate, maybe my unusual social surroundings – had been remarkably low throughout the stay, my loins virtually unstirred, my fantasies on a long snooze.

Not sure I was that happy about it – sexuality, after all, was part of creativity's energy.

No doubting it now, though. The company of two young attractive women had seen the return of the sex drive. Even if I hadn't driven anywhere.

BREAKFAST – porridge and honey, spaghetti on toast

LUNCH – pasta in tomato sauce

EVE MEAL – tuna in cheese sauce with spaghetti and rampant sex (sorry about that . . . only joking)

SUNDAY, 15 APRIL 2001 – DAY NINETY-TWO

The Egg Man Cometh – The Murderer of Plants

After spending nine weeks in hospital with two operations, an infection, a broken femur, after being discharged for only four days, news came through of my mother. She had taken another fall in the nursing home. Her leg was broken again. And she was back in hospital.

It was worse. My brother Alex, his wife Helen and my nephew Matthew were on holiday together in France. Which meant my mother was virtually alone.

The news pole-axed me.

I walked out of the house and into St Mary's church for the main Easter service, the Eucharist. This had been my plan and I couldn't think what else to do at that very moment. The church was packed, the queue for communion longer than at British Rail's enquiry windows. I couldn't think of God. Only my mother.

What was to be done?

The service was interrupted by the odd bawling baby or an errant infant whizzing Dinky cars up and down the aisle. The collecting plate came round. I wondered just where this tradition came from. I could understand passing round the hat for street theatre, for buskers, for the pub band – but for one of the country's biggest landlords?

My mother. Alone. Eighty-five years of age. A third operation in three months.

The final hymn was 'Rise in Christ'. Everyone stood up. When singing the chorus, many of the congregation held their right arm up in the air stiffly. I hadn't seen this before. It disconcerted me, like some right-wing political rally.

My status on the island was on the up. I had been invited to judge the Children's Easter Egg Competition at the Heritage Centre. This took my mind off my mother.

There were two categories. The under-fives. And the over-fives. On some of the former the age was written as '2', which suggested – given the sophistication of the decorated eggs – either an unprecedented number of child prodigies or some slight parental assistance.

As I studied the eggs on the table, a crowd of children gathered close. These were mainly the entrants and some slight coercion of the judge took place. One child tugged at my arm and pointed. 'That's mine!' he hissed. Another one ordered: 'Pick that one!'

As far as I could tell, no plain brown paper envelopes were involved, nor any offer to open an offshore account on my behalf, and because I was three times the size of those attempting coercion I was able to resist.

Some of the eggs were surreal. One character had eyebrows made of bread. Another egg had been turned into a terrifying black spider. The winners (and as I write I'm still waiting for a spot of the folding stuff in the post) included Alistair Brophy's Holy Island seal, which came complete with its own beach; Ryan Douglas's chicken – impossible to see the actual egg, such was the cosmetic quality; and Danielle Bishop's effort, which had not only transformed the egg into an astronaut but had also built a spaceship which looked fully capable of making Saturn.

My mind on this day was a mass of contrasting emotion; anticipation of my planned Third Tide for Cuthbert the next day and my long-awaited visit to Snook Tower on the Tuesday mixed with a giddy sense that I was within sight of my 100 days target. And confusion about my mother.

That night in the Ship I heard of a small, significant island incident.

A member of the God Squad had, that very weekend, had a row with a member of the farming community over damage to a vehicle. The farm person had been busy with a foot-and-mouth spray disinfecter when the spat blew up. As the argument escalated, he turned and sprayed the other from head to foot. Which gave a whole new emphasis to cleanliness being next to godliness.

I left the pub early, knowing my early rise.

The previous day Nelly had remarked how sick and wilting the plant on my writing desk looked. I now realised this applied to every single plant in the house, of which there were many but whose existence I had singularly failed to register over 92 days. Plants were my blind spot. Wherever I had lived, any attempt to keep plants had ended in disaster. I no more thought of watering plants than I did of retiling the roof. Plants, in my domiciles, became invisible as I had been those long months at the Two Kirstys bar. Their parched cries went unheard, as did their final death rattle. I rushed about that night in what was no doubt a far too late attempt at watery atonement. And I wrote a haiku.

Watering neglected plants.
In her hospital bed
my neglected mother

BREAKFAST – Craster kippers
LUNCH – cheese and onion on toast, yoghurt and honey
EVE MEAL – mashed spuds, fried eggs and peas

MONDAY, 16 APRIL 2001 –
DAY NINETY-THREE

Out of my Depth – The Coldest Judge

How else could I explain what happened this morning, except that I was distracted by my mother? The only other alternative is crass stupidity, which I'd prefer to dismiss.

I rose at 5.15 a.m., which probably not many could say on Easter Monday. High tide was at 9.42 a.m. and was only 3.6 metres, one of the lowest. This also was probably influential. The weather forecast was good.

I ate breakfast, made a flask of soup, packed melon slices, a Mars Bar, crisps, bread and butter, and forgot the binoculars.

I walked through the deserted village, still hunched in sleep. The keen wind was cold; the odd streak of light in the sky, much cloud. I walked through the churchyard and was halfway down Jenny Bell Lane when I was seized with a sudden panic.

The channel of water between the beach and the island was already more than wellie deep and was deepening by the minute.

I stood frozen by indecision. To wade through would be highly unpleasant. If I turned back, if I missed the Third Tide this day, the chance would probably be gone.

I hurried down to the shoreside. My heart was beating hard as I removed wellies and socks, rolled my trousers up above knee height, replaced wellies, stuck socks in my bag and plunged into the water.

It was above the wellie tops rapidly. It came up above my knees. Then up to my thighs. I kept going. By this time it was groin-high. I kept going. The water was now almost waist-high; I held my bag over my head like some escaping flood victim.

On and on, the freezing water swirling on its strong tidal route, the rock-strewn surface always likely to topple me. My trousers, leggings and pants were soaked, the shock of the cold water forcing from me small, quasi-orgasmic gasps. Several times I stumbled and steadied myself. I fought down the instinct to lose control, knew that if I stayed calm eventually the waters would drop. I plunged on. By this time the water had reached the bottom of my T-shirt, plus the shirt and jumper.

But like the motorist who'd driven across the flooded causeway, there was no going back. Only going on. It seemed an eternity but eventually the uneven ground began to slope upwards, the water levels slowly dropped and I emerged dripping, frozen, on to St Cuthbert's desolate wind-swept beach. I stumbled up the rocks, across the tufted grass and fell into the shallow dip of St Cuthbert's ruined cell.

Not everything was against me. The earliness of the hour meant there were no shore witnesses to see my stupidity. I also hoped no inhabitants of Fiddler's Green were scanning the island with binoculars as I shed trousers, leggings and pants – though a very powerful pair of binoculars, given the extreme temperature, would have been needed to see anything of significance. Modesty at such times takes a low priority.

There was something else to cheer me, too. In eight hours I could go back.

I wrung out the three items of clothing. The keen wind was north-easterly, which meant by the time it arrived it had already been well chilled by the sea.

I was shaking like a jellyfish – the cold, the shock. And there was no way I could prance round this island bottomless for more than a moment.

The slightly lesser evil was to put back on the pants, the leggings, the trousers, wet or not. Which I did and wondered what kind of a field day Arthur was having with all this.

Ironically, my socks, which on the previous day were the only articles of clothing to get wet, on this day were all that was completely dry. Plus the shoes. The dry socks and shoes were strangely comforting and again I used the binliners, wrapping my feet like toffee apples for extra insulation.

Michael Fish and his cohorts had been wrong on their forecast. There was no sun. The cloud was low, as was the temperature, and the wind continued to bite.

Part of Cuthbert's experiences on the island had been the suffering. Mine, too. Perhaps there was an inevitability to all this, that eventually St Cuthbert's Island would push me to an extreme. Whereas my first two tides had been active, walking the island, spotting birds, cars, people, this third one became a static, internalised affair. I was shrunk, foetus-like, in the shelter, scanning the sky for any small vestige of sun.

How much I needed that sun. Its absence was more than an absence of warmth. It was, on that day, as I sat through eight cold, wet hours, an absence of my father. He was not there for me. I imagined my mother in her hospital bed. I was not there for her either. She needed me and I wasn't there. And on that small, shivering island, as the great longing for my dead father took hold, I knew I had to travel the next day to Rotherham. The island had told me that.

I grew stiff and cold. I stood up and stomped about to aid circulation. Each time the chilling wind after a couple of minutes drove me back to the meagre shelter, so that I had little contact with the island itself, not the birds, not the seals, not the mainland, not Holy Island. I sealed myself into myself. I tried to read but couldn't concentrate. I swallowed some hot soup, whose heat, for a few moments at least, seemed to glow and pulse in my body. I ate the crisps and fruit and a slice of melon.

I realised that, unlike Holy Island proper, where I would leave a legacy of poems on rocks, bathroom walls, quilts and in pubs, on St Cuthbert's I had left nothing. This would not do. This was out of step with my rituals.

I tore off a small piece of paper from my notebook. On it I wrote the haiku '*To Cuthbert's/Island. The longest/Journey – Peter Mortimer, 16 April, 2001*'. Underneath I wrote, '*Please return this poem to its safe place when you have read it. Thank you.*' I took a dried melon pip to symbolise fertility and the future, folded it inside the paper and then folded that inside a piece of blue cellophane for protection. I inserted this between two of the cell's foundation stones close to where I lay, at the far end of the cross. Thus the conceit of the writer. Would it ever be read?

The hours passed. The tide reached its height, began its retreat. It slipped back from St Cuthbert's shoreline. One by one the nearby rocks rose from the water, the small southern beach slid into view, the channel narrowed.

For several hours I had focused in on myself. I had attempted to cast out the externals, the cold, the wet, the wind, just as much as Cuthbert had cast out his demons. He had stood neck-deep in the freezing waters. My own, less ambitious, purely accidental experience had been to hunch myself hours long in freezing wet clothes.

Cuthbert's suffering was by design. My experience was by chance. Or at least that's what I told myself. I had little idea. What is chance anyway? Maybe all things are meant and we have to learn from them.

At 2 p.m. the channel's width was about 30 metres. I decided to risk it, packed the bag, donned the wellies and stiffly and slowly made my way to the water's edge.

Once again I had misjudged it and the water came lapping into the wellies. The truth was I didn't care. I plunged on.

This was Easter Monday and several shoreline walkers witnessed this man plunging through the waters in his dayglo COASTGUARD coat. Not that the man was worried about them. The man could think only of home and warmth. And the man was aware only much later of the irony of what happened next. As he came ashore the very first thin sliver of sunlight on this freezing overcast day anointed his shoulder.

By the time I got home exposure was shaking me like a pneumatic drill. I poured the water out of my wellies, stripped off the various layers of wet clothing. A fish being skinned must have felt something similar to this sensation. I was stood starkers and shivering when the phone rang.

'Hello, Peter? It's the Heritage Centre. All the kids are waiting for you to judge the second Easter Egg Competition.'

I assured the caller I would be there in a few minutes and could they please have the kettle on? I splashed hot water all over myself, put on dry clothes and went off to do the judging.

At the centre they fed me piping hot tea which tasted better than Bollinger champagne (come to that, lots of things do). The young competitors, for whom the entire world at that moment revolved around the pending fortunes of their handiwork, looked slightly askance at the shivering, trembling judge trying hard not to drop their eggs.

Somehow winners were chosen: under-fives, Victoria Douglas's rabbit and Roseannah (surname unknown) with Knothead; over-fives, Laura Smith's Humpty Dumpty and Patrick Dillonthatcher's Itinerant.

My prize for the most welcome sight, the most uplifting spectacle in the whole affair, went to that steaming mug of tea. I felt I had survived St Cuthbert's Island at its most extreme. And through that, a necessary part of my island pattern had fallen into place.

I needed Banjo Bill's bonhomie that day. Plus his hospitality. In his warm kitchen I found myself drawn, that day in particular, to the large framed photograph above the fireplace. Two adults and ten children were on the lawn outside a grand-looking house. The children were sat on or gathered round a splendid rocking horse and they all had that bright-eyed innocence of young beings for whom the world is just beginning. One of the seated children, with a shock of blond hair, was Bill, aged three.

'All those children are dead now,' said Bill. 'Except me and the baby David.'

All those children are dead now . . . I stared again at those fresh faces. Had I not been in this room, had those words not been spoken by one of those same children, the impact may have not been so great.

The photo – in remarkably good condition – was from 1919. Jack Dempsey world heavyweight champion, World War One just finished. First non-stop Atlantic flight by Alcock and Brown. And there before me, the eager smiling faces of those children still waiting for life to make its mark. Life had now ceased for them.

'All those children are dead now.' Maybe it was the St Cuthbert's experience that brought such a strong sense of mortality. Whatever, the sentence resonated through me, haunted me and I found myself unable to stop staring at Banjo Bill.

BREAKFAST – tomato soup

LUNCH – soup, melon, crisps, fruit

EVE MEAL – Banjo Bill's mashed spuds, gravy and Yorkshire puds (no beef)

TUESDAY, 17 APRIL 2001 – DAY NINETY-FOUR

The Necessity of Snook – Rotherham Delirium

There was something strange about leaving the island six days before the end of my exile. It unsettled me and I needed to change plans, rejig things. In so doing, I felt the freneticism of my other life edging its way back in.

I rose early, grateful that Arthur hadn't thus far taken advantage of the previous day's long cold exposure. Eight hours of wet trousers is not the best recommended medicine for an arthritic hip.

My trip to Snook awaited. But also I had to deal with Gilbert. I'll forgive you for having totally forgotten about Gilbert. Gilbert was the stone dragged up from St Cuthbert's beach that at the first touch of a chisel had simply gone all to pieces, despite my two days of sanding.

Waste not, want not. Mike and Anne Burden wanted a Mortimer poem in their garden and I owed them several favours. I was confident Gilbert might show a stiffer resolve when faced with a paint-brush.

Anne and I decided on a rust-coloured acrylic paint. I applied this without problem till the 's' of the word 'longest' (the poem, by the way, was the St Cuthbert haiku). The letter looked like a burst sausage and no amount of cosmetics would improve it. I decided obliteration by sanding was the only course. But this would have to wait.

My need to go to Snook Tower stemmed from various things. I was fascinated by the place's remoteness, its total detachment from the rest of the island, and I also wanted to see what kind of person would own it. I also knew that Sue Ryland was a Buddhist and I felt the gentle, though powerful, influence of Buddhism during my stay. This was in direct contrast to religions in general and Christianity, in particular, which my island stay had alienated me from in a strange kind of enlightenment or moments of anti-epiphany, you might say. The closer I got to most religions, the less free I felt. This did not apply to Buddhism. And if St Cuthbert's had been the longest journey, this small one was also important.

I cycled along the causeway into a strong headwind. The road should have been flooded 40 minutes since but this tide was low and weak and lay exhausted some 30 metres away, too knackered to advance further.

If the causeway was hard going, no less so the flooded track to the tower, the mud and water at times bringing the bike to a full stop. Buddhism was making me work for my journey. I arrived breathless to see Sue Ryland running out of the dunes which surrounded Snook on three sides and secreted it away. In front was her black Labrador Tristan, with a giant toy dice in his mouth.

Sue was a tall attractive woman, slim, with a neat line in Thai hats and an extraordinary Art Garfunkel haircut. She was an historian, based 60 miles south on Wearside, and had bought Snook Tower ten years previously as little more than a shell. Attached to the tower was 'the barn' (her living-room), once used by the island fishermen and partly built with stone from the Priory.

Think of towers: the Martello Tower in Joyce, Byron's Dark Tower, all those fairy princesses locked in high towers. Towers were much too magical and mysterious to be built today. Think of Snook Tower. Nowhere near any damned thing.

Sue had put in a spiral staircase which twirled up past a balcony bedroom which jutted out over the living-room, past porthole windows, a bathroom, up and out on to the roof, whose solar panels provided the lighting.

From the roof both North and South Shores were visible, as were Lindisfarne and Bamburgh Castles, the Cheviot hills, the Kyloe Hills, the North Sea, Scotland and back towards the village. Everything was spread before me, my life of 100 days. And all seen from Snook Tower, peeping out from the sand dunes like a periscope, and noticed just as infrequently by those whizzing along the causeway. Walk in any direction from Snook Tower and you'd be at the sea soon enough.

Sue had marked out the flat land with a series of simple wooden posts (plans for a future fence), making it resemble the staked-out plot of some Wild West pioneer.

Down in the living-room (the barn) I flopped on exotic Eastern cushions. The hanging curtains were Eastern, too; there was a wood stove quietly pulsing heat as I stared up at heavy vaulted beams, drank tea and fancied staying not the single hour which my coming Rotherham trip dictated but maybe a month or so.

I wanted to ask Sue Ryland about her Buddhism (Tibetan variety), plus the isolation here and the silence, both of which attracted her. I wanted to ask her loads but her daughter Kate arrived with an entourage of kids and it was time to go. Too many things cramming in.

It must have been that tower, plus being close to a Buddhist, because for some reason I kept thinking of the meaning of life. Any *Hitchhikers' Guide* fan knows the answer to the meaning of life is 42 and maybe that was all there was to it. Except I kept thinking of the many people for whom life seemed to have no meaning; a succession of mechanical tasks, day following inconsequential day. And I realised that in one way life *did* have no meaning, that whatever religion taught us, whatever the ideas of some 'great plan', life was utterly devoid of meaning or purpose or objective; that it was a question of being born, living, dying and being forgotten.

This was only not true when an individual gave life meaning. Meaning was not an abstract imposed from on high, meaning was for each and every one of us to create, and if we did create it, then life became transformed.

This seemed like a simple truth never acknowledged (at least by me) as I whizzed down the east coast main line on the York train (one hour late). And spending a fortune on therapists or shovelling in the daily Prozac was a waste of time unless we took this on board. Discover what meaning your own life was meant to have, what gave it a purpose – whether this was sailing single-handed round the world, planting the street's best garden, running the local darts team, writing a novel or, indeed, spending 100 days on Holy Island – and you no longer worried about what the meaning of life was. It just was.

These were quite startling thoughts to have on the York–Doncaster train (ten minutes late) but I settled myself for the Doncaster–Rotherham connection, which was on time.

I couldn't look to God for the meaning of life. I had to look to myself. It was that simple. And that difficult.

In Rotherham General Hospital my mother's right leg was in a huge cast. She was half-hysterical, sobbing. She accused the hospital staff of lying to her or bringing her the same newspaper every day.

She had broken both fibula and tibia and at the age of 85 faced the third trip to the operating theatre in as many months. And in those same three months, she'd lost her husband of 60 years. This would have unsettled someone half her age. The fall and fracture had left her frightened, confused and alone. At the mention of my father, she burst into tears.

I spent nearly an hour calming her. Sometimes I spoke sweetly, sometimes I admonished her. I cuddled her, I brushed her hair. She shredded napkins endlessly and arranged and rearranged the jars and bottles at her bedside.

Something kept her going.

Bit by bit she grew calmer in that cheerless hospital room. She stopped biting her lip, her breathing became more measured. In this time I hardly saw a nurse, my mother left alone to rant and sob.

My niece Hannah arrived and we drove to the Rotherham council house she shared with husband Martin and their two-year-old daughter, Chloe. My bed for the night, after a visit to the local chippy, was the lounge settee; going through my brain the calm of the Buddhist tower, the pain of the hospital room.

BREAKFAST – cereal

LUNCH – cheese omelette

EVE MEAL – fish, chips and mushy peas

WEDNESDAY, 18 APRIL 2001 –
DAY NINETY-FIVE

Nine Nervous Writers – Camus on Lindisfarne

That morning, for the first time, my great-neice Chloe walked up to me with her bowl of cereal, held it out for me to feed her and said 'Pete'.

This was all the recognition anyone could want. I fed her and thought of my mother, three generations down the line. Probably someone was feeding her at this moment, too.

My mother was calmer that morning. We chatted for two hours. She was in a small ward of six elderly women, who'd obviously been listening in.

'I want to go to Holy Island too,' one of them spouted up.

'Right,' I said. 'Anyone else?'

Yes – everyone.

'This is the plan then,' I said. 'I'll get six wheelchairs, back the van up and we'll be halfway up the A1 before they've ever brought round the trolleys of mince.'

We all discussed the finer details of the plan for several minutes. It brought a smile to my mother's face which was as welcome as a ray of sunshine on St Cuthbert's Island.

Later, she grew more sombre.

'I'm going to die soon,' she said.

'Look,' I replied, 'if you die before this book is out I'll never speak to you again – all right? The book's dedicated to Dad, remember?'

My mother nodded.

And I journeyed – definitely for the last time – back to Holy Island and my final five days, a postscript almost, a tailpiece, a strange appendage.

The three return trains showed great consistency. Each one was late. Chris and Derek whisked me from Berwick station back to the island, where the tardiness gave me no more time than to drop the overnight bag, pick up a folder and walk to the writers' workshop I'd been asked to run at the Heritage Centre.

Nine hopeful scribes had turned up with a variety of poetry, prose, drama and a spot of porn. Why did they look at me like that? I knew why. It was the same way I had looked at professional writers running workshops before I'd given up proper work to scribble full time.

It was the belief of all aspirant writers (as with all aspirant footballers, rock stars or whatever) that if only they could do for a living what they now did for a pastime – in this case, write – all their troubles would be ended.

Which, actually, isn't quite the case.

Later, in the Manor House bar, I noticed my cabbage poem had been set, mounted, framed and hung. It was upside down but only in the middle of my spluttering complaint did the loud laughter all around me bring the realisation I was being wound up. And so easily.

I'd finished the ninth of the books given me by northern writers for Holy Island mental sustenance. This was from playwright Steve Chambers and was the novel *The Plague* by Albert Camus. All we 1960s students had read Camus, and his French stable-mate Sartre, and if we weren't *exactly* sure what existentialism meant, we at least knew it offered some alternative to the stuff we were being spoon-fed by our government and the mass media. We yearned for another voice and these French writers seemed to supply it. It was an age when novels were supposed to be philosophical, not marketing opportunities; when publishers looked for more than the laddish or the bimboesque.

With idealism now dead, both Sartre and Camus were unfashionable. Neither fitted with a culture that promoted a quiz show called *Greed* or considered leisure time best spent watching a group of sad telly wannabes picking their noses in a sealed house.

But stimulating the intellect wasn't the only reason I was grateful to have been given Camus's book. The novel tells of the plague's visitation to the small fictional French town of Oran in the 1940s and is usually taken as a parable of the German wartime occupation. Camus himself fought in the resistance, though I don't think this featured in 'Allo 'Allo. But even a slight glance makes the similarities with the UK in 2001 apparent.

'The epidemic spelt the ruin of the tourist trade.'

There are funeral pyres, mass burials, eerie descriptions of the foul, stinking smoke of corpses. Throughout the book runs the question – should vaccination be used or not? The official line is that everything is under control. In fact, it's chaos. The main character, Dr Rieux, is swamped by the number of victims and estranged from his wife. The society is bewildered, frightened, the veneer of civilisation breaking down before an invisible enemy.

The Plague has been interpreted on many levels. In foot-and-mouth Britain comes an extra one.

One small section especially stays in the mind. The audience at the town opera house are gathered for some musical escapism from the dreadful external reality. A cast member collapses. The pestilence has invaded their fantasy land, too. Camus resists milking the situation. Silently, the audience rises and files out of the theatre – the subdued tone rendering the episode yet more harrowing.

It was 30 years since I'd read *The Plague*. It couldn't simply be chance I was rereading it at this moment.

BREAKFAST – Shredded Wheat, toast
LUNCH – GNER tuna and tomato rolls
EVE MEAL – nothing – no time

THURSDAY, 19 APRIL 2001 – DAY NINETY-SIX

Day of the Stone – Telly Time

A ll day Tyne-Tees Television filmed. It was the day of the stone. For the cameras I secured it in the ground. Not really secured, of course. Television was an illusion.

They left. I wrote 1,000 words about their visit. Then threw them all away. I was writing about an illusion. And what was left to write?

FRIDAY, 20 APRIL 2001 – DAY NINETY-SEVEN

Day ninety-seven
the last ballpoint
running dry

T he day Kitty returned. I tracked her progress across the causeway, the exact spot, 97 days previously, I had tracked her departure. Polly the pooch leapt and licked. Something slackened, loosened off. The island's grip. Already it had begun. Distancing itself; leaving me little to write.

My final parish council meeting. At the house of Ian and Helen McGregor, me and Kitty gave a reading. In the evening a curry with Margo and Stuart Moffitt. The stone properly secured by Jimmy Middlemiss. A pivotal moment. And nothing more to say. Ghosts in the wind.

SATURDAY, 21 APRIL 2001 –
DAY NINETY-EIGHT

Day ninety-eight
in the bathroom
a second toothbrush

This about the Holy Island wind, which scarcely knows when or how to cease; 'it is an ill wind, bastard progeny of tempest and fury. It lacks all grace, being disfigured by malevolence.' Not my words – those of Michael Watkins in his 1981 book, *The English*.

Time is almost up. The island knows this. Just as I know the island wind. Not always disfigured.

These days write white on the page.

SUNDAY, 22 APRIL 2001 – DAY NINETY-NINE

Before emptying the
house, I fill
the house

At the Cuddy House, the farewell party. Islanders, fishermen, incomers, shopkeepers, publicans, solicitors, handymen, hoteliers, masseuses, schoolteachers, weekenders, musicians.

Come one, come all.

Come tempest and fury.

Almost. A fight looms in the kitchen. I step in. But why? I don't know.

MONDAY, 23 APRIL 2001 – DAY ONE HUNDRED

Cleaning out the fire
I will never
light again

After the party the house was full of spectres. Everyone I had known on this island.

I took my final wash in the bathroom. The final stripping of the bed. Shirts yanked off hangers, clothes and towels gathered up, the writing desk folded away for the last time. Me and Kitty washing the floor; the rubbish put out, memory hoovered away.

And like the island, the house knew the time had come.

The day was grey and misty, wrapping round itself once more, secreting itself, reclaiming itself from intruders.

What were these 100 days?

The flicker of an eyelid, a single breath, a heartbeat barely measured. Two hundred tides, a tiny weathering of statues, a small encroachment of sand. A frozen sea, an opening bud.

Farewell to Banjo Bill, farewell to Ross and Jean Peart, farewell to Caitlin White, to Molly and Joel, farewell, to Malcolm Patterson, farewell (and a handshake).

And up to the village's highest point with Stuart McMurdo and painter Nick Skinner – the old coastguard look-out on top of the Heugh. Up high once more, like Snook Tower, with my island history spread out beneath us. Except the mist obscured that history.

And then down, walking back through Shanty Town. And on this misty and murky final Holy Island day, a small moment, an instant of significance to no one but myself.

Framed in the doorway of a battered Shanty Town shed were two native islanders, Maggie and Goff (see nicknames). Stuart McMurdo hailed them. A muffled greeting was returned.

Their shapes were ill-defined in the gloom. In that doorway they were removed, just as they and many other islanders had been removed through my 100 days. Half-visible vague figures in a doorway, ever a mystery to me.

Because, despite all the glossy tourist board brochures, despite the islanders' welcoming video messages in the Heritage Centre, much of this indigenous culture was only half-seen, half-grasped by any outsider. A small culture which knew itself inside out. But what did the rest of the world know of it? And what did it know of the rest of the world? It clung to a cultural self-sufficiency that no amount of satellite dishes nor tens of thousands of visitors could penetrate. And if its days were numbered, then so were all days numbered.

The image of these two shadowy islanders burnt into my retina. Inside a shed which I could never enter.

Kitty, Polly and I drove over the causeway. I clung to Kitty's hand, clung to the bunch of daffodils – the farewell present from Joel and Molly in the school.

The mist lowered itself further, obliterating all distance. We reached the mainland, drove the few miles to the busy A1, turned south where, a few miles later, I looked out across the North Sea for that familiar island shape. But it simply wasn't there.

AFTERMATH

One hundred days spent walking across some vast continent might have been an easier book to write, if harder on the feet. The very smallness of Holy Island, the same landscape, people and buildings day after day after day, my sense of confinement and removal from the world at large combined to make me feel simultaneously entrenched and unrooted.

Back home in Cullercoats my immediate behaviour was strange. I found myself taking long solitary walks, not on the splendid coastline that lay just round the corner but along suburban streets, the world of bay-windowed semis. I wanted to look at the neatly trimmed lawns, the freshly washed cars in the drive, I wanted to study the DFS sofas in the well-arranged living-rooms, the very stuff of well-ordered domesticity, as if the urban man in me was wildly over-reacting, was seeking the sheer mundanity of suburbia as some kind of antidote to my 100 days' exposure on that small outcrop.

The island had produced various unusual reactions in me. The sense of not 'belonging' created an insecurity which forced me to leave my mark in a way that is natural to me – as a writer. Thus I carved poems on to rocks, painted them on to stones and bathroom walls, left them in gardens and framed on pub walls.

This knowledge that I wasn't 'of' the island the way other people were pushed me to extreme acts which those same other people had never experienced. Thus I could lay some claim to ownership because I had isolated myself in the refuge box, spent three long tides on St Cuthbert's Island, dragged my poem stone three miles over the sand dunes, walked right out on to the vast unvisited wastes to the north, home only to rotting wrecks.

I took a duck to supper, I found strangely comforting the sessions with the school's population of two, where I was never judged. I deliberately exposed myself to more Christian religion than over the past 20 years. I liked most of the practitioners but felt alienated from what they practised.

I long to rid the world of religion but fear the destabilising vacuum that might immediately ensue. I find bizarre the concept of some remote superior being we are supposed to worship.

On the spur of the moment I gave up meat after 57 years as a voraciously gulping carnivore.

And here, in spring 2002, I remain 95 per cent vegetarian. Purists may scoff at the five per cent but the knowledge I can indulge just the occasional bacon sandwich or chicken dinner saves me from the unhappiness total abstinence was dropping me into.

I took with me to Holy Island a great emptiness from the death of my father a few days previously, also the sense of guilt over my sick 85-year-old mother. This guilt saw me three times fleeing from the island to console her as she faced a hat-trick of operations.

In my early days I had to really convince myself that being on the island served any purpose whatsoever – and it was the writer's instincts which came to my aid.

Why did I go in the first place? Possibly to escape a country increasingly ill at ease with itself, sullen, dysfunctional, polarised. Except people can't simply escape.

Or maybe it was the challenge, to discover if from the rough material of the everyday winter life of this small community I could hew a book of some worth. In many ways the whole idea was an enormous conceit. People, places, experiences often take decades to work themselves through a writer. I was planning to go and one year later produce a 100,000-word book.

And I realised the following: go to Holy Island for two days with a film crew and you'd probably feel you'd captured it. Spend 100 days there with a notebook and you'd be less sure. Ten years would probably remove all confidence at having found the essence. Such is the nature of things.

The work sits somewhere between literature and journalism, without the fictional freedom of the former but allowing more reflection than the latter; an ambition to distil, as against merely recording experience.

Nothing much else occupied my time during 2001: three months on the island, nine months writing about it. No holidays, few diversions. This semi-monasticism at times pissed me off but also brought the sensation – which some may dismiss as plain daft – that I was doing what I was 'meant' to do. The island is often a sensitive, touchy place, wary of the likes of me (though, to be fair, none of the many previous Holy Island books is like this one).

Nothing is more guaranteed than that some islanders will take exception to some of the things I've written, though without the support and kindness of most of them my stay would have been intolerable. In his book, *Pieces of Land – Journeys to Eight Islands*, Kevin Crossley-Holland writes: 'My impression is that few native Holy Islanders will welcome anything written about them, irrespective of truth or quality, unless of course there's money in it.'

In June 2001 I returned for the Jazz & Blues Festival, which, despite the torrential rain all day, was a huge success. Unburdened by my '100 Days' yoke I felt more relaxed with the islanders and sensed they returned the compliment.

And I was able to view the place with more of the delight with which the visitor views it, a different perspective to the resident. Life was proceeding.

Banjo Bill got second place in the Blackpool National George Formby Song Competition. The Dutchman Harm was banned from a second pub. Foot-and-mouth restrictions were eventually lifted without, as far as I could tell, any island business going into bankruptcy.

My various poems are still *in situ* and, I imagine, in the main unread.

Back on Tyneside, in the autumn I attended, with many other writers, the funeral of poet Andrew Waterhouse, a suicide that left many of us in a state of shock. Soon after his death his pamphlet *Good News from a Small Island* was published and because of its poignancy and its connection to my own experience I'm reprinting here his splendid poem.

>On St Cuthberts Island
>(for Stella)
>
>A nervous scramble over wracks
>to this small acre of dolerite
>and scurvy grass to crouch together
>out of the wind and under the cross,
>
>where his invisible enemies
>may have been defeated by fasting
>and prayer and we clutch at each other
>as a mist comes in with a useless
>
>new moon and the village lights
>appear and fade and the sleet
>starts and our faces are numbed,
>which is what finally forces us
>
>to give in and carry his love and devils
>and hunger back to the mainland.
>
>Andrew Waterhouse
>Reprinted from *Good News from a Small Island* by Andrew Waterhouse
>(MidNag Arts Group, 2001)

I write this in March 2002, and my Boots Shaving Bowl is incredibly still in use, 15 months on.

And as for Arthur . . . I spent several months being passed round doctors, physios and consultants to little effect and eventually, and glumly, asked to be stuck on the long hip-replacement waiting list, as the pain and lack of movement worsened. Only in the last few weeks have I encountered a chiropractor who scoffs at the inevitability of such a move and feels I have at least a fighting chance of combating the worst excesses without drugs and by using my own body as a weapon. It may come to nothing. But the challenge, psychologically, is energising.

And in the middle of writing the book September 11 happened, an atrocity of such shattering magnitude that it seems almost impossible to be writing of a time *before* that event occurred. Yet it seems also to be an event from which the USA has learnt nothing, except how to be even more gung-ho and to give carte blanche to the morally bankrupt policies of its president.

Maybe a book such as this says more about its author than its subject matter. It is intended in no way as a guide book, nor as a social, historical or religious survey of that remarkable lump of rock and sand cast adrift in the North Sea.

In truth, there is no way I can define it except to say – here it is. I wrote various small poems during my 100 days and finish with another tiddler completed soon after my return, an image that stayed in my mind and in some ways reinforces the fact that I can never belong to, yet will never be free of, that small huddled island which is simultaneously well known and yet not known at all.

On the Cullercoats carpet
my yanked-off boots
spill North Shore sand.